**Consumer advocates, industry leade.. .
praise *How to Fund the Life You Want***

'If you're serious about getting things right with your money – and
avoiding costly mistakes – then set time aside to work through this
excellent book. You will end up better off. No question.'

Paul Lewis, Freelance Presenter, Money Box BBC Radio 4

'This book possibly has the most heart of any finance book ever
written. It gets right to the nub of why mastering the management
of our finances for ourselves is so crucial – but also so difficult. Robin
and Jonathan skilfully blend excellent tips with helpful exercises,
relatable anecdotes and decades of wisdom. Their understanding of
behavioural psychology underpins their very human approach, and
the result is that topics are accessible in a way that I would venture
has never been achieved in a finance book before.'

Becky O'Connor, Head of Pensions and Savings,
Interactive Investor

'Wonderfully researched, jargon-free, thought-provoking, interactive
and engages the reader from start to finish.'

Jeff Prestridge, Personal Finance Editor, Mail on Sunday

'I'm often asked to recommend a good, essential book on investments
within the UK tax and legal system. Until now, there wasn't one.
This book is now my go-to pick.'

Steve Conley, CEO, Academy of Life Planning, and
former Head of Investments, HSBC

'Anyone who wants to get started in the world of investing faces
information overload. This book offers a great solution – it's written
by experienced authors that you can trust and it's set out in a clear
and highly digestible format.'

Moira O'Neill, Investing columnist, Financial Times

'This is not just another book about investing. It is a comprehensive financial lifestyle manual relevant to people of all ages and walks of life.'

Mark Northway, Director, ShareSoc

'I welcome this much-needed book, here to help anyone make sense of their money and pensions. With their human touch, no-nonsense language and a relentlessly practical approach, Robin and Jonathan have written the "missing manual" for everyday investors.'

Jackie Leiper, Managing Director, Pensions &
Stockbroking at Lloyds Banking Group

'This book is an antidote to the misleading messaging and hype that some parts of the industry have been putting out for decades, to consumers' detriment.'

Andy Agathangelou, Founder, Transparency Task Force

'Jonathan and Robin are refreshingly clear about a complex subject, offering a straightforward, evidence-based approach to retirement planning. Great for the everyday investor who wants to cut through the jargon and make good decisions for the future.'

Diane Maxwell, former Retirement Commissioner for New Zealand

'There are many books about how to get rich fast. Their authors certainly get rich, readers less so. Much more useful and a lot rarer are books that help you to grow your money steadily and avoid losing your savings – this book achieves this. It is very precious!'

Ludovic Phalippou, Professor of Financial Economics,
University of Oxford Saïd Business School

'This is such a valuable guide to DIY investing, I recommend you make this book your first investment.'

Claer Barrett, Consumer Editor, Financial Times

HOW TO FUND THE LIFE YOU WANT

What everyone needs to know about savings, pensions and investments

ROBIN POWELL AND JONATHAN HOLLOW

WITH A FOREWORD BY IONA BAIN

BLOOMSBURY BUSINESS
LONDON · OXFORD · NEW YORK · NEW DELHI · SYDNEY

BLOOMSBURY BUSINESS
Bloomsbury Publishing Plc
50 Bedford Square, London, WC1B 3DP, UK
29 Earlsfort Terrace, Dublin 2, Ireland

BLOOMSBURY, BLOOMSBURY BUSINESS and the Diana logo are trademarks of
Bloomsbury Publishing Plc

First published in Great Britain 2022

A catalogue record for this book is available from the British Library

Library of Congress Cataloguing-in-Publication data has been applied for

ISBN: 978-1-3994-0460-0; eBook: 978-1-3994-0459-4

2 4 6 8 10 9 7 5 3

Typeset in Bembo Std by Deanta Global Publishing Services, Chennai, India

Printed and bound in Great Britain by CPI Group (UK) Ltd, Croydon CR0 4YY

To find out more about our authors and books visit www.bloomsbury.com
and sign up for our newsletters

Contents

About the Authors

Robin Powell studied at the University of Oxford, then worked as a print, radio and television journalist and founded a media production company. He now focuses exclusively on financial content and is the founding editor of *The Evidence-Based Investor*, a blog that works to dispel the myths surrounding investing and challenges the vested interests in the asset management industry. He has interviewed and co-authored content with some of the most distinguished practitioners and researchers in the field, including several Nobel Prize winners. He is an Ambassador for the Transparency Task Force, a campaign group that holds the financial services sector to account for the fees it charges. He is also head of client education for the financial planning firm RockWealth.

Jonathan Hollow studied at the University of Cambridge. He then worked in publishing and digital content production, then later strategy and innovation for a wide range of charitable and public service causes. He has specialized in plain English and turning complex regulations into practical information people can use. More recently, he worked for the UK government's Money Advice Service (now rebranded MoneyHelper), and after this, the Money and Pensions Service. He worked with leaders from across government, regulators and the financial services industry. Together, they created the *UK Strategy for Financial Wellbeing*. He also worked on the Chartered Institute of Insurance's *Insuring Women's Futures* taskforce. This aimed to understand, and begin to solve, some of the scandalous differences in financial outcomes between women and men.

Foreword by Iona Bain

I only started investing in the last few years, as a self-employed woman hurtling towards her thirties. Well, we all have to learn as we go and make our own mistakes but I can honestly say I would love to have had this guide in front of me before I embarked on the journey. That's because it's all too easy nowadays to be lured by the bright lights of the share trading revolution. It's a world where, for all the fancy sliders and emojis, education and enlightenment are in short supply.

Yes, it's great that we now have apps which open up the world of investing to anyone with a phone. Anyone with money to put aside for the long term must understand that inflation is outpacing today's savings rates. But it's even more important to learn the difference between trading for *fun*, which is akin to gambling, and *investing*, which is a programme of care for your future self. A programme needs rules and rules must be based on the best possible science or evidence.

The problem is that there is a big investment industry out there, which in many ways is out to befuddle us and blind us to science. It is constantly suggesting new ideas, themes, angles and solutions, which will offer a route to riches. In reality, this is promotional material – what this book calls 'the investing equivalent of fast fashion'. I know, because when I opened my first share trading account, I plucked out a bunch of shares and funds which appealed to me, based on ideas picked up from financial media. I didn't think much about how they all hung together, or whether the tips could be backed up with convincing research.

As a journalist constantly engaged with financial news, it's tough to ignore the zeitgeist. But the authors' suggestion that following too much news about investing is a bad idea has really struck home with me. Might it actually make far more sense to use a set of evidence-based rules to build my little portfolio (or to find an adviser, one who is firm on evidence-based investing, who can take it on for me)? Then just walk away and leave it to grow ...

Women are said to be more cautious investors than men but that can be an unhelpful idea. It suggests that men are prepared to take more risk and will therefore achieve better returns. But this book underlines that while attitudes to managing money may differ, women and men have the same emotional and intellectual potential to be successful investors.

I also like Robin and Jonathan's reminder that capitalism will not go out of fashion any time soon. Investing is an act of faith in the spirit of human enterprise, in the way entrepreneurs and companies adapt and innovate – for instance, in response to climate change policies.

In my own book, *Own It! How Our Generation Can Invest Our Way to a Better Future*, I called investing an act of 'practical hope'. This book proves why there's plenty of cause for it. So I recommend you settle in and make time to read – and enjoy! This friendly, no-fuss book will help you to pay attention to the evidence, not the headlines. And it gives you the tools you need to put its smart rules into practice, setting you on a path to long-term financial freedom.

Iona Bain is an award-winning speaker, author, writer and broadcaster on a mission to help people, especially younger people, get to grips with personal finance.

Introduction

This book distils the evidence and experience we have both gained in the field of money management. Our aim is to help you and thousands of other readers plan for a better financial future. You could take your choice among numerous other books addressing this topic – there's no shortage! So why one more, and why this one?

There are many other great books and many writers and bloggers we admire but neither of us could find a single book that hit all our marks:

- We wanted to take as much fear and complexity as we could out of the pensions system, and the rollercoaster rides of markets.
- We didn't want a book that makes money management sound easier than it is or that leaves you 'high and dry' at the level of theoretical principles. For example, planning for your financial future involves not just what you earn and how you invest it, but how it is taxed. No government has managed to make taxation simple! Addressing this and other topics has led us into practical detail, more than other books.
- We wanted a book that worked hand-in-glove for readers in the UK. Many of the best books on this topic are written for readers in the US. Much of what they say is transferable, but not all of it.
- Above all, we wanted it to be based on evidence. Not anecdote and not folk wisdom. With something as precious as your financial future, you need it to rest on solid foundations.

Robin writes: My investing wake-up call

As the celebrated investor Warren Buffett once said, risk comes from not knowing what you're doing. In my experience, there are plenty of people who *think* they know about investing but actually don't have a clue. They're taking big risks – not least the risk that they'll outlive their savings and end up relying on the state or their loved ones to support them financially in their later years.

For many years, I was one of them. I devoured the money sections in the weekend papers. I regularly checked the FTSE 100 Index and the price of the shares I owned. I fancied myself as a bit of an expert. In fact, I was making mistake after mistake. It was only in 2010, while making an online documentary about investing, that I realized how deluded I had become. I was shocked to learn that, since the 1950s, there's been a broad academic consensus on how to invest successfully, yet most investors do virtually the opposite. Worse still, those same investors are actively encouraged to do so by financial professionals, most of whom are either unaware of the peer-reviewed evidence or simply choose to ignore it.

Had I known what I know about investing now when I was 21, I would be far better off today. In fact, I would probably have retired some years ago. And that's precisely what inspired me to start my blog, The Evidence-Based Investor, to promote financial literacy and to campaign for a fairer, more transparent industry. It's also why I'm working with Jonathan on this book. Life is short and earning money is a means to an end, not an end in itself. This book presents, simply and accessibly, the most reliable and efficient way to fund the life you want to lead. Enjoy it, learn from it, but most of all, *act on it*. Your future self will be forever grateful.

You will have seen from our biographies that neither of us has a background as a financial adviser or a professional investor. Over a working life of about 30 years, we have both been through the painful process of moving from baffled outsiders to careful explainers of the financial system.

Jonathan writes: A French view on our financial system

My family has long connections with a family in France. These go back to a French exchange my father made from a grey and gloomy Bristol in 1947, across the Channel to explore the wonders of Versailles. That penfriend and language exchange has spanned two generations.

One of the family members of my generation I'll call Jean-Pierre. We have known each other since the 1970s. He is a great Anglophile and when he married, it was to an Englishwoman. I was very happy and intrigued when after so many years of visiting the UK, he finally moved and began a professional life here. Sometime in the early years of that new period in his life I asked him what he had learned about the UK from the inside. What had he not known or understood about our country despite all his holidays and brief visits?

Jean-Pierre could have addressed any topic at all, but his response intrigued me: he said that in contrast to France, he was astonished by the complexity of the UK's system for retirement planning and the burdens it put on people of all levels of education and background.

'What burdens?' I asked.

He answered: the burden of taking life-changing financial decisions, decisions that then play out on the shifting sands of financial markets. And with the backdrop that nobody knows how long they will live. Jean-Pierre felt that even as a well-educated professional, he was finding these burdens quite difficult. He was concerned about what it must be like for people with fewer opportunities and less money to spare.

This conversation has never left me and is one of the reasons I am so passionate about making it easier to deal with those burdens. There will always be natural uncertainty about the future. Why does our system make that even harder by adding complexity and confusion to the mix? That is not to say, by the way, that I think the solution to your retirement problems is to move to France! France has a retirement system that still puts much more responsibility on the state rather than the individual, but there are deep questions about its sustainability. By contrast, the UK has lost most of its guaranteed company pension schemes and it has the worst state pension of any comparable country. So as a country, we load much more onto individuals than we did even 15 years ago, let alone 50.

As part of my work for the UK government on these matters, I came into contact with specialists from banks, regulators and financial education from many countries around the world. The systems I came to admire the most were those of the Netherlands, New Zealand, Australia and Sweden. The systems in the UK and the US are not dreadful, but they're not exemplary either – they're just dotted with pros and cons. There is no doubt though that in the UK, enormous responsibility falls on you and that is why we want to make this book as helpful and practical as possible, so it can help you to live with those responsibilities.

So we want this book to change people's lives and we hope it will change yours. That's a big ambition, but too many people are wrestling with money and pensions and that's got to change. We have written this book for people in the UK who feel they don't know enough about pensions and investing to plan for their retirement. Or who feel they know a reasonable amount, but aren't doing everything they can to put it into practice. If you *don't* live in the UK, you will still find a great deal of useful learning here, but be aware that everything we say about taxes and product rules (as opposed to the basic principles of investing) will be different in your country.

If *any* part of your retirement plan will depend on savings and investments (rather than a guaranteed income from an employer's or state pension), we are here to help you. We have road-tested this book – everyone who read it said they made a change to their money management as a result. The changes you make may be small, or they may be large, but we believe that reading what we say should not be an exercise in theory. When you reach the end, we want you to be able to take action:

- You will see how money fits into a happy life, according to the best evidence available about human psychology.
- You will understand what you *can* control about your future finances and what you *can't*. You will therefore be able to focus on what you *should* worry about – because you *can* change it!
- You will understand the rules of the game we all have to play in: the laws, regulations and taxes affecting markets, and therefore you.
- You will understand the best and latest evidence about how to get your money to grow as much as possible while you worry about it as little as possible. The great news is that this can be distilled to six simple rules. (If you like spoilers, we set out these rules at the end of this book, alongside a downloadable workbook that brings together all our practical steps.)
- You will understand how financial advisers can help you to check your thinking. There are certainly times when it's cheaper and at least as effective to go to other people or sort things yourself, as to visit a financial adviser. But whoever you do it with, checking your thinking about retirement planning is a very important follow-on from using this book. And we have a vital message that covers this in a bit more detail at the end of Chapter 2 (*Invest in ... Yourself*, pages 35–7).
- The final section of this book introduces a workbook designed to help you take action. It will help you to take stock of your financial situation, map future life goals and put together a high-level plan to achieve them.

Don't expect to read this book in one sitting. If you alternate the chapters with the tasks from the downloadable workbook, it will take a little while – especially if you have to gather information about current pensions from financial providers. We believe that the work in the workbook (see page 233) will take most people about three days to complete. That's not just the work you'll need to do, but also talking it through with a friend or partner. That may sound a lot so it's a good idea to break it into chunks and do it as you go through the chapters. And what is an 'investment' of three days against the reward of setting your future life after work – which might be as long as 20, 30 or even 40 years – on firm foundations?

The best way to start is to start

Taking control of your financial future might seem complex and it may be something you've put off for a good while. If you're worried that you might just read the book and still put off taking action, we suggest you take some steps to prevent that:

1 Thumb through the rest of the book and work out how long it will take you to read Chapters 1–9.
2 Thumb through the final section, and download the workbook, to see what it involves.
3 Pre-commit. Write down somewhere (on a calendar, in an email to a partner or friend, or in a prominent place where you can see it) the dates when you plan to a) read the main chapters of the book and b) finish the workbook.

You might wish to book a weekend in your diary to go through most of the downloadable workbook. That way, you have a built-in deadline. And you can co-ordinate with a partner to make sure you are both available and aligned at the same time.

Experimental evidence suggests that pre-commitment deadlines like these are effective in helping people who may be tempted to put off complex and demanding tasks. A 2002 study by Dan Ariely of the Massachusetts Institute of Technology (MIT) and Klaus Wertenbroch of INSEAD demonstrated this.[*1] It set students tasks and let them

---

*This is an evidence-based book, so we wanted you to be able to look up any facts and figures we quote. So at the back of the book, you will also find endnotes that give references for every fact and source we cite in the book. As well as the numbers, a text snippet guides your eye to the right note.

In the endnotes you will also find the hyperlinks to all the external sites and tools we mention. And if you download the PDF of our workbook, it has live, clickable links to all the key tools.

For readers of the eBook, to keep the main chapters of the book less busy, we have not put in hyperlinks in to every source and reference, but we have linked to key tools and a few key sites – the ones that will help you to take action.

choose whether they gave themselves deadlines earlier than end-of-term. There were penalties for late submission and for poorer work. The students who chose to take an earlier and harder route did better. Most people who pre-committed to earlier deadlines than strictly required received higher grades. By contrast, students who were given naturally spaced deadlines, or who only worked to the last deadline at the end of term, scored less well. You may do even better if you pre-commit to someone other than yourself. Is there somebody you would trust not only with a deadline, but with whom you could talk through financial matters as you work through this book? We strongly recommend you try to find such a person.

Jonathan writes: Talking about money – the British problem?

My work at the Money Advice Service (now MoneyHelper) meant that a lot of excellent research crossed my desk. A recurring theme is the embarrassment that stops people in the UK from talking to their family, friends or even their partner about money.

This creates serious problems. The most striking example is when people have serious debts that they can't manage. An independent review of debt advice quoted the charity Christians Against Poverty, which helps people who have unmanageable debts. Christians Against Poverty found that 33 per cent of their highly indebted clients had waited more than three years before seeking help, 51 per cent had waited more than two years and 66 per cent had waited over a year. Among them, 49 per cent stated the reason for delay was embarrassment or shame and 43 per cent because they thought no one could help.[2] Needless to say, by the time clients had waited between one and three years to address serious debt problems, the debts had mounted. So their problem was significantly harder to address. But even in less extreme cases than problem debt, the confusion and mystery around good financial planning and management is simply increased by the lack of talk. We don't talk about money so how can we learn from others?

If you can find someone with whom you will feel comfortable talking about the contents of this book, you will gain in many ways. You can test your assumptions with them, they can check your maths and they can help you to find further ways to commit and take action.

A word about choices

In this book we're going to cover a wide range of mainstream choices that people can make about their pensions and investments. Of course we know that a big factor, perhaps the biggest one shaping your choices, is how much money you have. We talk about investing in other accounts as well as a pension, or building up a cash reserve outside your pension. Some readers will know that their money won't stretch that far. We mention this upfront because we have to strike a difficult balance – between being realistic and encouraging people to set their sights as high as they can.

We try to write with humility and sensitivity, knowing that this book needs to be useful to a wide range of readers. Our readers will have different incomes, different levels of wealth and different spending and saving needs.

We hope that if you can't take up all the choices set out here, you will be able to make the best of the choices you do have and that your knowledge about the other choices will be useful later in life. What seems impossible now may become a possibility in the future. Above all, we ask you not to be discouraged. We talk about 'climbing a pensions mountain' in Chapter 3 (*Manage Your Money*, see pages 42–66). That is often how it feels – a long, exhausting slog with the summit seemingly as distant as ever. But if you have climbed a mountain, you'll know that you can often lose sight of the summit for most of the climb and then it will appear, near at hand, when you least expect it.

How we ask you to approach this book

There are two people you need to think about as you read through these pages. You will hear us talking about both of them – and they are both yourself! The person that most people find it harder to help is their *future self*. The future seems very distant; people aren't certain that they will reach it and they don't know what it will look like, so there is a natural urge to prioritize another person: your current self. Your current needs are urgent and if you satisfy them, gratification comes a lot sooner. But as we will set out in Chapter 2 (*Invest in ... Yourself*, see pages 27–41), these two selves can and should come to a mutually beneficial understanding. We will try to help you work that out as you work through the book.

We hope and intend this book will help you to base your future financial plans on evidence. The flipside is: we ask you to set aside what you think you know about money and financial planning as you read it. You may be very well informed about the evidence or you may have been more influenced by the myths and dreams peddled by the investment management industry. These tend to help middlemen to get rich from your savings. More on this later! Either way, we ask that you start with a 'beginner's mindset' so leave behind your knowledge and preconceptions as you journey through the topics.

What we mean by evidence

For us, there are four important questions you should ask when presented with anything purporting to be research on how to invest. You should ask these about what you read in this book – and even more about what you read outside it.

Is the evidence genuinely independent?
New studies are being published all the time that appear to support a particular investment strategy or course of action but all too often these reports are produced, or else commissioned and paid for, by companies with a commercial interest in publicizing the outcome. Many academics, on the other hand, are truly independent. They don't have an agenda or a point to prove. Instead they leave it to financial practitioners to act on their findings or not.

Is it based on robust data analysis?
We all know the old adage about lies, damned lies and statistics. Abuse of data can be very misleading. Often findings are based on

too short a time period or a sample that's too small. Sometimes the fund industry ignores survivorship bias; in other words, it overlooks those funds that performed so poorly that they no longer exist. At other times it compares returns to the wrong benchmark or quotes performance figures before the full impact of fees and charges. Sometimes it simply gets the maths wrong.

Has it been peer-reviewed?

To test whether their findings are reliable, academics publish their research in credible academic journals. This gives other academics the chance to agree or disagree on whether the results are sound. Again, caution is required – some journals are less credible than others. But evidence that has been properly peer-reviewed should carry far more weight with investors than otherwise.

Have the results been reproduced?

The fourth and final characteristic of findings you can depend on is that they've been tested across multiple environments and timeframes. There is some disagreement on the extent to which academic finance is properly scientific. Asset prices, for example, never move in exactly the same way as they have done in the past. However, there needs to be a strong element of repeatability. This demonstrates that the findings of a particular study weren't just down to random luck or else reached through selective 'data mining'.

Everywhere we possibly can, we use this kind of evidence in this book. In other words, independent and based on robust data analysis; furthermore, the findings have been peer-reviewed and have also been reproduced. Some of our sources don't meet that test but we only include evidence we think is strongly worth considering. We have put endnotes at the back of the book so you can follow up on the evidence yourself if you want to.

If the evidence is so strong, why doesn't everyone follow it?

You might wonder why there is still a battle between evidence and myth in the field of financial planning and investment. Why is the financial services industry still full of people making promises they can't keep? Promises about 'beating the market', picking the best stocks, market timing and guaranteed returns? The answer is pretty simple, really. Although there's academic evidence to back up the point that people warp their reasoning because of their motivations,[3] the answer has been pithily summarized by the writer Upton Sinclair: 'It is difficult to get a man to understand something when his salary depends on his not understanding it.'

Many, many salaries depend on promoting the lines of thought that this book is trying to combat with evidence. By contrast, we, as authors, consider our job is to give you the simplest guide we can, based on the best-regarded evidence. The only financial relationship we have with you is in your buying the book – we won't be making any money out of your investments.

Our six rules

To help make this book simple and memorable, we have distilled the principles to six simple rules. If you want to know what they are right now, turn to page 229, the section that introduces our workbook. But that's not essential. We will gradually introduce them as you go through the content. They will then become more meaningful in the context of the evidence and explanations we give.

By the time you put the book down, we think you will have internalized the meaning of the six rules. You will be able to re-use them time and again.

In Chapters 1–3, we'll help you ground your thinking about your future money in the context of your life. We'll start with what makes life matter, then move on to the financial pressures you face every day and how to master them. In Chapters 4–9, we will go into more detail about how those rules shape investing and managing your money for retirement.

Let's begin that journey.

I

Your Money or Your Life?

This is a book about funding your future life, but for this first chapter, we want you to think through much more than money: this chapter is about your life. After all, money is only a means to an end – living. So what's the point of sorting out your money, only to fund the wrong life?

The key message here is that a happy life is made up of experiences, relationships and time. If you're aiming for money as an end goal, you've got the wrong target.

Your current time pays for your future life

Assuming you are still in your working career, at some point you will need or want to work less, or stop working altogether. At that point, unless you can depend on somebody else's income, you will need to draw on money previously earned or received in order to live. So everyone looking at funding their future life has to strike a balance. How long should they work for? How much should they try to earn while they are working? When should they start to spend it down and live their future life?

You may feel not in control of your day-to-day money in the here and now. In Chapter 3 (*Manage Your Money*, see pages 42–66), we'll set out a simple system that will help you to manage it better, if that's the case. But whatever your here and now is like, you still have choices to make about your future self and the life you hope to have.

Retirement used to be an event. Now, you can choose to make it a gradual process. In the UK, age discrimination legislation means no one can tell you when to stop working. Even if you don't need to continue to earn, you may choose to, for the satisfaction your job brings. Or you may be in a stressful situation precisely because you're trying so hard to earn enough to fund a future life.

So, what's the right balance between the two?

Benjamin Franklin gives food for thought in this marvellous quotation:

Dost thou love life? Then do not squander time, for that's the stuff life is made of.

If time is the stuff of life, how much is your 'now' worth to you and what value do you want to put on your later life?

The case of Jonathan Frostick caught attention during the Covid pandemic.[1] An IT worker for a big UK bank, he was working very long days and one particular Sunday sat down at 4 p.m. to prepare for the week ahead. He then suffered a heart attack.

He recorded the thoughts that struck him at the moment of his heart attack:

- His first two thoughts were anxieties about his immediate work problems.
- Only fourth in the sequence of his thoughts was the fear that his wife might find him dead.

Jonathan Frostick was shocked, and many people caught his sense of shock, that work claimed his first two thoughts in his potentially dying moments. Happily, he survived. Among his reconsidered thoughts during recovery were these:

1 I'm not spending all day on Zoom anymore;
2 I'm restructuring my approach to work;
3 I'm really not going to be putting up with any s#%t at work ever again – life literally is too short.

Perhaps these thoughts and feelings ring bells for you, or perhaps not. Either way, this book will encourage you to think about what's really important for your future and how to pay for it.

This takes us to our first rule. A purpose, a plan and a method to achieve them are the essential foundations of a successful financial

Rule 1: Have a purpose, a plan and a method

future. The first three chapters will walk you through these different dimensions of the rule. The workbook will help you to put them into practice.

How long will you live?

Make a start by thinking about this question. It's a question that is vitally important, challenging to think about, yet as Jonathan Frostick's case underlines, with no certain answer.

People tend to underestimate their likely lifespan. Research by Alison O'Connell, an independent researcher and actuary, looked at population-level estimates of 'subjective lifespan' in six countries.[2] Averaging out, she found that men were likely to live four years longer than they thought they would. Women were likely to live six years longer than their expectations.

What does that longevity look like these days?

- According to the UK's Office for National Statistics, a man aged 50 is likely to live to 81 and a 50-year-old woman is likely to live to 84.[3] But men who live to 70 are likely to live until they are 84 and women until they are 87.
- You will be pleased and perhaps surprised to learn that, on average, a woman now aged 87 is expected to live not just a couple more years, but six more – to age 93. After that age, life expectancy drops down year by year. Only when you get to 100 does an extra two years become the average.

So, the good news is that you may have plenty of 'the stuff of life' to play with. The bad news, of course, is that it all needs paying for and you might end up with too much or too little when it is all over.

A good way to think this through for yourself is to visit livingto100.com. It has a very detailed lifestyle questionnaire that enables the site to estimate how long you will live. Or, if you want a more statistical view, look at longevityillustrator.org. This site is run by the American Academy of Actuaries and the Society of Actuaries. It gives a helpful view of the probability of living beyond a certain number of years.

As we the authors are of the same age and health, it gives us both a 16 per cent probability of living beyond age 95 (we were surprised by how high this was). And we have a 5 per cent probability of living beyond 100. Of course, these are educated guesses but they are quite likely to be better than your own guess, given the evidence noted above.

When planning, it's certainly better to die with too much money than to run out. As a contingency, you could add six or seven years to any final estimate you make of your life expectancy (but remember, you could still be wrong even then and live well beyond your 100th birthday).

Purpose and priorities

A good financial adviser or planner will start by asking you what your purpose and priorities are for later life. They will then work backwards from there to your financial needs, as should you. As the finance writer and cartoonist Carl Richards puts it: 'wise investments are pieces of a larger puzzle.'

Many people thinking about retirement focus on their financial needs and expect the enjoyment of the fruits of their labours to take care of itself. A 2017 YouGov survey found that just 17 per cent of Britons said they 'loved' their job, and almost the same number (16 per cent) said they 'disliked' or 'hated' it.[4] The majority had an attitude either of neutrality, or of 'somewhat' liking their job. Another survey bluntly asserted that 34 per cent of Britons were unhappy in their current jobs.[5] But when the stresses and strains of the here and now are front and foremost in our minds, it's easy to think that the blank canvas of retirement will automatically be better. In fact, it's a canvas that everyone should plan to fill.

If you know your purpose in later life, and are able to articulate your priorities, you'll be better able to answer the question 'how much is my "enough"?' To help you think about purpose, we have studied the evidence on sources of happiness. Obviously a hugely complex and multidimensional question, it touches on fundamental issues that run all the way from basic human impulses to spiritual quests. But we think three themes are definitely worth anyone's consideration. These are the links between *money* and happiness, *time* and happiness, and *experiences* and happiness.

What is the link between money and happiness?

It's a cliché, of course, that money can't buy happiness. Can it be that simple? Like many clichés, it does have some truth behind it, but the simplicity and memorability masks what's really going on.

In the 1970s, the economist Richard Easterlin demonstrated that although the material *wealth* of the United States had changed a great deal in the previous decades, levels of *happiness* had barely improved.[6] This has led to decades of debate. Should governments focus on economic growth if it doesn't make people any happier? If not, what is their point?

Easterlin's work triggered an explosion of surveys and studies. The best available evidence suggests that it told us something true about developed countries, yet it is false for developing countries. As Janusz Czapiński of the University of Warsaw puts it in his paper surveying all this evidence, 'The economics of happiness and the psychology of wealth':

> In poor societies and individuals, income affects well-being but in wealthy societies and individuals, the direction of the relationship is reversed: well-being determines income. Money buys happiness when income is too low to satisfy basic needs, and happiness brings money when income satisfies basic needs.[7]

What does Czapiński mean by 'happiness brings money'? His view of the evidence is that when a society reaches a certain level of economic development, and most people's basic needs are met, that society begins to more comprehensively support collaboration, entrepreneurship and greater economic growth. This is not just because of the efforts of individuals, but a web of connections (and education) they can depend on, sometimes called 'social capital'.

If you are reading this book in the UK or one of the other more affluent countries, the practical upshot is that if you pursue more and more money, it is likely to be subject to a law of diminishing returns. Provided your basic needs are already satisfied, for every extra pound or dollar you get, your happiness *might* increase. But it will increase *less* than it would for someone in a poorer country. To quote another study: 'money buys happiness, but it buys less than most people think.'[8] And there's more. In their paper, 'If Money Doesn't Make You Happy, Consider Time', Jennifer L. Aaker, Melanie Rudd and Cassie Mogilner point out:

> A growing number of studies show that simply thinking about money fosters behaviors that are misaligned with happiness. The mere mention of money leads individuals to be less likely to help others, donate to charity, and socialize with friends and family – behaviors that are tied to personal happiness. Priming money also motivates individuals to work more, which – although productive – tends to be associated with the least happy part of one's day. Finally, subtle reminders of wealth impair people's ability to savor everyday experiences.[9]

That's all very well, but you already knew deep down that you need to think about much more than money. So what do these last three authors have to say about the role of *time* in happiness?

Time and happiness

In their paper, Aaker, Rudd and Mogilner review a variety of psychological evidence from different countries and come up with some very interesting conclusions about time. They say: 'in spite of the belief that money is the resource most central to America's pursuit of happiness, increased happiness requires attention to time.'

Why? In what ways should we pay attention to time?

Well, as they point out, 'time spent is unable to be regained.' This is not true of money – if you've spent it, you could earn, or be given, its replacement. But more fundamentally, they note that time is filled with personal meaning.

Meaningful connections with others can only come about through investment of time. Indeed, there needs to be joint investment of the *same amount* of time. Both personal meaning (memories) and interpersonal connection are much stronger drivers of human happiness than wealth, or spending it. Above all, using time to strengthen relationships with friends and family is likely to bring happiness.

Many authors on happiness (and on retirement) also focus on the often-overlooked happiness of helping others outside our circle of friends and family. Volunteering, working for a charity, becoming a trustee of a charity – all these are ways in which we can not only increase our happiness, but they also increase our sense of control over the time we have.

Control, or freedom, is another crucial dimension of human happiness. It's true that money can help to buy freedom. If you don't like doing the dishes, money will buy you freedom from that in the form of a dishwasher, or even someone to come and do it for you. But it's also true that if you can meet your basic needs in retirement, what you will end up with is much greater *control over your time*. More than money could buy you at any point during your working life. So it's worth thinking about how to make the most of the control that you will end up having over your time – a fundamental freedom that needn't cost you any more money.

Experiences and happiness

A highly influential piece of academic thinking about experiences and happiness is the paper 'If Money Doesn't Make You Happy Then You Probably Aren't Spending It Right' by Elizabeth W. Dunn, Daniel T. Gilbert, and Timothy D. Wilson.[10] Dunn has expanded the thinking into a very good book: *Happy Money: the Science of Smarter Spending*. The original paper starts with a bang:

Wealthy people don't just have better toys; they have better nutrition and better medical care, more free time and more meaningful labor – more of just about every ingredient in the recipe for a happy life. And yet, they aren't that much happier than those who have less. If money can buy happiness, then why doesn't it?

Because people don't spend it right. Most people don't know the basic scientific facts about happiness – about what brings it and what sustains it – and so they don't know how to use their money to acquire it. It is not surprising when wealthy people who know nothing about wine end up with cellars that aren't that much better stocked than their neighbors', and it should not be surprising when wealthy people who know nothing about happiness end up with lives that aren't that much happier than anyone else's.

To justify this opener, they cite evidence that shows people are generally made much happier by spending money on *experiences* than on *things*. One key reason is that most material items hardly change at all. Because they stay the same, we adapt to them quite quickly (they become 'part of the furniture', so to speak). By contrast, good *experiences* not only live in our memory, but can change, and give new pleasure, through the prism of repeated recollection. And this is easily demonstrated. When was the last time you took pleasure in recollecting and savouring the memory of a *thing*, rather than an experience?

(It is true, and the authors point out, there can be a fuzzy line between the two. If you buy an open-top car, will your memories be about the vehicle, or the experiences it gave you? Probably a blend of the two. But more often than not, there is a meaningful dividing line between the two.)

Dunn, Gilbert and Wilson are also advocates of what they call *'pro-social'* spending: money spent on others (be it gifts or shared experiences), or by giving money to charity. They cite research that shows people *overestimate* how much spending money on themselves will make them happy. They also *underestimate* the benefits they will personally derive from spending on others. (In our downloadable workbook, we give 'blank canvases' for your future life, to encourage you to think through this.)

Dunn and co. also advocate a reversal of the credit-card driven culture of 'consume now, pay later'. They argue that by consuming *before* we pay, we lose the benefit of pleasurable anticipation. Pleasurable anticipation increases the happiness we get from buying a thing. And as a side benefit, a more drawn-out approach may divert us from buying, on a whim, things we don't need or won't value.

'Inconspicuous consumption'

A phrase that usefully binds these reflections on money, time and experiences is 'inconspicuous consumption'. We owe this phrase to Robert Frank, who reflected on a great deal of research about happiness and drew many threads together. In his article 'How not to buy happiness' he notes:

> Consumption spending has much in common with a military arms race. A family can choose how much of its own money to spend, but it cannot choose how much others spend. Buying a smaller-than-average vehicle means greater risk of dying in an accident. Spending less on an interview suit means a greater risk of not landing the best job. Yet when all spend more on heavier cars and more finely tailored suits, the results tend to be mutually offsetting, just as when all nations spend more on armaments.[11]

This brings out a key difficulty with material purchases. Not only do we adapt to them much more quickly than we expect, but material things are much more easily compared to what others have. We are psychologically inclined to make such comparisons, and we then find ourselves less satisfied if other people have better things.

What does Frank mean by 'inconspicuous consumption'? Above all, he means the collective and connecting experiences with family and friends noted above and the ways in which we can take better control of our time. But he expands this thinking to (for example) better working hours, shorter commutes and better environmental conditions.

Some of these, of course, are outside our individual control. They need social investment that we would all need to vote for and direct. But those are worth thinking about too. Whatever you earn in your retirement, a simply enormous portion of it will be taken in taxes. You could passively 'pay and forget' this small fortune in taxes, or you could consider it as the kind of spending that enables you to increase happiness for yourself and others. Accordingly, you could try to influence how it is spent. We will have much more to say about this in Chapter 7 (*Manage Your Mix*, see pages 152–86).

Purpose and priorities: think outside the box

There is a further area we invite you to consider as you review your purpose and priorities for your future way of living. It is good to challenge received wisdom about the biggest variables that will affect your money. Making radical choices about all these variables is, of course, much easier if it's just you that you are answerable to, but you can also bring your family into your outside-the-box thinking.

Received wisdom is correct, of course, that you can't control the variable of when you will die, but you can positively or negatively influence it through diet and exercise. Then there are other major variables you can wholly control. Your future life doesn't have to be shaped only by the absolute amount of money you think you will be able to draw on each year and the date of your death.

You have choices you can make about your inheritance. If you want to prioritize leaving money to others, this will dampen down the money you can plan to spend. Or you can prioritize giving your children good financial habits and keep your money for your own life. At the end of Chapter 3 (*Manage Your Money*, see pages 64–6), we give food for thought about why giving children good money habits is more valuable than an inheritance.

You can choose to work for longer, part-time or full-time, for financial or emotional reasons. And indeed, if you are one of those people who have left it very late, and have very little saved, this might be the main decision you need to take about your finances in retirement.

If and when you own a home, you have options. You can downsize, or even rent, in order to release some capital to fund your retirement. Or you can treat it as the piggy bank you may need to pay for social care. More on this also in Chapter 7 (*Manage Your Mix*, see pages 152–86).

You also have choices about where that home is going to be. If you have a UK or US passport, congratulations! In the Henley Passport Ranking Index (a global ranking of passports according to the travel freedom they give their holders), either passport scores seventh equal in a list of 130 countries.[12] This means that you have more options to travel (and in many cases live, whether for a short or a long while) than people from most other countries in the world.

You may be surprised by how many countries both have an excellent standard of living and are substantially cheaper to live in than the UK.

- For example, living in the beautiful town of Porto in Portugal costs about 75 per cent of what the same standard of living will cost in Birmingham, England.
- In Cuenca, the second city of Ecuador, these comparative costs are down to 45 per cent.
- In the vibrant capital of Georgia, Tbilisi, living costs about 38 per cent of a similar standard in the UK.[13]

Take some time to imagine the effect on your retirement planning if you could live on just 40–50 per cent of the costs that apply where you live now. You can visit the numbeo.com site and play around with places that interest you to see what results you find. And you can use Numbeo to compare the cost of living between different cities in the UK, as well. That doesn't mean you have to up sticks and move abroad for the rest of your life. It could be a carefully thought-through emergency plan ('break glass in case of financial difficulty', so to speak). Or it might be a temporary adventure. You could live and learn for two, three, five years as part of a financial and emotional experiment to start (or vary) your retirement years. These are just a few of the major variables – there may be more you can think of that are personal to you.

Jonathan writes: Women's money and women's lives

I want to take a turn into the options and constraints that women face as they think about their future lives. This is a vital topic for both men and women to consider.

In 2019 and 2020 I took part in an investigation run by the Chartered Institute of Insurance called *Insuring Women's Futures*. Although it came from the chartered body for insurance, it looked at women's finances in the round. It shone a light on an enduring scandal. Throughout their financial lives, women are accumulating financial disadvantage after disadvantage. The most striking figure this culminates in is the difference between the average pension pot for women and men at age 65. The average pension pot belonging to a 65-year-old woman in the UK is £35,800 – just one fifth of the average pot of a man the same age.[14] Pensions are pretty much the final scorecard from a lifetime's work. So what does this tell us about how we reward women's working lives?

Now, as ever, the truth is complicated. Not least because some of the disadvantages are equalizing between women in their twenties and thirties and men of the same age. But far from all their disadvantages are fading away. The gender pay gap – women still earn, on average, 15.4 per cent less than men for every hour worked – is the biggest root cause.[15] But suppose the gender pay gap disappeared tomorrow. From what I've seen, I don't believe men and women's financial outcomes would rapidly converge.

Women tend to accumulate financial disadvantages because they miss out on pension contributions when taking time to have children and care for parents. They don't get their fair share of pensions on divorce and they receive male-centric advice from a male-dominated investment industry. Then there are still older women who lack financial confidence, because of the marital and family role society moulded for them. Let's not forget that until 1975, women still had to get their husband or father to sign their credit applications. Unbelievably, they were not viewed as capable of full financial independence.

Women readers will not have missed the irony of two men writing a book and raising these points. But men must be part of any solution. I was proud to be invited by the Chartered Insurance Institute (CII) to help their work and I'm very passionate in raising what I learned in this book.

We have tried to make this book as helpful to women as it is for men (if not more so) and have asked women to read it before publishing it, with that goal in mind. Happily, almost all the thinking here has no different application to women from men, or from same-sex to opposite-sex couples. However, out of those readings and conversations with women readers of this book, I'm taking a moment to address some pension considerations that arise from having a baby.

A working woman who takes maternity leave should check that her employer is living up to their legal obligation on pensions. Employers must make pension contributions over the same period that they are paying statutory maternity pay (and for longer than that if the employment contract is more generous).

After the baby is born, there are obviously lots of choices about the balance between a woman's and any partner's career when it comes to raising and nurturing. These will be very personal. However, the evidence suggests *all* mothers – and their partners – should particularly consider these financial factors:

- Taking a career break, and/or returning to part-time and lesser-paid roles have been the causes of major differences in women's pension outcomes. If you are earning less than you were before the baby came along, consider if you or your partner can fund your pension contributions to keep them at their previous level. A partner (let us suppose one who is working full-time, or earning more) is entitled to pay contributions into your pension *as well as their own*. This means that you can both benefit from your taxable allowance as well as your partner's.
- If you are not working at all, you are still entitled to open a personal pension, or contribute to an existing pension, at the rate of up to £2,880 a year at the time of writing. A valuable tax subsidy will be added, even if an employer is not contributing.

- Up to a child's 12th birthday, the UK government gives non-working mothers National Insurance credits towards their state pension. After that birthday if they want to continue adding contribution years to their state pension, they have to return to work.

It's a minefield of personal, financial and relationship trade-offs but for this reason, everyone it affects should think about it carefully. It could greatly affect their future financial self.

On a separate point, anyone in a marriage should be aware that if divorce occurs, the pensions accumulated may well be the marriage's most valuable assets. Often they can be far more valuable than equity in a property.

More generally, I hope to encourage female readers of this book to own the simple rules it offers and to think very decisively about how they can maximize money and get the widest range of options for their future lives. Common sense would tell you this, but it is also underlined by hard evidence: while there may be differences in attitudes and behaviours between men and women towards managing their money, there are no differences in their emotional and intellectual potential to do so with great success.

Now take action

In our workbook, you have a place to record your thoughts on:

- Your purpose and goals for later life.
- Your thoughts on the major variables: what kind of work you want to do for how long, what kind of place you want to live in, where you want to live and what you hope to leave to others.
- Initial thoughts on what those might mean for your financial needs.
- Your best estimate of how long you will live.

These are big questions and big decisions so take your time to discuss them with those you hold dear. Writing things down is powerful, but revising them after deeper thought even more so.

2

Invest in ... Yourself

In the last chapter, we asked you to forget about money and think about life. Here, we want you to look beyond investing in money and markets and think about your investment in ... yourself.

In our introduction, we wrote about the challenge of meeting the money needs of both your current and future selves. Most people find it easier to spend more on their current life, putting off any sacrifices they need for the future. But your two selves need to reach a mutually beneficial understanding. The key message of this chapter is that if you are happy, stable and financially well-organized, and as skilled and productive as you can be, this is the most fertile ground to sow the harvest that your future self will need.

This is 'our view' because we will be straight with you. Unlike the other chapters in this book, the evidence for what we propose here is somewhat contradictory and uncertain. It stands to reason that increasing your skills, knowledge and connections, educating yourself and stabilizing your finances (which we cover in the next chapter) will all increase your potential earnings. What the jury is out on – from the evidence we have seen – is how much of that is in your direct control. And to the extent that it's not, is it actually in the hands of power networks that surround you? For example, the networks of existing wealth, of hierarchy and of social and racial privilege.

There is a lively academic debate about the return on investment from investing in yourself. We won't divert things with too much of it but as a well-known example, it used to be well accepted that getting a university education gave someone a lifetime earnings 'premium'.

But as the number of people going to university rises, this 'graduate premium' nearly halved over the 25 years to 2016.[1] There's plenty of reason to think it will keep on falling.

Is that an argument *not* to get a degree, provided it's something you aspire to anyway? We don't think so. A degree isn't for everyone. But for those who do study at university, there should be plenty of non-financial benefits alongside the potential for higher pay. So this chapter rests on a commonsense principle: expand your possibilities and keep yourself up to date. We can't provide an evidence-based rule on how far that will take you but we're sure it will take you further than not trying at all.

Invest in ... your earning power

You must *have* money to *invest* money. Unless you are independently wealthy, or stand to receive a life-changing inheritance, we assume that your current earning power is what will fund your future life. Here's the stark fact: every time you get paid, your current self and your future self *both* need to live off it. There's good news, though: you are not alone. You have three additional co-investors (maybe even three-and-a-half) to help you with the important task of investing in your future life. They will help you out in proportion to the amount that you yourself invest so it makes sense to maximize their contribution as much as you can.

Your first co-investor: compound interest
Compound interest is your most valuable co-investor. You don't have to save all the money you need in retirement, because compound interest can earn very large amounts of it for you. Einstein is reputed to have called compound interest 'the eighth wonder of the world'. Even if the attribution is mythical, there are good reasons it has stuck to him. The full quote attributed to him is: 'Compound interest is the eighth wonder of the world. He who understands it, earns it. He who doesn't, pays it.'

Here's a simple example: £50 a month for 50 years. Suppose you are aged 20 and you start putting away just £50 a month, and you do that for 50 years (increasing your contribution of £50 in line with

2 per cent inflation, so it keeps its value). You will have put away £30,000 in today's money by the time you are 70. But if you can earn an 8 per cent return on those savings for that same 50-year period, the compounding from reinvestment will add more than £149,000. In fact, it will have gifted you 83 per cent of the final amount of £179,000 (in today's money) you can call on after 50 years.

An 8 per cent return, racing ahead of 2 per cent inflation, may sound extremely fanciful. Certainly, if you invest cash in a savings account, it's quite inconceivable. But US micro-caps, an accessible class of investment in shares, have a long-term average rate of return of 14.8 per cent,[2] so 8 per cent is a very cautious view of what is achievable over that extremely long run.

Were you to achieve 14.8 per cent over 50 years, your final booty would be more than £2,700,000 in today's money – from the £30,000 you put in!

Your second co-investor: time

And this introduces us to your second great co-investor – time. Compound interest depends on time for its magic, the more the merrier. But the great additional benefit of time is that it smooths out risk. Although an investment in micro-cap shares has a fantastic 14.8 per cent historical average return, in the short term, it's alarmingly risky. It comes with wild 'mood swings' – returns may soar by as much as 20 per cent, or plummet by 20 per cent.

Over a short period, say, five years, this is likely to offer a rollercoaster ride that will drain the blood out of the average investor's face. But year by year, over the much longer term, wild swings will get smoothed out. You will be increasingly likely to get a return that approaches the long-term average.

Now if you are in your forties or fifties, you may be thinking: 'But time is not on my side!' If so, a very significant change took place in the UK in 2015 that probably should alter your view. Before 2015, if you had invested money for retirement, the rules in place made you *cash it all at once*, and worse, at the *beginning* of your retirement. Most people could only choose to buy an 'annuity' once they wanted to retire. That is, they gave their stock-market based savings to a pension company, all in one immense payment. In return, the pension company gave them a guaranteed, usually inflation-proofed, income for the rest of their life.

You can still choose to buy an annuity but since the dramatic change to the rules in 2015, you don't have to (and annuities have provided progressively worse value since then). Now you can keep your pension money invested in the stock market so it can keep on growing.

This 2015 change to the UK law changes the significance of time for older people too – even if you are now in your fifties or sixties. If you are keeping your pension money invested in the stock market from age 65, you need to consider 25 to 35 years of investment.

Now it's true that because you will be spending down your pension investments, as well as letting the rest of it grow, the smoothing effects of time on risk don't leave you in quite as carefree a state as they would do while you are still earning but the key fact remains: you are investing for a very long time. And time is therefore a vital co-investor when it comes to compounding growth and reducing risk.

Your third co-investors: your employer (and the tax man)
If you have an employer, as of 2021 they are legally required to make contributions to your pension when you earn more than £6,240 per year. They must contribute 3 per cent of the value of your salary to your pension, provided you also contribute 5 per cent. But your 5 per cent is deducted *from* your salary. The employer pays 3 per cent *in addition* to your salary.

Some employers will voluntarily contribute even more than the 3 per cent the law requires of them. Or they may apply 3 per cent if you earn more than £50,270, which the law doesn't require them to do.[3]

Robin writes: A word about 'final salary' pensions

We need to divert for a quick jargon buster here ...

A very small number of employers still offer a guaranteed pension. This is sometimes called a 'final salary' pension, or a 'defined benefit' (DB) pension. Either way, the point is that it gives a guaranteed income (like an annuity). What you will get is

---

linked – there are various ways – to the salary you earned with your employer during your career. We have little to say about this type of pension in this book, because they are very simple and very attractive – they solve the problem of uncertainty.

If you have access to one of these pensions, take it. If you are confident it will pay you enough to live on, you will probably get most value from just the first three chapters of this book and Chapter 5 (*Avoid Charlatans and Sharks*, see pages 87–113). A more likely scenario is that you don't have access to a DB pension. Or if you do, you realize that although very attractive, it will only provide a proportion of what you need to live on in your future life.

If your DB pension is good, but not good enough, the rest of this book is still highly relevant. You will need to supplement it with other investments. If you invest these in a pension (and that is the most effective way of investing for almost everyone who is employed), then the jargon for your invested pension (virtually everyone's pension these days) will be a 'defined contribution' (DC) pension. (You will see the letters DB and DC again and again in this book.)

The pensions world is full of fancy language. In this case the jargon masks an uncomfortable truth. DC means you will know how much you have put in, but you can't be certain how much you will get out. And there's plenty more jargon. We have tried to get rid of as much as possible, but when you interface with products and advisers, it will rear its ugly head again so we will explain key terms the first time we use them. In case anyone is still lost, we've included a glossary, or 'jargon buster' at the back of the book (see pages 235–42). And there is also an index at page 261.

A 3 per cent contribution from your employer to a defined contribution pension may not sound like a lot but it's not to be sniffed at. In Chapter 4 of this book (*Capture Market Returns*, see pages 67–86), you will see what a difference even 0.5 per cent (half of 1 per cent) will make to your future wealth. A 3 per cent uplift is a huge gift.

You also get tax relief – in effect, an extra contribution from HMRC of 20 per cent, or more, of the contributions you make. We have more to say about this in later chapters. It benefits from the magic of compounding, so it is also an investor, but as you are taxed when you finally withdraw your pension, it's not a free gift to quite the same extent as your employer's contribution.

Jonathan writes: Two murky secrets of UK pensions policy

Bringing together some previous threads in this chapter, I see fundamental contradictions and problems in the way our retirement saving system is now set up. Despite many improvements, based on well-meaning efforts, the system still has traps set for the savers it's trying to help. Here's how they affect you.

Before 2015, a system of 'auto-enrolment' in pensions was gradually established. This makes employers pay 3 per cent and employees pay 5 per cent. By default, that's what's there for most people. But it's optional. You can opt out of your auto-enrolment into a pension and stop all payments. We wouldn't suggest you do, but you can.

Auto-enrolment therefore relies to a large degree on blissful ignorance. It has been hugely successful, in these terms, because far fewer people have chosen to opt out than anyone ever expected. Millions have accepted the default position. A significant minority probably don't even know they *are* contributing to a pension. This means that the number of people saving for their retirement has gone up by tens of millions. Which is, of course, in everyone's interest. The previous situation was unsustainable.

Despite this success, there are still two rather grubby secrets. The first is this: contributing 5 per cent of your salary for retirement, though set as the default by the government and supplemented by both employers and a tax subsidy, is unlikely to be enough to fund the life you want. It may be if you start at 18, because of the magic of compound interest. But if you start even a handful of years later, it's likely more will be needed. Unfortunately, most people reading this book will need to think about contributing more than 10 per cent.

Given that auto-enrolment relies on you *not* making choices and *not* thinking about your pension, that's not a great situation. Most people probably think they are on the right track already. And if the 5 per cent rule is backed by the government, why wouldn't they? But here's the second secret: the sudden switch people need to make from *not* thinking, to thinking hard! The 'pension freedoms' changes in 2015 mean that to get the best out of the system, from the day you retire you need to turn into some sort of investment manager. It gives you ultimate control over what will be for most people, the largest and least certain investment you've ever made.

Those wanting to retire as early as the law allows must switch from blissful ignorance aged 54 to being a successful manager of a portfolio of investments from the day of their 55th birthday. (From 2028, there will be a jump of two years and it will be age 57.) How can people turn on this sixpence and turn into capable money managers, if they have hardly considered how their pension is being invested for the whole time money has been going in? That's a key reason why I wrote this book: I want to help you engage and understand, rather than be carried along as a passive bystander.

Take stock

With these three co-investors (perhaps four depending on your view of HMRC) at your side, it makes sense for you to maximize your current earning power. You will want to contribute as much as possible to fund your future life alongside your present life. And this will tend to maximize what your employer pays, too.

This isn't a careers book, so we won't try to tell you how to do that. But we do highly recommend Brian Fetherstonhaugh's book *The Long View*, a powerful general look at how to maximize your career.[4] Brian points to the US *Survey of Consumer Finances*, which indicates that 85–90 per cent of people's wealth is accumulated *after* their 40th birthday. A dramatic and strangely heartening figure! (It would appear from the 2018 Household Wealth and Assets Survey that the UK figure might be nearer 80 per cent, but that's still pretty dramatic too.)[5] This helps Brian articulate an important theme, which is that you should treat your career itself as a long-term investment.

We assume that you are not necessarily reading this book with the intention of joining the FIRE ('Financial Independence, Retire Early') movement. This is a loose grouping of people with overlapping habits and beliefs, who save at extraordinarily aggressive rates in order to stop working at 45, 40 or even 35. Their plan is to save what they trust will last them for the rest of their lives. (If that's your choice, you will indeed be able to apply lessons from the later chapters to your own circumstances.) We're not against FIRE but we're assuming that for most readers FIRE will be too risky or ambitious – so most readers of this book will have a more typical working lifespan of 30+ years. For people with that working lifespan, we don't advocate that you should simply focus on earning as much as you can, as early as you can. There could be bad life consequences to accompany the higher earnings. You might burn out; you could choose the wrong path. You might miss out on family and relationships.

We echo Brian's very sensible view that it's a good idea, for the first phase of your career, which may well last until your 40th birthday, to *experiment with different things.* Find out what you are really good at, and how you can work most effectively with other people. If you do that, you can move into the highest-earning phase of your career knowing your worth. Moreover, that worth will rest on a solid foundation of achievement and happiness. Recognize, however, that by experimenting in your career, your earnings might not progress in a straight line.

Many writers on retirement have advocated a rule of thumb about how many multiples of your current salary you should have saved by certain ages for your retirement. We will go into planning how much you need for your retirement in more detail in the next chapter. There is no perfect rule but Fidelity advocated a simple rule of thumb and it's useful to introduce it now for you to consider. Note that it was designed for savers in the United States but we still think it's a valuable stimulus for UK readers.

By age...	30	40	50	60	67
	I x	3 x	6 x	8 x	10 x
Aim to save	*the value of your gross salary (the salary you earn at each age above), in savings set aside wholly for your retirement — and invested for growth*				

Source: Fidelity[6]

Some of the test readers of this book found Fidelity's view horribly daunting but remember, most people acquire most of their wealth *after* age 40. And you also have control over all sorts of major variables (look back to the last chapter – *Your Money or Your Life?*, see pages 13–26). Fidelity are setting out what they think will give the optimum results for the average person. You may not need those optimum results for your particular circumstances.

Fidelity's thinking builds in the power of compound interest. What you need by your sixties, as we've stated above, doesn't have to be saved directly from your pocket, provided you are investing for growth. But of course, the later you start, the less compound interest will help and the bigger the role your own contributions will need to play.

Whatever you think about Fidelity's high-level principles, we hope you agree that it underlines the second part of Rule 1. You

Rule 1: Have a purpose, a plan and a method

need a plan, even if you decide not to aim as high as Fidelity recommends. That's what our workbook will help you to sort out.

Robin and Jonathan write: An important word about putting this book into practice

We want you to make good use of the recommendations in this book, but we can't know your circumstances so you will need to make sure they are right for you and adapt them accordingly. If you receive regulated financial advice in the UK, your adviser will be liable for any bad advice they give. The idea is that they should get to know your circumstances in some detail. They can then give you specific recommendations about what you should do with your money, including investments.

Obviously, this book, although it does set up an intimate relationship between writers and reader, can't possibly replicate that one-to-one interaction. There's not much symmetry to our relationship! You will learn quite a lot about us, but by the end of writing this book, it's still impossible for us to know about your *individual* circumstances.

The traditional way that books such as this one have dealt with this issue is to get lawyers to write a disclaimer. These are usually hard to understand but to the extent that they make any sense, they look like they are undermining the very purpose of the book. We didn't want to leave you to make sense of a disclaimer, we decided to use this page to draw these commonsense points to your attention:

- This aims to be a practical book, setting out simple general rules you can use to plan your finances, to fund your future life. It also gives you access to a downloadable workbook. The principal purpose of the workbook is to help you answer your own key questions, against the backdrop of your own circumstances.
- By their very nature, simple rules apply to *most* people's circumstances, *most* of the time.
- Your circumstances may need an adaptation of our general rules. Or, critical circumstances of the law, tax, or money system may change after we have published this book. (All the facts in this book have been checked as of April 2022.)
- For all these reasons, this book therefore cannot offer you regulated financial *advice* – and won't try! But it's still, we hope, a very useful book. We intend that you will be able to use it to learn about money management, how our rules could apply to your individual circumstances and then how to double-check your thinking. We devote all of the final chapter (Find a

First-Rate Adviser, see pages 202–28), to all the different ways you could do this very important double-check.

And with that said to give it meaningful context, here is the inescapable legal bit:

While every effort has been made to ensure that information in this book is accurate, no liability can be accepted for any loss incurred in any way whatsoever by any person relying solely on the information contained herein.

No responsibility for loss occasioned to any person or corporate body acting or refraining to act as a result of reading material in this book can be accepted by the authors, or anyone working for them. The authors do not have any control over nor any responsibility for any third-party websites or other information sources referred to in this book.

Keep your income safe

Given the life-changing importance of your future income, you might think that taking out insurance against losing it would be quite popular. In fact, according to *Which?*, just 9 per cent of the people they surveyed had this kind of insurance.[7] By contrast, nearly twice as many had private health insurance. Objectively, it's a strange choice. If you have a major health crisis, the NHS will give you pretty much unlimited support but if you suffer a permanent inability to earn, the UK's social security system will only offer you the most meagre replacement.

For young people in particular, their *human capital* – in other words, the cumulative value of their potential future income from work – is the single most valuable asset they possess. The bottom line is, short of winning the lottery or receiving a large inheritance, you're going to need a regular income to cover your outgoings – including your regular savings and investments. Protecting that human capital from the risk of a prolonged illness or disability should be an absolute priority.

We would say that your mid-forties onwards is a particular danger zone. You will be reaching your highest earning potential yet you may find it especially hard to find a similar higher-earning job if you are made redundant. People over 50 are three times more likely to find themselves being among the 'long-term' unemployed, seeking work for two years or more.[8]

The first step, then, is to check whether you are covered by a staff income protection insurance policy through your employer. If you are not, or if you are self-employed, you should consider buying a personal income protection policy.

If you have children or a partner who is financially dependent on you, you should also have a life insurance policy. It should provide for them and repay any debts not covered by your assets in the event of your premature death. But a word of warning here: whether it's income protection or life insurance you are buying, the jargon to look out for is a straightforward *term assurance* policy. *Term* means when it ends. For example, you can set your income protection to end at your likely retirement age, or your life insurance to end when your youngest child finishes university.

Some policies offer an element of insurance *and* investment, and pay you a cash amount even if there is never a claim. Such policies might seem attractive, but most people should avoid them. Products that try to do two very different things well either cost too much or do both badly.

Finally, once you've secured the best deal and set up a direct debit, see it as money well spent and enjoy the peace of mind it gives you. Ideally, you and your loved ones will never have to benefit from the insurer paying out. But, if the worst happens, you or they will be very glad you made provision.

Invest in ... your knowledge about investing

There's one special form of life-long investment in yourself that we want to draw your attention to as this chapter closes. That is our recommendation that you continually keep your knowledge up to date about what's happening in the world of money.

It's very important to note what we're *not* saying here. We have a lot more to say about successful investing in later chapters but the key thought to hold in your mind is that successful investing is much more about history and psychology than it is about the shifting sands of economic *news*.

There is an enormous industry of communications professionals and journalists who make a living out of promoting financial ideas. We view these as the investing equivalent of 'fast fashion'. Yet they find an audience. There are too many investors who read the press, then keep on fidgeting around with their investment portfolio to fix *this* problem or grasp *that* opportunity, which they've read out about in the news that morning. They rack up huge transaction costs – but by the law of averages, they won't outsmart the market.

So by and large, following too much *news* about investing is a bad idea. The better way is to apply evidence-based *rules* and leave your investments to grow. We believe our six rules come from that thinking and so they are evergreen but the circumstances in which they need to be *applied* will change a little every month. We're talking here less about the world of investing and more about the world of everyday money management – and tax. New regulations and laws reshape markets and consumer behaviours. New digital products disrupt banks and other traditional providers. Brilliant new tools come into existence that can help you manage your money with ever more sophistication and at ever lower cost.

It's just possible, in the long run, that there will be new forms of money. Bitcoin (currently a highly speculative 'lottery ticket' – not an investment!) was predicted to disappear in a puff of virtual smoke but through many ups and downs, it's lasted a decade. In 2022 it sank fast, disproving the belief that it had become a store of value, like gold. It's very unlikely that this will reverse, but over a very long period of investing, it's at least worth being aware of new trends, especially when they endure for a decade or more. (But *not* in order to get in early.)

The great news about your life-long learning is that you've already made a fantastic start – you're already on page 39 of this book.

We recommend the Saturday 'Money' section of *The Financial Times* as a moderate weekly diet. Your mileage may vary – its editorial values may change, although they haven't shifted dramatically for many years. Below, Jonathan writes to set out why he currently values it so much.

Jonathan writes: The weird and wonderful world of The Financial Times *and the solid score from* The Evidence-Based Investor

On weekdays, *The Financial Times*, uniquely among national newspapers, appears to be written for those who live on another planet. Of course, the people who need to read what it says find it very valuable, so this is rather cheeky of me, but as someone with my feet firmly on planet Earth, there's definitely a limit to how much I can read about companies and markets.

The Saturday edition of *The Financial Times* is a very different beast. The main part of the paper still has long and strange lists of financial figures and intricate stories about companies in Uzbekistan that are broadening their offer beyond cement – but the other sections take you in a much more colourful direction. There is *How to Spend It*, an impossibly glossy supplement full of adverts for unimaginably expensive things – private jets and yachts, or heli-skiing tours of the Kamchatka Peninsula in Russia. But its sheer surrealism (and visual panache) gives me a great deal of voyeuristic entertainment.

Then there is the *FT Money* section. I find this to be very balanced, very informative, and it features lively writers who will give you lots of useful detail. I believe I have learned 80 per cent of what I know about money management from reading this section over the last 15 years of my life. It is true that this section has content for the super-rich, so it ventures into areas such as private family trusts that most of us will never have any need for. But even these articles touch on basic principles of tax and money management. These are useful points for mere mortals to have drummed into them again and again. Plus, rich people's problems are much more interesting than their yachts...

If you want one mainstream media source to keep up to date with money, tax and investment, a Saturday routine with *FT Money* is as good a place to start as any.

And one more thing. There is *one* constantly updated source about investing that I do suggest you keep up to date with, if only to help yourself stay on the straight-and-narrow path. My co-author Robin refused to blow his own trumpet for it, but I will happily do so!

I'm talking about Robin's website, *The Evidence-Based Investor*. He's much too modest about this treasure trove of information and highly informed views, with an archive going back to 2015. And it's free! Following Robin on social media will mean that you are updated with all the latest information that goes onto his site. This site will point you to the best new books on money management and investment. We are great believers in books. If you only consume financial information from media and newspaper outlets, you should be continually cautious. Media have a constant need to say something new and they will tend to say it based on press releases provided by people with products to sell.

Now take action

Where are you in your career?

- How long would you like to work and what would you ideally like to be earning by the time you retire?
- What have you set aside to fund your retirement already and how does that match up to Fidelity's rule-of-thumb principles?
- How do you think your career and your earning power still need to develop?
- What skills and knowledge do you think you need to improve your career and earning power?
- How are you investing in people and connections to put you in a good place for future work and earnings?
- Have you thought through whether and how you should secure your income with insurance?

Only you can answer these questions, so you can use our downloadable workbook to reflect on them.

3

Manage Your Money

Processing and taking action on what we said in the last chapter will, of course, take a while but this chapter will take as its starting point the assumption that you *will* do what you can to maximize your income and then make plans to see what you can do to maximize it further in the future. That done, you will still need to make the most of *all* the money you have flowing in. You need to squeeze as much as possible out of every payday – and pay your future self in a fair way, alongside your current self. You need ... a method.

In many chapters of this book, we hope you will learn some things that are totally new to you. We should warn you – in *this* chapter, you will already know and understand the basic principles. *Everyone* knows that it's good to budget and that out of that budget they should set aside money for saving. The difficulty many people have is not about knowing *what* to do, it's about doing it. Here, we aim to give you the tools to do what you know you need to do.

This is a really important chapter for you if you:

- feel you are not on top of your money;
- don't have a budget;
- or don't separate out key categories of spending and saving like household bills, holidays and a fund for emergencies.

If you do indeed do all that already, we recommend you at least skim these pages to see if you can pick up something new. (But if you decide to skip forward, turn to the subsection of this chapter titled 'How much money do I need in retirement?' on page 53.)

If you are *not* on top of your day-to-day money management, the good news is it's never been easier to automate it, so it's never

Rule 1: Have a purpose, a plan and a method

been less tedious to keep on top of it all. Automate everything you possibly can. That way, you can focus on life, rather than money.

If you've not automated everything you can think of, we hope you will learn new things in this chapter too.

Jonathan writes: From muddle to Monzo

I am reasonably good at it now, but I have not always been on top of money management. In my twenties and thirties and even until my early forties, any estimate I made about how much was in my bank account was likely to be plus or minus several hundred pounds. I bounced in and out of overdrafts as a result, paying a small fortune in fees. And I didn't have a financial plan.

I saw my father laboriously keeping all his receipts and entering them into a spreadsheet, then reconciling them every month against his bank statement. What an example he set! Yet I could never have replicated his patience. I was too lazy for that ... Luckily, I earned a decent salary. And I was (following instinct rather than any of the simple rules set out here) investing in property, which turned out reasonably well. This meant that through luck, I avoided the worst consequences of my money management mistakes and omissions. However, I do wonder how much my money management would have improved if banking technologies were still exactly the same today as they were 15 years ago. It is now vastly easier to keep track of your money and to automate payments. These have made an enormous difference to me, because they have taken away a lot of the tedium.

When I first started banking, it was with First Direct, which was very advanced for its time. It was a telephone bank! Finally, you didn't need to queue inside a branch (and in those days, branches closed in the mid-afternoon) to make something happen. This was immensely liberating. But to get stuff done, you still needed

43

to telephone somebody and therefore go through some irksome security questions. Postal statements and then cash machines were the most natural way of finding out how much money was in your account. As a result, I was usually behind reality.

The game-changer for me has been mobile phone banking and biometric identification (first by fingerprint, but more recently, facial recognition). The means of managing your money is on your phone, a finger-swipe away. So many barriers that were excuses for not doing it have more or less evaporated. And in the UK, we are lucky to have one of the most vibrant 'fintech' (financial technology) industries in the world. This has led to a flowering of innovation. And most of it is free at the point of use. This really is a golden age for better money management.

Monzo Bank has been one the most influential fintech 'challengers' to mainstream banks. We say more about bank-based budgeting apps below. Monzo is not the only bank that offers a great budgeting service. By the time you read this, there may be better ones. In my case, I learned about Monzo because of research done by the Money Advice Service (the government body for which I worked). People who were struggling to manage their money spoke about the bank and its app in glowing terms. I decided to give it a try and I've never looked back. So in contributing to this chapter, I'm drawing on hard-won personal experience. I'm also drawing on research I've encountered about what most helps people to manage their money well from day to day.

The good news is: you're not born good at it, so you can always learn and in this book, you can learn from our mistakes. Indeed, if someone as lazy as me about admin can get on top of it, I must have found a way that is relatively pain-free!

This chapter sets out our recipe for managing your money day-to-day based on eight keywords. We are suggesting that you **accept, divide, track, stabilize, prioritize, trim, maximize** (and **teach**). That may sound like a lot but one will flow into another and we hope you will find it an easy and logical flow. Let's take each in turn.

Accept

Money has lots of complicated feelings attached. If you are not managing your everyday money to the best of your knowledge, you are probably battling difficult feelings. These could include *guilt* about things you know you should have done but have not done to date, *worry* or even *panic* about the consequences that you fear are building up and *regret* about opportunities that you think you should have already taken.

Shelley H. Carson and Ellen J. Langer of Harvard University, in their research paper 'Mindfulness and Self-Acceptance', talk about the 'trap' of thinking in 'rigid categories' and how this limits our ability to find self-acceptance.[1] They make a distinction between looking at your past experiences in a 'mindful' versus a 'mindless' way. The 'mindless' way, they say, sees the past through rigid categorizations. It frames past behaviours and mistakes as absolutely right or absolutely wrong. In that way it dramatizes and cements the pain and power they can still cause.

A 'mindful' way leaves behind these rigid categories. People using a 'mindful' approach *explore* past experiences and mistakes from multiple perspectives. This makes it easier for them to both accept what has happened, then move beyond it.

Are you finding it difficult to move beyond strong emotions and a feeling of helplessness about your money situation? If so, it may be helpful for you to look at what you have done both from a critical perspective – what are the difficult consequences that have flowed from not managing your money? But just as importantly, try out a forgiving perspective. What are all the reasons why it was perfectly natural for you to behave in the way that you did?

Try looking at your decisions and behaviours from the point of view of multiple other people, including your harshest critics and your most supportive friends. And remind yourself that the consumer societies we live in create multiple, sophisticated pressures to prioritize our present over our future. We are encouraged every day to use credit instead of saving for something, to treat spending as leisure and saving and self-restraint as boring and unfashionable. You might say that almost all of the advertising industry is designed to apply these pressures to you. Almost all of it exists to tempt you into current consumption. That's billions of pounds of persuasion a year, up against your will and intellect.

Use the approach above to explore and accept your feelings about these pressures and what you may consider to be previous money mistakes. We make a place for you to record these in the workbook.

A recurring theme of this book is to encourage you not to worry about things you can't control (Rule 5). What you have done in the past, and your current situation up to now, fall into exactly that category. Look at them in a mindful way and then move to take action.

Jonathan writes: Help is available for unmanageable debt

Working for the Money Advice Service, I learned a great deal about problem debt. That organization (and the Money and Pensions Service, which succeeded it) was responsible for distributing tens of millions of pounds of funding to debt advice charities every year. I learned that about a tenth of the UK population were in debt so deep, they needed to take independent advice about how to deal with it. By 2021, that number had risen to nine million.[2] I heard heartbreaking stories about the relationship breakdowns, mental health problems and physical health problems that result from overwhelming debt.

The government measures the number of people who are over-indebted by surveying how many people either feel their debts are a heavy burden, or have missed paying two or more essential bills in the last six months. Only you can tell whether your debts are indeed unmanageable but if you can say yes to either of these red flags, you should certainly explore getting the independent view of a debt adviser – who will work for you. For free.

Thanks to government funding, everyone can get free, impartial debt advice. As part of that advice, the adviser can contact your creditors and renegotiate the payment schedule for your debt. In some cases, creditors will write off part of your debts as part of the renegotiation.

It will be extremely difficult to fund your future life if you are managing a large amount of higher-interest debt that you are not repaying at a steady, affordable rate. Except for pension contributions that trigger the maximum contributions from your employer, any further money that you might be tempted to put aside into a pension will almost certainly be better spent reducing your debt. Otherwise the penalties you will pay in debt interest will wipe out any investment gains from your pension pot.

If you are seriously over-indebted, it is probably better to return to this book as soon as you have taken stock of your situation with an independent, impartial debt adviser funded by charity or government. A free tool to help you find a debt adviser is available on the MoneyHelper website.

Divide

Do you have just one bank account? If so, we ask you to make two, to move on to our next step in managing your money. Keep your main account, the one that your earnings go into, to pay household bills, rent and the like. If you don't have a second account, apply for one. It will help you to divide, and therefore track your variable spending.

If you already have a second account (with a payment card), you can repurpose it to help you with this step but it may be useful to explore opening an account with a new provider. There are many better account providers for this step than some of the traditional banks. Monzo Bank is a good place to start, but it has strong rivals such as Starling Bank. Even mainstream banks such as Barclays and HSBC are beginning to build budgeting tools into their current accounts. At a bare minimum, all you need to do is ask your bank if you can have a second account for spending purposes. If they won't give it to you at no cost, approach one that will – moneysavingexpert.com has a regularly updated guide to the 'Best bank accounts'.[3] Then make sure that you can very easily access the second account – ideally through your mobile phone. Remove as many barriers as possible to logging in to it (for example, by setting up fingerprint or face identification if your phone supports that).

Track

The next step in the journey to managing your current money is to track it. There's a quick way of doing this and a lazy way that takes longer.

The quick way
Download your last three months of bank statements for all your spending and go through them with three marker pens. Use different colours to highlight each transaction: one colour for what you paid for bills, a different colour for any variable spending, another for holidays. Then you will need to add up the total for each colour. When that's done, proceed to the next step in the 'Stabilize' section below. This will take a couple of hours of careful effort.

The alternative is what we call the lazy way.

The lazy way
Automation makes this tracking incredibly easy for lazy people, but the trade-off is that it will take longer. The automated route is this: when you get the card for your extra account, set yourself a simple rule and stick to it rigidly. For the next three months, for anything other than a bill, you always pay for it using the payment card for your second account. Food, entertainment, holidays, presents – if it's not a bill, put all your spending on that one account. So that you record as much detail as possible, use as little cash as possible. If you need to get some, withdraw it in small amounts from that same account.

If you have credit cards, or other accounts, put the other cards away in an envelope so that you're not tempted to pay from different accounts. This would fragment your spending record and make tracking more difficult.

You *will* need to guesstimate how much money you have to feed into the new account in order not to run into an overdraft. But don't worry about this too much. Put a reasonable amount in based on a guess, then check it frequently and feed it frequently. This doesn't take much foresight – just monitoring. Transfers from one account to another usually take minutes.

Get a card for your partner if it needs to be a new joint account and be sure they understand why you are asking them to follow the same rule.

Why does this discipline matter so much? Because it will make it easy to build up a comprehensive account of your more unpredictable spending in *one place*. By running it for three months, the picture will be reasonably representative and rounded.

Many banks have extra features that make this tracking even easier. Monzo automatically bundles up your spending into categories based on where you bought from. So if it's from a cinema, your spending gets filed under a category of 'entertainment'.

(Monzo also pops up an alert on your phone every time you pay. This sounds inconsequential, but you'd be amazed at the difference it makes to have a visible signal of the cost of spending, every time you spend. Without this signal, you get the gratification of buying and receiving what you have paid for, but you're not reminded that money has gone out of your account to pay for it. Monzo creates a better balance between the two.)

After three months, you should have a good set of data to look at. Many banks will let you download it in some form that you can pull into a spreadsheet. Now you have three months of data, you can stabilize your finances.

Stabilize

The first thing that you need to do to stabilize is to work out the average monthly spend for your variable spending, your bills and pick out your holiday costs. Just add up the totals for the three months and divide by three.

Holidays are a significant proportion of people's expenditure and people find it hard to plan for and predict the costs. That's why it's a good idea to hive off your holiday and leisure travel costs into a separate sum. (This might be better worked out as an annual sum and then divided by 12 if you need to gradually fund it out of your monthly income.) Then think about whether there has been any unusual event in the three months that means you should adjust the average a little.

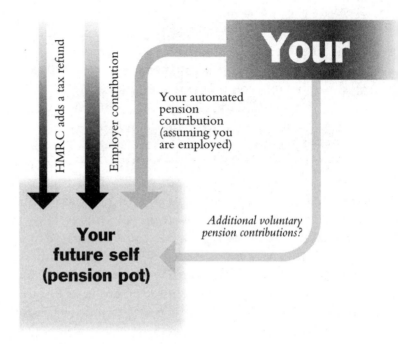

Our recommendation is to bundle up in your 'bills' calculation not just utilities and council tax, but subscriptions, car MOT costs, recurring insurance, mortgage – *everything* that is predictable and recurring on a monthly or annual basis. You should end up with three numbers:

- the amounts you need to pay your monthly and annual bills and expenses;
- your monthly variable expenses and;
- your annual (built up monthly) holiday expenses.

Prioritize

Now we invite you to think about the big picture of your finances, not just for your current self, but your future self. The diagram above can help you to visualize it all.

On the left, you have the money that needs to flow regularly to fund your future self. For most people that will go into some kind of pension fund. If you are employed, you will likely be set up with a

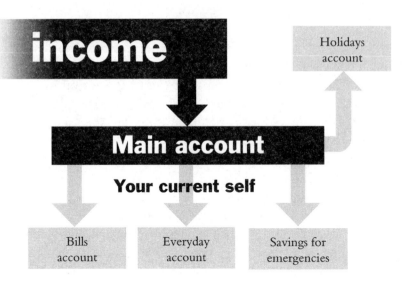

default pension contribution (explained in Chapter 2 – *Invest in ... Yourself*, see pages 27–41). If so, your employer, and HMRC via tax relief, will also be putting money into your pension pot.

If your employer is offering to pay money into a pension, but you have opted out of contributing, we recommend that you fix that immediately. As you can see, you are missing out on contributions from two extra sources. (And if you are self-employed, you would still be missing out on the HMRC additional funding.)

On the right, you have the money for your current self. We recommend you now create a further three accounts so that you can manage your current money most effectively. The system works like this:

- Your salary gets paid into your main account.
- From this, you then set up an automated monthly debit to pay the average amount you need for your household bills into a 'bills account'. This means that you will have a very clear ring-fenced view of those bills. This will give you peace of mind that you can pay them. It will also help you to focus on keeping the total cost of the bills low as you review

them annually. Rent or mortgage should also be paid from this account.

- The new account you set up to track your spending now becomes your 'everyday account'. From your main account, set up another automated payment – to fund the monthly spending that you estimate you need for this everyday account. That way, if you overspend on everyday spending, you will need to actively add more from your main account. This is better than digging into the extra money without particularly knowing or noticing.

- We also recommend that you set up a 'holiday account' and make regular payments into this too. Use the payment card from that account for all your holiday spending, from booking travel to paying for everything, wherever you holiday. We recommend separating a holiday account mainly because people tend not to plan for how much they spend on holidays, or keep up with costs when they do. But there is an additional good reason to have a separate account: you may save money if you use a completely different bank or provider. Some specialist providers offer much lower transaction costs for dealing in foreign money than traditional banks – whether you are converting it, withdrawing cash or spending on a card while you are abroad. Wise (formerly Transferwise) is a good example at the time of writing: if you convert money into the local currency, then pay with the Wise card abroad – you will have no further processing fees for each payment. Revolut is a rival with a similar offer.

- Finally, we recommend that you have a separate savings account (or accounts) – for emergencies, at the very least. It is best if those earn interest, so there are options, which we discuss below in the 'maximize' section.

If you use this system, you will be dividing up your money into separate pots and you will automatically, each month, be transferring the optimum amount from your main account into each individual pot. This is a 'natural' method of budgeting – no spreadsheets are required. All you need to do is keep an eye on it at the level of the four or five automated payments each month and whether they need tweaking.

If you're worried about what you are spending *within* a pot, just scroll through the statement for that account to see what you've spent it on. If you overspend within that pot, you will have to actively top it up from your main account. This is healthy and helpful – you will have to notice and so you will have to think about it.

This book won't try to make firm recommendations about how to handle these accounts if you have a spouse or partner. That will very much depend on your feelings about money and how you view relationships. Given Chapters 1 and 2, we obviously view a happy long-term relationship as a key part of a successful future life so even though we don't dedicate much space in this book to the question of money and relationships, that's not because we don't think it's important. It would make our book have lots of highways and byways if we tried at every turn to account for all the different ways people might handle money in a relationship. It's simpler for you to act on this book, we believe, if we suggest rules that work for an individual. They can easily be adapted to the dynamic of your relationship once you understand how best they will work for you. However, Robin does give his own experience on this a little later in this chapter.

Some people choose to share everything, some to keep everything separate and many choose a hybrid but if your money with your partner is a bit of a blur and a muddle, our system is very easy to adapt both to include them and to make things simpler and clearer. If you want to keep some of your money separate from your partner, but to share key joint expenses, they can be joint holder of some – or all – of the subsidiary accounts. You can each make regular payments into them, while your own main accounts will be separate. But as you set up these automated monthly amounts, now is a time to prioritize. Ask yourself: do you need to tilt the balance further away from funding your current self and towards your future self?

How much money do I need in retirement?

We touched on Fidelity's view of how much you need to save for retirement as a first thought in Chapter 2 (*Invest in … Yourself*, see pages 34–5). Here it is below, as a reminder. But we are now going to go more deeply into this question.

By age...	30	40	50	60	67
Aim to save	I x	3 x	6 x	8 x	10 x
	the value of your gross salary (the salary you earn at each age above), in savings set aside wholly for your retirement – and invested for growth				

Source: Fidelity

Fidelity doesn't have a monopoly of wisdom. We are going to bring in two further and overlapping perspectives here. Both are from trusted, independent sources.

Which? for the Consumer Association surveyed thousands of retired people and looked at how much they spent.[4] Crucially, *Which?* included housing costs in these calculations. The assumption that people will fully own a house by the time they retire is, sadly, very outdated now.

An alternative view is provided by a trade body, the Pensions and Lifetime Savings Association: what they call the Retirement Living Standards.[5] This was also based on crunching a lot of data, but the data was more about what things cost than what people say they are spending. PLSA did not include housing costs – but interestingly, still came up with higher amounts, in some cases, than *Which?*

Both sets of findings are full of detail. In the downloadable workbook we link you to the full sites, so that you can explore how the budget breakdowns underneath the headline figure might apply to you. But we thought it would be helpful to draw together their findings in a single table on page 56 so that you can look at them side by side.

Rather confusingly, although both sets of findings look at three different levels of lifestyle, both use the label 'comfortable', but PLSA uses it to mean the *highest* level of living and *Which?* uses it to mean a *middle* level of living. Turn forward to see the diagrams a couple of pages ahead. Some points to consider as you look at them are:

- The amounts in the table are what people *spend*, so the tax you will pay must be added on top to create a total *income*. We will come back to tax in more detail in Chapter 7 (*Manage Your Mix*, see pages 152–86). However, we have made some simple and crude assumptions about tax to give the figures in 'mountain' graphic on page 57. They are *very* approximate, but they do include what you need to pay taxes. They assume you have only state and a Defined Contribution (DC) pension and make use of the 25 per cent tax-free drawdown available to you.

- The 'middle' and 'highest' standards over-simplify. Most people don't spend as much on day-to-day living and travel in the later years of their retirement as they do in earlier years. But this is quite helpful for planning. If you live a long time, your average spending per year is likely to be lower. Choose a target number that represents a good standard of living for you in the year you retire. If you then base your calculations for your whole retirement on this starting number, this gives you a bit of room for error.

- If you will be getting the full state pension (just above £9,300), you are probably already aware that it pays less than the 'essential' or 'minimum' amounts for a single person – although not by very much. But it does help quite a lot. It needs to be subtracted from the figures in the table to give you an idea of what you will have to fund yourself. But in the mountain graphic, we have assumed you/a couple get the full state pension.

- So our 'mountain' gives an *approximate* sum for the pensions 'mountain' you will need to climb to achieve different standards of living. You will need to reach your desired resting point on the path towards the summit by the time you retire. Our graphic can only be very approximate because it has to make quite a few assumptions but hopefully it begins to give you at least a sense of *scale* and to help you think about what the challenge looks like for you. Our workbook will step you through the maths to generate a figure more tailored to your own circumstances.

- Whether you will still have a mortgage or rent to pay will make a major difference.

- By managing your money using the system of accounts we propose in this chapter, you will get an accurate and clear picture of your budget. You will have years of records for the cost of your basic needs and your expectations for non-essentials, holidays, etc. So if you stick to our system, by the time you reach retirement you should have built up an excellent idea of the fit between your spending needs and your post-tax income. This will remove a big anxiety for you, compared to those who don't budget!

	'Essential' (*Which?*) 'Minimum' (PLSA)		'Comfortable' (*Which?*) 'Moderate' (PLSA)		'Luxurious' (*Which?*) 'Comfortable' (PLSA)		*Notes*
	Single person's annual spending	**Couple's annual spending**	*Single person's annual spending*	**Couple's annual spending**	*Single person's annual spending*	**Couple's annual spending**	
Which?	£13,000	£18,000	£19,000	£26,000	£31,000	£41,000	Dated February 2021. Includes housing but excludes social care.
PLSA	£10,900	£16,700	£20,800	£30,600	£33,600	£49,700	Dated 2021. Excludes housing and social care.

Sources: Which?, the Pensions and Lifetime Savings Association

The pensions mountain:
approximating the pot size needed

This aims to give an initial impression. Our workbook is designed to help you calculate a sum closer to your own circumstances.

£860,000 for a couple needed for the average of the *Which?*/ PLSA highest levels

£290,000 for a couple needed for the average of the *Which?*/PLSA middle levels

£80,000 for a single person needed for the average of the *Which?*/PLSA lowest levels

Includes/assumes:

... no other private pensions, but full state pension(s) ... little or no rent/mortgage ... income tax payments (using the 25 per cent tax-free allowance for DC pensions – explained in Chapter 7) ... 3.3 per cent withdrawal rate that should keep your pension pot going until you die (explained in Chapter 6) and excludes social care costs (explained in Chapter 7).

- Neither the table nor our 'mountain' graphic includes the cost of paying for social care, if it is needed at the end of your life. We return to this difficult topic in Chapter 7 (*Manage Your Mix*, see pages 180–4).

Is it time to rebalance towards your future self?

Let's return to the bigger picture: how much you need to tilt your spending away from your current self and towards your future self depends on where you want to position yourself up this mountain. And on how far you are up on the path towards it. So, returning to the logic of the left-hand side of the graphic on page 50, think now very carefully about how much you should be putting away to fund your *future* self.

Can you, and should you, increase the contributions automatically deducted from your salary to fund your pension? (If you're not paying everything your employer encourages you to, you may be missing out on the maximum employer and tax contributions.) This is a good route to take if you can. It will be completely automated and will rise relatively painlessly in step with your income. But if you are already paying the maximum (the most that your employer will then add to), should you think about making additional pension contributions anyway? They don't have to be regular. You could make them if you have had a good year, or only when you have had a pay rise.

The best free online calculator we have found that will help you model whether your current contributions are enough to fund the pension pot you need is run by PensionBee. And the best free calculator that looks at how much you can get out of your eventual pot (assuming you don't buy an annuity) is run by *Which?*[6] We highly recommend that at this stage you at least use the PensionBee calculator. Plug in your present situation and see where it may get you by your desired retirement age. Our workbook will help you use these tools as part of a larger plan.

Some people will find it difficult to pull all the information together because they have several pensions left behind after different jobs. They can benefit from consolidating them into one single account. We'll come back to the practicalities of this in Chapter 7 (*Manage Your Mix*, see pages 152–86). If you decide you can't increase pension payments now, should you set yourself a review point each year when you reconsider?

Robin writes: Money in marriage

Married couples are a team and as with any other team, things go better when you're pulling in the same direction. That certainly applies to money and investing. Team Powell would never win any trophies for it, but I'm pleased to say my wife and I have handled our finances pretty well. We're still learning (you always are), but here are the biggest lessons I've learned so far. I'm not saying this is the way every couple should manage their money, but I thought it would help to share some experiences and ideas in case they inspire you.

Work out what's important – together! This is a huge subject I know, but it's amazing how many of us go through life without working out what we value and what we want to do with our lives. Do our downloadable workbook and talk it through together.

Have a joint current account. There are different schools of thought on this, but although I do understand the merits of having your income paid to a sole account, I can't understand the logic for then keeping *all* your bank accounts separate. Having a slice of both your incomes going to the same account relieves the stress of working out who pays for what.

Share a spreadsheet. Both of you should know how much money is coming in, and how much going out, on a monthly basis. If you haven't yet done so, create and share a spreadsheet for your income and expenditure and keep it up to date.

Play to your strengths. My wife likes to focus on detail. So, for example, checking the bank account and ensuring we aren't overpaying for groceries or utilities are her responsibilities. I'm a big picture person – it's my role to keep us on track to reach our financial goals.

Talk about your expenditure. Spending money is an important part of life, yet many people don't like discussing it, even with their partner. You need to agree between you what your priorities are. If you're considering a large purchase or perhaps feel aggrieved at one your partner has made, *talk about it together.*

Invest at least 15 per cent of your income. Business magnate Warren Buffett once described investing as 'an activity in which consumption today is foregone in an attempt to allow greater consumption at a later date'. For couples, it's a joint commitment and a shared sacrifice. Invest as much as you can each month and jointly agree that, whenever your income increases, so will the amount of money you put away.

Cut yourselves some slack. As long as you stick to whatever percentage you decide to invest each month, don't feel guilty about spending the money that's left. Money, after all, is a means to an end, not an end in itself. Prioritize holidays and shared adventures. If your spouse enjoys a little luxury now and again, leave them to it. Life is short, enjoy it while it lasts.

Trim

Can you trim your spending to fund more of your future life? You have three months' spending data for your variable spending. Now is a good time to comb through it and take a careful look at your spending patterns.

You may not want to look in detail at every transaction but you can bundle together *types* of spend and take a step back. Above all, were you getting pleasure or utility from everything you spent? (Answering this question can help focus your thinking.)

Are there areas where you feel you could reasonably, or even painlessly, cut back? Tot up your supermarket spending, for example. Could you have saved significant sums by switching to a cheaper supermarket? Are there one-off rentals or subscriptions you took on but didn't make the most of?

Loyalty cards shave a per cent or so off supermarket and other bills. Keeping up with them often seems like a lot of trouble. But if you spend an afternoon setting it all up in the most efficient way, you can reap the benefits for many years. There's a trade-off as the cards offer you savings in return for gathering data about you. There's no such thing as a free lunch.

But if you want to trim, and you feel relaxed about this trade-off, it's worth thinking about spending an afternoon setting up a phone app like Stocard. This is another helpful way of automating what would otherwise be a fiddly process. It allows you to store all the barcodes needed to claim loyalty points in one place on your phone. Sign up to all the stores and petrol stations you regularly use then say goodbye to that fiddly sheaf of physical plastic cards! You can swipe using the app. It's pretty painless – and will add up. If you could add 1 per cent of the value of your supermarket bills to your pension every month, over the years that would make a useful difference. And could your essentials and everyday commodities have been bought more cheaply? They are boring – can they also come at a low cost?

We recommend that for all your recurring bills, you review them. Start now, then again every 12 months. Look to see if switching to a new provider can save you money, or whether there are subscriptions you are no longer using and should cancel. There is the potential to save a fair amount each year if you do this for all your different regular bills.

You can automate this process too. Look After My Bills, Switchcraft and WeFlip are just a few of a new generation of switching providers that will take on the boredom of doing energy comparisons for you and take the switching decisions out of your hands.[7] Moneysavingexpert.com offers a similar service. These are just for energy; there are other providers that will go further, including raking over subscriptions to check with you whether you still need them.

Maximize

You can maximize your spare cash by helping it grow and shielding it from tax. The choices about maximizing that are best for you will vary for each person, depending on your income and how close your expenditure comes to using it all up each month.

This principle – maximize – is asking you to think about some overlapping concepts. The first is that you should ideally save up an emergency fund of cash. You need it to help you deal with unexpected expenses and emergencies. The smaller that reserve is, the less interest it can earn, so if it's a very small amount then there may not be much you can, or should do, to maximize it. In the simplest scenario, you could try to plan so that there are always a few hundred pounds left over in your main account after the other accounts have all been 'fed'.

But this will only cover the least demanding of emergencies, such as a fridge breaking down.

Can you build your emergency reserve towards the ideal amount? This is widely considered to be three months' salary (or at least three months' spending). If you can, you will begin to have a reasonable sum of money sitting around, so keeping it in your main bank account, where you are unlikely to earn any meaningful interest, is less attractive.

There are too many different options here for us to set out a standard path. The general principle we recommend is to strike a balance between keeping the cash reasonably accessible and getting it to grow as much as possible. These two aims are usually in tension – and interest rates change all the time.

It's not hard to find best buy tables of savings accounts, which tell you how easily you can access your money. The 'Top Savings Accounts' page at moneysavingexpert.com is always up to date. It's a very good place to start. But the rates for instant-access cash, at the time of publishing this book, are miserably low. (Muslim investors who want to save according to Sharia-compliant principles do not use traditional interest-bearing accounts. But however their money grows, the same principle applies – don't let your spare cash be idle.)

Some other options to consider include Premium Bonds. They are almost as good as cash; you can turn them back into cash at any time and because they are backed by the UK Treasury, they are as safe as pretty much anything can be. They can pay something approximating a market rate of interest, but it comes as prizes in a random draw, where every bond you hold is a 'ticket'. If you're interested in understanding the odds better, there is a brilliant Premium Bonds explainer on the moneysavingexpert.com site. But the key point to understand is that the closer you get to holding the maximum £50,000 in bonds, the closer you will get to earning (winning) the headline interest rate. For amounts less than £25,000, you should expect your bad luck to disappoint you, but compared to a bank account paying next to zero interest, Premium Bonds may still be a better bet. It's just possible that you will win a meaningful sum. And if you do, it will be even more exciting as you won't pay any tax on it.

Another aspect of maximization is to make sure you reap as many tax advantages as you can. Individual Savings Accounts (ISAs) are the leading tax-exempt option in the UK. A cash ISA, or a stocks and shares ISA, allows you to squirrel away £20,000 a year. This amount is the maximum you can spread across all your ISAs. Or you can put it all into just one 'flavour' of ISA. That £20,000 can grow if you invest it – and none of the growth will be subject to tax.

Investing some of your shorter-term cash in a stocks and shares ISA is an option if you have quite a lot of it. For example, the limit of what you can put into a pension is currently £40,000 a year. If you have more cash than that to put aside for your future years, consider a stocks and shares ISA as a place to park it.

Cash ISAs offer low interest rates. There is already a reasonably generous tax allowance for the interest you can earn outside an ISA so cash ISAs have never been less attractive. We say more about the ISA option in Chapter 7 (*Manage Your Mix*, see pages 156–60).

For stocks and shares ISAs, provided you use an affordable, usable platform (see Chapter 4 – *Capture Market Returns*, pages 67–86), you can sell a chunk of what you hold within days to realize any cash you need. We would not recommend this if you have only a few thousand pounds of spare cash, because stocks and shares go up and down in the short term. You might be caught short with less cash than you need. But if your savings outside your pension are growing beyond the tens of thousands, and particularly beyond three months' salary or spending, the amount you might need to call on at short notice will be a relatively small portion of the whole – the rest could therefore work harder.

We have a lot more to say about investing in stocks and shares in later chapters, so this is just a taster of that thinking. But the key thing to think about is this: you want as little as possible of your cash sitting in any account where it will not grow. For any excess, you will need to trade access (locking it away for two or three years) to get growth. Or you will need to trade risk (investing in stocks and shares) to get growth.

One final point about maximization and tax. If you are a higher-rate taxpayer, and you are contributing to a workplace pension, you are likely to be able to claim further tax relief on your payments. HMRC only add *basic rate* tax relief to pension payments.

If you pay higher rate tax, you can reclaim the difference between the basic rate tax and the higher rate. The only way of doing this is through the annual self-assessment process. Nobody will nudge you to do it. If you don't claim it, you lose it. The repayment can amount to hundreds or even thousands of pounds a year, depending on how much you pay into your pension contributions. About 80 per cent of higher rate taxpayers miss out on this money.[8] This saves the government nearly three-quarters of a billion pounds each year. Get your slice if you are eligible for it!

Teach

Our final keyword in this chapter is 'teach'. This is mainly directed at people who have children, so we'll write it from that point of view. But everyone has contact with young people and so everyone has a possibility of influencing. If you don't have children, perhaps there is nonetheless some young person in your life who could benefit from these lessons.

If you've read this far you will have seen that managing money doesn't come naturally and is fraught with emotional challenges. But it can be learned. So, children do need to learn it and you can do a lot of good by passing on life lessons about money management. The Money Advice Service did a great deal of good research into what is happening with money and children.[9] What it found was this:

- Less than half the children in the UK have a positive memory of any financial education at school so don't rely on schools to do all the teaching about money. For one thing, because they are reasonably representative of society as a whole, teachers themselves can have just as many hang-ups about money as their peers have. This can affect the way they teach – or whether they sidestep teaching financial education at all.
- In any case, what happens in the home is at least as important as what happens at school.
- And the financial education that does happen at home or at school usually comes too late. Critical attitudes to money management are formed when children are surprisingly young. It's perfectly sensible to start introducing them to the simplest concepts (and attitudes) about money before the age of five. By age seven, lots of their attitudes are well-formed and will have a big influence in later life.

The Money Advice Service also found that, in the home, the most important positive behaviours were to ensure that:

- Children see and handle money from an early age. (This is harder than it sounds in an age of digital cash.)
- Money is talked about in the home – what it's worth, what it's used for and how to manage it.
- Children receive money regularly and take responsibility for what to do with it.

This last point raises the spectre of 'pocket money' and all the middle-class anxieties about giving children too much or too little – but its life lesson can be perfectly effectively fulfilled without giving them any pocket money at all. A child could be given money that is already part of household spending and be asked to spend it themselves, accompanied or unaccompanied. For example, on regular supplies of milk or bread.

The above points are the three crucial lessons that children need to experience. How much more you do than that will depend a lot on your individual circumstances and how much money you have to spare. But echoing our discussion of the options you have for your retirement at the end of Chapter 1 (*Your Money or Your Life?*, see pages 22–6), we believe that helping your children into both good habits and helpful attitudes so that they can fund their own financial future is much more valuable to them than any legacy you could hope to leave them. For a start, legacies are always subject to inheritance tax and nobody can predict how radically that will change in the future. But more fundamentally than that, to make good plans for a happy financial future, children need to learn to handle money well *now*. This will give them peace of mind now – not just when you die. And if they can't manage their money well now, they might not handle your legacy any better.

A final key lesson from the Money Advice Service's research, and this relates to adults as well, is the importance of a regular savings habit as the critical 'lead indicator' for virtually every other positive money management behaviour.[10] This was based on an 'Adult Financial Capability Survey', a survey of more than 5,000 adults across the UK. It looked not just at what money people had, but their attitudes towards it, it tested their skills with various simple money questions and checked their beliefs. This led to a multidimensional, cross-checked view of whether what people do, say and know is consistent.

If people saved regularly, all their other indicators of money management were more likely to tilt towards the positive measures. And the interesting finding was that it didn't matter whether they regularly saved only a tiny amount, or a lot. It was the habit itself that counted. Whether this is cause or effect is still open to question but it's worth applying to your own money management and to any support you give to children and young people. The habit of saving regularly is a cornerstone. Put that in place and you increase the chances of it supporting everything else.

We now go back to our compound interest example from Chapter 2 (*Invest in ... Yourself*, see pages 28–9): saving £50 a month for 50 years, compounding to £179,000. Imagine setting a young person on that path and what difference that £179,000 would make to them. As we have seen from the pensions 'mountain' graphic earlier in this chapter, that won't fund a future life for everyone, but it will set anyone well on the way to climbing their own mountain. And not many people know that as a parent of a child aged below 18, you can start contributing to a pension for them and claim tax relief on your contributions. So if you can afford to make that very early start, what you pay in will be augmented by HMRC. An early start to a regular savings and investment habit is the best gift you could possibly give to your child or a young person you know.

Now take action

Our workbook will help you work through all the issues covered in this chapter:

- What are your feelings about your past money management and what do you want them to be from now on?
- Do you have unmanageable debts that should currently take priority over pensions?
- Now is the time to accept, divide, track, stabilize, prioritize, trim, maximize and teach.

4

Capture Market Returns

It's hard to escape the 'drama' of financial markets. Every day the prices of hundreds of securities are listed in the press. There are daily, if not hourly, updates on radio stations, entire TV channels dedicated to bringing us the latest news from the trading floor. The impression given is that to be a good investor, you need to keep abreast of the markets, and what the experts are saying about them, all of the time.

But the truth is very different.

From an investor's point of view, the gyrations of the markets are quite irrelevant. Jack Bogle, a businessman and author who has helped to revolutionize the investment industry in the US, refers to markets as 'a giant distraction from the business of investing'. Paul Krugman, the Nobel-prize winning economist, puts it this way: 'No matter how many times we keep on saying the stock market is not the economy, people won't believe it, but it isn't, [– it's] about one piece of the economy – corporate profits – and it's not even about the current or near-future level of corporate profits, it's about corporate profits over a somewhat longish horizon.'[1]

Essentially, investing in the stock market is about sharing in these, the profits of capitalism. Companies distribute their profits

> **Rule 2: Take a slice of everyone's business**

and this distribution is called 'dividends'. Companies generally pay higher dividends when they're doing well and lower dividends when they're not. When the market expects future profits for a particular company to rise, the price of its shares tends to rise as well. When profits are expected to fall, so does the price. As a result, the value of our investments in shares, or equities as they're also known, constantly rises and falls. In the short term particularly, it can fluctuate wildly. But if you believe, by and large, that human enterprise works and that in the long term, there will continue to be a demand for goods and services, and so companies will carry on making profits, then it makes sense to benefit from this process yourself. And so this takes us to our second rule. We will come back to it again and again throughout this book.

Of course, the world faces huge risks, such as climate change and terrorism. Nor can we rule out the possibility of a cataclysmic event, such as a nuclear war or an asteroid strike. This book is not going to try to adapt your future finances to outsmart events such as these. That would require an entirely different kind of attitude and mindset. It rests on a central assumption: that, as throughout history, the spirit of human enterprise will prove resilient so market-based economies will continue to prosper. Governments will set new rules to adapt our way of living to mitigate global warming. Markets and companies will respond with change and innovation.

The author and financial adviser Mark Hebner sums it up like this: 'With a total market capitalisation of over 51 trillion dollars, annual profits of over two trillion dollars, more than 13 thousand CEOs worldwide, and more than 82 million employees selling products in 195 countries, it simply isn't reasonable to believe that Capitalism Inc. will go out of business.'[2]

So what are your options for investing in all this activity? And what are the evidence-based rules about how to go about it?

Two ways to invest

As an investor, there are essentially two things you can do with your money to make it grow. You can either lend it to someone by investing in bonds, or you can become a part-owner of a company by investing in shares. Bonds and shares are referred to as different types of assets, or 'asset classes'.

Bonds are lending. When you buy a bond, you are lending money, either to a business or government. The returns you receive include the interest paid on the loan (the 'coupon') and the expected capital return (bonds vary in price, so their capital value can go up or down). As a creditor, you're nearer the front of the queue, should the bond issuer go bust. For this reason, bonds are seen as safer than shares, but also at the cost of a lower expected return.

Shares are owning. When you buy a share, you're getting part-ownership of a business. Your returns in this case come from the share of the profits paid out (dividends) and, hopefully, a capital return (an increase in the share price). Being a share owner, you rank behind the creditors if the company goes bust. For this reason, you expect a premium for investing in shares over bonds.

So, different asset classes come with different risks and different rates of return. Generally, cash is seen as the safest, but it also delivers the lowest returns. You can take on slightly more risk and invest in the highest-rated government bonds. These will give a higher return than just cash. Corporate bonds are another step up on this risk 'ladder'. And, finally, at the top of that risk ladder, you can target the highest expected return by investing in equities or shares. Within shares, there are additional premiums available from smaller and cheaper companies.

However, inflation is not just a risk, it's a fact of life. If you leave your money in cash, and it is earning little or no interest, its purchasing power will fall each year. Because inflation is usually less dramatic than a stock-market plunge, its effects are insidious. People are less worried about them because they notice them less. But over a very long period – the duration of your retirement, for example – the effect of inflation on your standard of living could be enormous.

The flipside of the higher returns you get from investing is greater volatility from year to year. As we have already noted, shares offer a bumpier ride. But the longer your investment horizon, the less these ups and downs matter. And you can moderate the bumps and increase the reliability by diversifying, as we will see later in Chapters 6 and 7.

What is the right portfolio for you? It depends on a range of factors, including your individual circumstances, risk appetite and time horizon. For example, Muslim readers who intend to invest according to the principles of Sharia-compliant finance will need portfolios that avoid Western-style bonds (sukuk bonds

A risk 'ladder' for common assets

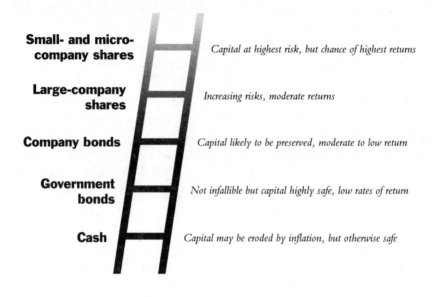

Small- and micro-company shares — *Capital at highest risk, but chance of highest returns*

Large-company shares — *Increasing risks, moderate returns*

Company bonds — *Capital likely to be preserved, moderate to low return*

Government bonds — *Not infallible but capital highly safe, low rates of return*

Cash — *Capital may be eroded by inflation, but otherwise safe*

are an alternative), and choose shares carefully.[3] This is because of the principle in Islamic finance that you shouldn't make money solely out of other money. In practice, this means avoiding interest payments to the greatest extent possible, and so investing in intrinsically productive activities. We have more to say about this on page 171. But they will not be alone in having personal factors that need to shape their portfolio choices.

Ultimately, the best portfolio is the one you are able to stick with, even when markets are at their most turbulent. This is a good

> **Rule 3: To dilute your risks, add lots of time**

place to introduce our third and fourth rules. What we do know is that over time markets have a history of rewarding investors who exercise patience and discipline, and who can live with the risk in expectation of the return. Much of the remainder of this book will be devoted to this 'patience principle'! Rule 3 underlines the importance of it.

Rule 4 is then about sticking the course and trying to avoid impulsive decisions and reactions. You may need help to do so.

Rule 4: Phone a friend, especially when times are taxing

Friends, family or an adviser can help you exercise this patience. We will have a lot more to say about this later in Chapters 8 and 9.

What drives returns on your assets?

Over several decades, financial academics have discovered a number of factors that drive returns in the long term. These factors are evident in markets around the world and over long periods.

Your chosen market: there is a return available from investing in a globally diversified portfolio of shares as opposed to putting all your money in the safest government bonds. This is called the 'market premium'. Shares are more volatile than bonds, but with the offer of a higher expected return.

Size, relative price, profitability: within the share market itself, there are three other sources of higher returns, or 'premiums'. Smaller companies have been shown to offer a higher expected return than large companies over time. Likewise, low relative price or 'value' stocks have delivered a long-term premium over high relative price or 'growth' stocks. Finally, more profitable companies have delivered a long-term premium over less profitable ones. Like the equity premium itself, these size, value and profitability premiums come and go.

Term and credit: within the bond market, there are two drivers of returns – term and credit. 'Term' refers to how long the bond has until it matures or comes due. This can range from a few months to 30 years or more. Generally, the longer the term, the higher the expected return. The credit factor refers to the likelihood of the bond defaulting. Generally, there is a higher return for investing in governments or companies that have a lower credit score. However, these term and credit returns (as with the equity, size, value and profitability returns) are not constant over time.

In summary, financial economists have built a strong sense of what drives returns over the long term. Investors can build diverse portfolios around these long-term drivers. You can trade off risk and return according to your tolerances, circumstances, goals and time horizons. These will lead you to choose a mix of assets and a mix of risks.

There is broad agreement among academics that asset allocation is the most important decision you will make as an investor. It's important when buying or selling to try to 'time' when a market is going to rise or fall.

The most commonly cited academic paper is one from 1986 by Gary Brinson, Randolph Hood and Gilbert Beebower, which concludes that asset allocation explained 93.6 per cent of the variation in a portfolio's quarterly returns.[4] This was later revised to 91.7 per cent. Like all academic papers, there have been further refinements and challenges, but our view is that their fundamental sense of priority holds good today.

In Chapters 6 and 7, we will set out the choices you can make about asset allocation and about rebalancing them as your pension fund grows. First, we need to talk about how to invest in assets at all. We will start with a fundamental difference – the difference between two styles of investing, commonly known as 'active' or 'passive' investing.

It's one of the most important lessons in our book.

Active versus passive investing: what's the difference?

For most of the history of stock markets, all investing was active. This meant that a human being was *actively choosing* investments – whether the investment was in the asset class of shares (also known as 'equities') or the asset class of bonds. This person could have been an individual investor, but because of the difficulty of picking investments they were more likely to be an intermediary. In other words, some kind of investment manager.

More recently, a different style of investing came about. This is called passive investing. Other very common names for it are indexing or index tracking. It's doubtful that this style of investing would have come about without the computer revolution. It depends for its evidence on crunching large amounts of data and the reason why it is so easy and cost-effective to implement is because computers do so much of the work.

There are different types of index funds, but they're all based on a fixed set of rules. Instead of choosing individual securities, they simply invest in every stock or bond in a particular market. Or indeed, they may target a particular segment of a market.

Most of them are weighted by market capitalization ('market cap' for short). In other words, the price of an individual share is multiplied by the number of stocks or bonds issued. The securities with the biggest market cap are allocated the biggest weighting and those with the smallest market cap are given the smallest weighting.

An index fund manager's job is to ensure that the fund is as close as possible to being a miniaturized representation of the market being targeted. Indexes themselves are managed by an index provider such as S&P Dow Jones, MSCI or FTSE Russell. Each index is governed by different rules. To qualify for inclusion, a stock or bond must meet specific criteria.

In the case of the S&P 500, for example, which includes 500 of the largest US companies, there's an index committee that convenes periodically to discuss its makeup. If there's a stock outside the index whose market cap has overtaken that of an index constituent, the committee decides whether to replace one with the other. Whenever it does so, all index funds that track the S&P 500 must buy the stock that enters the index and sell the one that drops out.

You can see why this approach is a very good match to Rule 2. Instead of picking a handful of winners, you invest in enormous

Rule 2: Take a slice of everyone's business

numbers of businesses and seek to capture the returns from them all. Although the computation and data behind this approach are immensely sophisticated, for you as an investor, it couldn't be simpler. You don't have to worry about analysing the balance sheets of individual companies or whether some part of a sector such as energy or plastics is on the up or down; you simply track the market. When you need to sell your investments to fund your future life, you sell a little bit of all of them (still staying invested in the whole market with what remains in your portfolio).

Industry very rarely promotes index funds. Why? Because it makes far more money out of selling actively managed ones. And, from a journalistic point of view, active funds are far more exciting to read and write about.

Index funds, in our view, are the best innovation in asset management since investment funds were invented in the 1770s. They're simple, transparent and, most important of all, very much cheaper than actively managed funds. And don't just take our word for it that index funds are the way to go. Warren Buffett, the most famous and successful investor of the modern era, has consistently said that the majority of investors should be using them. But if that sounds a bit too good to be true, let's set out some of the evidence that backs it up.

Why does passive investing work better than active investing?

The case for avoiding the high-fee, actively managed funds that the investing industry overwhelmingly wants to sell us is ultimately based on two simple pieces of maths.

The first mathematical point is about averages and markets; the second concerns the cost of fees. Neither is very complex (and neither of us would describe ourselves as a natural mathematician!).

Averages and markets
Active funds and passive funds are investing in the same markets but in different ways. Unfortunately, each market is a zero–sum game so for one active manager to win, another must lose.

Active managers aim to be better than average – to beat the market return. They do this in two ways. First, they buy the securities they think will provide the best returns. Second, they attempt to 'time the market' – in other words, they try to buy and sell assets at the right time.

Some active managers will beat the market, some won't, while others will hover around the average return. The problem is, they all charge fulsome fees. Active management is not cheap and almost without exception, you pay the fees regardless of how well or badly managers perform. And here's the rub: it's very hard to tell, in advance, which camp your chosen manager will turn out to be in. Of course, they will claim to be able to beat the market, but – by the law of averages – it's just as likely that they won't.

Passive managers, as we've seen, invest in the whole market and aim to deliver the market return. They also avoid any attempt to time the market. Again, there are fees to pay, but they're notably lower. The active fund industry doesn't like passive investing. Why? Because it represents an existential threat. Consequently, it tends to exaggerate the supposed benefits of active investing while at the same time discrediting index funds.

An argument you often hear from advocates of active management is that when the market falls, so does the value of your index fund. Active managers, on the other hand, have the flexibility to limit your losses. In theory, that's right: they do have the potential to limit the damage. What they don't tell you is that, in practice, they're very bad at predicting when the market is about to fall, or that, in a falling market, active funds often fall further than the broader index. There is broad and rich evidence to support this point and we'll walk you through the highlights of it in the next chapter. Nor do they tell you that by reducing their risk exposure in anticipation of a crash that never comes, they tend to lose out to index funds when markets suddenly rise, too. Again, it comes down to averages. No active manager likes to admit being below average, but half of them have to be.

And then there are the fees
The second piece of simple arithmetic is explained by the Nobel Prize-winning economist William Sharpe in his very readable 1991 paper, 'The Arithmetic of Active Management'.[5] Here's the abbreviated summary:

- The investing community is divided into active and passive investors.
- *Before* fees, the return on any average actively managed pound of shares in 'Company ABC' will be exactly the same as the return on the average passively managed pound in the same company.

- Active investors are people who need salaries, support teams, research and marketing, and so they charge *higher fees* than those implementing simple rules, largely using computers.
- *After* fees, the return on the average actively managed pound in 'Company ABC' will be less than the return on the average passively managed pound.

Therefore, the average active investor must – no ifs or maybes, *must* – *underperform* the average passive investor. Period. To quote Professor Sharpe: 'These assertions will hold for any time period. Moreover, they depend only on the laws of addition, subtraction, multiplication and division. Nothing else is required.'

We should also point out that we're not talking about minor differences in cost. Once you factor in all the different fees and charges, active investors are typically paying in the region of 10 times more to invest than their passive peers. You wouldn't dream of paying £5 for a pint of milk, or £15 for a litre to fill up your car with fuel, but most people similarly overpay to have their money managed and aren't even aware of it.

As Vanguard founder Jack Bogle has said, it all boils down to 'the relentless rules of humble arithmetic' – a phrase he used for the title of a 2005 paper for *The Financial Analysts Journal*.[6] In it, he says: 'The overarching reality is simple: Gross returns in the financial markets minus the costs of financial intermediation equal the net returns actually delivered to investors.'

Our experience is that most investors, and indeed many advisers and investment journalists, are simply unaware of the impact of compounded investment fees and charges over the long term. In his 2005 paper, Bogle stated that in the US at that time '50 per cent or more of the real return on stocks can be consumed by costs'. In the UK, where the cost of investing is higher, the effect of charges can typically reduce your potential returns by two-thirds.

These are staggering numbers. Of course, you cannot eradicate costs altogether and, for many people, dispensing with a financial adviser is definitely a bad idea. But costs are the one thing that you as an investor can control. Keep them to a minimum and you'll end up with bigger returns than the vast majority of your peers.

Just how efficient are the markets?

In his famous book, *Winning the Loser's Game*, Charles Ellis used a tennis analogy to explain why active investing – whether you pick the stocks yourself or pay a fund manager to do it for you – is a losing proposition.[7]

For amateurs, winning at tennis is all about avoiding errors: the player who makes the fewest usually wins the match. It's only brilliant players who win by playing brilliant shots. Professionals win points, while amateurs lose them.

It's the same with investing. For most people, the best strategy is to minimize mistakes. The vast majority of stocks don't even outperform government bonds; the bulk of equity returns are driven by only around 4 per cent of public companies. Identifying just one of those companies, in advance, is like playing an unreturnable tennis shot; identifying all of them, let's face it, just isn't going to happen.

You can own all of those top-performing stocks simply by investing in an index fund. The returns they generate will far outweigh the fact that you also own the losers. Yet most investors still insist on trying to compete with the professionals, with all their experience and all the information and technology they have at their disposal. The truth is that even the pros rarely beat an index fund in the long run. Why? Because they're competing with so many other pros, each with similar resources to their own. The chances of any one of them having an edge over all of the others are extremely slim.

In short, markets are highly efficient. Prices reflect the very latest information and the combined wisdom of the entire market. The market is like a giant super-computer that aggregates all known information about every publicly-listed stock. There are millions of trades every day and each one reflects the very latest opinion on what each security is worth.

It's *new* information that causes prices to rise or fall, and, by definition, news is impossible to predict. So, buying a stock because you think it's cheap, or selling one because you think it's overpriced, is effectively betting against that market. It's either a brave or foolish thing to do. Of course, that doesn't mean that markets are always perfectly efficient. Investors are prone to human emotions like fear and greed, and sentiment can change very quickly, which is why markets can fall and rise very sharply. But outguessing the market at any one point in time is a formidable challenge.

The market, in short, is a very tough opponent and the choice is yours. You can either accept the fact and take the market return, in which case your net returns will be substantially higher than average. Or you can have a go at trying to beat the market, in which case, best of luck, because you're certainly going to need it. It'll be less like a gentle knock-up with your mates at the local court than trading volleys with Federer and Djokovic at Wimbledon.

You *can* control costs

You might have thought you have heard enough about costs and fees from us. Sorry – not yet! We think it's worth visualizing

Rule 5: Only focus on what you can control

this point to hammer it home. This brings us to Rule 5. Costs are something we definitely do encourage you to worry about, because you *can* control them.

Everyone who deals with your money will need to be paid. Fair enough. But every payment you make to them reduces the chances of you capturing the *full* returns from the market.

Whether the market will rise or fall is completely uncertain but it is extremely unusual for costs to be based on anything other than the *total amount you have invested* – your capital, or 'principal'. So you will suffer more or less the same costs whatever happens, because your capital will always drive the largest mathematical proportion of the fees you pay.

(And this is very interesting, because you would have thought that active money managers, if they were confident they could beat the market, would only charge you higher costs when they actually achieve their stated aim of giving you higher-than-average returns.)

The other insidious factor is that your costs are nearly always quoted in tens or hundredths of a percentage point (known as 'basis points'). How can anyone get worked up about hundredths of a percentage point? The graphic on the next page aims to make this as clear as we can.

Our example is a pension pot with a nice round number. It's a healthy £1 million. The person holding it has agreed to pay costs of 1.2 per cent of the value of the pot at the start of each year, or 120 basis points. However, by the end of this year, the growth has not been great – only 2.5 per cent. If the pension holder chooses only to take that growth as her income, she's limited to taking £25,000.

But look carefully under the microscope. The 1.2 per cent costs, which seemed pretty trivial against the grand scheme of 100 per cent, are £12,000. If the pension-holder doesn't want to take more than her growth, she has to take £12,000 out of her £25,000. So she pays her intermediaries 48 per cent of the income the pension pot has created that year. As a result, she is left with just £13,000 (52 per cent). If she had agreed to fees amounting to 1.3 per cent, she'd be getting less than half of the growth. Because she limited her fees to a (still rather high) 1.2 per cent, she's at least getting the lion's share.

Because your growth is *always likely to be in the very low digits*, costs are *pretty much guaranteed to claim a high proportion of your growth*. This is why you need to keep them as low as you possibly can.

How low can you go? Well, the area of costs is a minefield because there is a real problem with transparency. Costs generally come in four layers. The good news is that you can avoid paying for at least some of these layers if you shop around.

You will see from the costs table that follows the graphic that if you were to go for having your money managed by an adviser and they were to choose the most expensive fee options, you could easily rack up fees totalling 3.5–4.5 per cent of your investments each year. Given that you will be doing well if your investments consistently achieve above 5 per cent growth, you can see how disastrous this would be for your future life. Your investments would be providing a much better living for advisers and intermediaries than they were for you.

Why costs must always be under your microscope

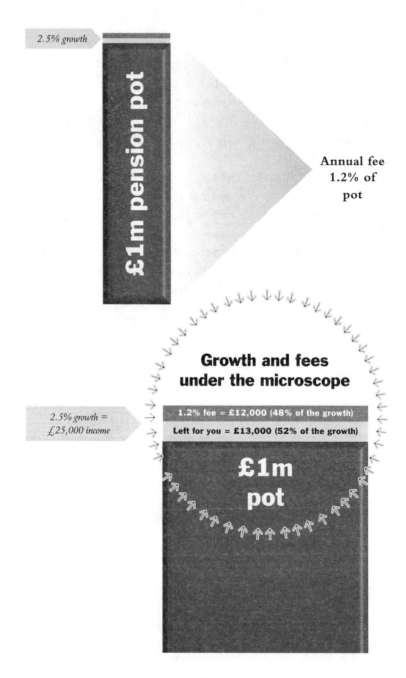

Area of cost	What this means	Using a 'supermarket' analogy	What kind of charges are there?	Things to consider
Platform fee	**You must pay a fee, directly or indirectly, to gain ongoing access to the trading environment where your stocks, shares and bonds can be bought and sold. Platforms are needed for saving into a pension, or into a stocks and shares ISA.**	*It's a bit like paying for entry to a supermarket. You would certainly want to be sure it has a wide range of affordable goods on sale before you go in.*	Vanguard charge 0.15 per cent of the first £250,000 you put on its platform and zero for anything above that. This is a very low fee. By contrast, Hargreaves Lansdown, a very well-known brand, charge three times as much (0.45 per cent). These figures are taken from Monevator, which provides a useful comparison site for broker fees.[8]	If you use a money manager (see below) they may conceal this fee in their overall charges so it is worth quizzing them on it. It's good to have a very low platform fee but you need to make sure your platform works for you. It needs to be easy to log in, secure, easy to use and have a wide range of choices on its 'supermarket shelves'.
Fund annual management charge (AMC)	**If you buy into an index fund, it will usually (but not always) have its own price – on top of the platform fee.**	*It's a bit like the cost of buying a product in the supermarket, but the key difference is you will pay it every year.*	Some pension providers, such as Aviva and Nest, do not impose extra fund charges. Essentially, you pay for access to their platform and that's it. So the AMC can be as low as zero.	If you can, it's best to have the majority of your investments in funds that charge no extra AMC. But to diversify (for example, into emerging

Area of cost	What this means	Using a 'supermarket' analogy	What kind of charges are there?	Things to consider
			These are more likely to be in passive funds. But a lot of popular and highly marketed funds (above all, actively managed funds) have fees that rise as high as 1–2 per cent. This is a lot to pay. In our experience, active financial advisors tend to buy these kinds of funds on your behalf, so you tend to get a double dose of high fees.	markets), you are likely to have to accept higher fees on smaller chunks of your pension pot.
Transaction fees	**When you buy and sell parts of a fund, there is a fee per transaction.**	*It's a bit like paying a credit card fee when you pay for your product in the supermarket.*	Transaction fees tend to be in absolute pound numbers rather than a percentage of the value of the transaction, so they are mostly in the low pounds or even pence.	We don't think these are a big area of concern, because we recommend that you trade infrequently. Apply Rule 5 – *only worry about what you can control.*

Area of cost	What this means	Using a 'supermarket' analogy	What kind of charges are there?	Things to consider
Adviser or money manager fee	**We devote a whole chapter (Chapter 9 – Find a First-Rate Adviser, see pages 202–28) to this layer of costs. The fundamental dilemma you have is whether or not to manage your money yourself, or ask someone else to do it for you. If they do, your fees will significantly increase so you will pay a significant slice of your investment income to them.**	*It's a bit like having a personal shopper go round and do all your shopping in the supermarket. By and large, their cost will be additional to all the costs above.*	A small number of advisers charge by the hour but most charge as a percentage of your portfolio. It's unusual to find an adviser who won't add at least a 0.8 per cent fee onto the costs above, rain or shine, if they are managing your money all the time.	See Chapter 9 for a discussion of all the ins and outs of this.

At the lowest end of costs, they are 'free'. There are apps on the market that offer trading without any transaction fees at all, knocking out at least one of the four layers of costs above. Robinhood is one of the most controversial ones – but it is currently available only to US customers. The comparable app Freetrade is available to UK users and has a product that can hold your pension savings. But this pension product has a monthly cost, so effectively you pay an annual management charge (AMC). Others in the same space include Revolut and Dodl.

This generation of apps is new, fast-moving and some among them *may* represent a less stable place to put your money. Their business models are evolving and they all will need to make money out of you somehow. They are unlikely to focus on long-term, low-frequency pension transactions. If their business model drives them to encourage you to trade frequently, we don't think this is a good idea unless you are able to resist it.

If you are interested in using one of these apps, first check that they are fully regulated by the Financial Conduct Authority and its related compensation scheme. If so, you can be quite certain that if a provider went bust, your money would be held separately from their business expenses. And of course, work out whether the trade-offs you have to make in return for 'free' are suitable for you.

But all this shows that it pays to shop around. We think it will pay to keep on exploring ways in which you can keep fees as low as possible and computers will continue to reduce the costs of investing. Above all, the costs of passive investing. You need to find the right position for you on this spectrum. But remember that 'free' exists as a healthy counterpoint to the high costs you will routinely encounter.

It is worth pointing out that a platform called Interactive Investor has a different business model from most of the above. They charge platform and trading fees, but all their fees are flat – the fees don't vary according to how much you have invested. This makes it quite difficult to compare them with most other providers, but the obvious point to make is that the higher the amount you invest with them, the more chance you have of saving money compared to other providers, especially if you trade infrequently.

Robin writes: The battle for transparency

One of the reasons why investor outcomes have been so consistently poor for so long is the industry's lack of transparency. Regardless of the sector, consumers need to know how much they're paying and that the product they're buying is worth paying for. Investors can be sure of neither.

Cost, as we've explained, is hugely important. The less you pay in fees and charges, the better your outcome is likely to be. But fund managers go to great lengths to *disguise* how much investors actually pay.

The explicit cost, i.e. the annual management fee, is only part of it. Our table is only a starter-for-ten on all the implicit costs – transaction costs, custody charges, brokerage fees, foreign exchange fees, platform fees and performance fees ... Calculating the total cost of investing is extremely difficult; in my experience, even fund management companies are unaware of how much their clients are paying. Of course, the exact amount will differ from product to product. However, research by my colleagues at the Transparency Task Force (for which I'm an ambassador) has found that it's typically as much as 3–4 per cent a year.

Then there's the question of quality. How do we know that we're buying a 'good' fund? Past performance tells us very little about future performance, yet there are several ways that fund managers can, and do, make their past performance appear better than it really is. Typically, for example, they choose a time period that excludes a particularly bad year. Or they compare their performance to an inappropriate benchmark.

Although we've made some progress in improving transparency around costs and performance, the likes of the Transparency Task Force and the True and Fair Campaign continue to meet huge resistance from the industry. The onus will always be on consumers to do their due diligence. So, remember, no matter how sceptical you are about the claims that investment professionals and their glossy brochures make... you probably aren't sceptical enough.

Now take action

Our downloadable workbook has a spot for you to write in the fees you are paying for your money to be managed at the moment. They also set you the task of thinking about a target number that you would like your money management costs to come in at, over the long term. We also point you to the best tools from the workbook. Monevator provides an up-to-date, free-to-access fees comparison table. *Which?* also provides, behind a paywall for its members, a guide to 'What is the cheapest investment platform?'.

A fees grand total of 0.5 per cent is not a difficult place to aim for if you are willing to manage your investments yourself. If you are self-managing and your fees are totting up to more than 0.7 per cent, take a long hard look at what you are getting for your money. If someone else is managing your money, Chapter 9 (*Find a First-Rate Adviser*, see pages 202–28) will help you to think through what you need and what you are getting.

5

Avoid Charlatans and Sharks

In the last chapter, we set out the general approach to how you can capture market returns, the fruits of profit and innovation from companies all over the world. In the next two chapters, we'll go deep into the practical detail. We'll tell you *how* you can set up and manage your portfolio of diversified assets that should grow and grow to fund your future. But before we go there, a detour, and for a very good reason. We want to warn you about the serious threats to your future finances that are always, and increasingly, preying on you when you make choices about money. If you are smart enough to build substantial savings for the future, you will be an alarmingly attractive target for charlatans and sharks.

In this chapter, we want to help you understand why and see some of the pitfalls to avoid. The last thing we want is for charlatans or sharks to be dipping their hands in your carefully constructed pensions and savings pots. The danger they pose to their victims can be far larger than the consequences of poor investment choices.

In the first half of this chapter, we'll discuss some of the *frauds* you may encounter – committed by outright *charlatans*. In the second half, we'll talk about legitimate, regulated financial intermediaries who we are going to call *sharks*. Because although their products are expensive and unsuited to your needs, they'll try as hard as they can to sell you them. Then we'll look at charlatans and sharks who tell you 'this time it's different'. And then, for the sake of full transparency, we'll turn the spotlight on ourselves.

Our world has become a paradise for lazy charlatans

Imagine if you wanted to defraud somebody 50 or even 20 years ago. You would likely have to get off your backside ... to travel somewhere to meet your unfortunate victim. Then you would have to persuade them in person of your scam, looking exactly like the person you purported to be. Then they would likely have to make their own journey to a bank to pay you. And at every step along the way, you were at risk of being caught red-handed by the police.

In that distant era, there were all sorts of frauds, but a very common and easy one was the driveway scam. The scammer would knock on somebody's door, say they were doing somebody's drive nearby. Would the householder like to have their own resurfaced for a bargain price, cash in hand? After the money was paid, the driveway would be done to a very poor standard – or not at all.

Think about the difference: back then, the scammers even needed capital investment and stock – mixers, tarmac and gravel. That looks like a great deal of hard labour compared to the charlatan's paradise in which we now live. Today's fraudsters are living off the fat of two big changes.

The first, of course, is the digitization of communications, bank accounts and money. Now a fraudster can sit at the comfort of their computer and orchestrate scams to their heart's content. They can create a myriad of false identities, moving swiftly on if someone is not biting. They need a very low investment of time and effort, and they can be a continent away from the scene of the crime.

The second is the generally increasing wealth of the pensioner population. Relative to decades ago, pensioners are better-off. And just as importantly, the pensions freedoms we discussed in Chapter 2 (*Invest in ...Yourself*, see pages 27–41) mean that instead of having a small annuity income each year, pensioners increasingly have control over enormous pots of money. This makes them horribly tempting targets.

Hence the explosion of fraud. Of course, it's not only directed at pensioners.

Worse, it's getting increasingly sophisticated. So it's harder and harder to spot.

End-to-end digital fraud

The ideal type of fraud (from the fraudster's perspective) takes place without having to persuade anyone of anything. Ideally, they would like to get access to your bank or savings account directly and commit fraud that is enabled end-to-end by computers. This is usually accomplished because of weak security, but sometimes, the fraudster has to persuade bank employees to reset account details in their favour. Digital security is therefore absolutely fundamental. We recommend that you:

- Either use a commercial, highly secure password manager, or choose your own very long passwords (at least 10 characters long) for your most important money accounts.[1] A good trick is to use book or film titles, or lines from poetry or pop songs that only you will know and remember, as the 'DNA' at the centre of each password. You can take the first letter of each word, or better still, the second, or last, to generate the 'DNA'. You'll need to make sure there is a number, a capital letter and a non-alphabetic character swapped in (or naturally occurring) in each of these memorable lines. And it's safer to use a different line for each related group of money accounts and services. For example, you could associate your bank with a book title, your pension fund with a pop song, and so on. Then when you have memorized these 'DNA' lines, you can choose a consistent approach to topping or tailing each one with some letters triggered by individual service names – the name of the site for which you are creating the password. This way, you will have unique, random-looking passwords that you never need to write down.
- Protect your phone with a PIN, or better still, a biometric ID such as your face or fingerprint.
- Set up two-factor authentication on every account that holds money – and very importantly, on your email account. This means that websites will require authentication from an SMS message or better still, an authentication app on your phone.
- Check with your mobile phone provider whether, if somebody asks for your phone number to be reassigned to

a new SIM card, you will have to give permission *from your old SIM card* first. Because in some cases even two-factor authentication has been breached. This has happened because of lax phone company security standards. Such a flaw can throw wide open the digital gateways to so much of our lives.

- Hold on to the same mobile phone number so that criminals can't crack two-factor authentication by 'recycling' your old number. (If you have to change numbers, unlink the old number from any accounts it has been used to authenticate.)
- Do not make your date of birth widely known beyond your circle of trusted friends.

Impersonation fraud

Not many people fall for the scam emails from the purported Nigerian prince who wants to deposit £30 million in your bank account. Nor are too many people fooled by automated telephone calls that threaten court action from HMRC. But unfortunately, there are much more sophisticated impersonations around. Two of the most worrying are invoice interception fraud and push payment fraud.

Invoice interception fraud can happen when someone gets access to your email account. They then patiently monitor it until you need to pay a major bill to a tradesman, or worse, make some kind of major transfer to a solicitor. They then strike – emailing you a very lifelike fake invoice, purporting to be from your solicitor or tradesman. This will substitute the fraudster's bank details as the destination for a substantial transfer of money.

Although it is harder for this to succeed now that UK banks have introduced checks to ensure that account names and numbers match, we're quite certain new versions of this fraud will continue to develop. Sally Flood lost £95,000 of her inheritance money because she transferred it to a scammer, instead of her solicitor, during a property purchase. What made her tale so horrifying is just how plausible every step of the process seemed.[2]

If you are making a major payment, even if the person it's meant to go to has already sent you their bank details by email, it is always best to ring them and ask them to confirm, say, the last four digits of their bank account number. And of course, do everything you can to secure your email account in the first place.

Authorized push payment fraud takes many forms, but a very common type is when someone rings you purporting to be from your bank, then asks you to help your bank catch (ironically, but very cleverly) … fraudsters or money launderers. These fraudsters have particularly clever tricks that spoof official bank telephone numbers. They ask to ring your bank to verify that what's going on is official, then they *stay on the line* so that their call with you is, in fact, never interrupted. They impersonate your bank's call centre and reassure you that you are, indeed, helping the bank and performing a valuable public service. Once you believe that, they proceed to drain your account through a series of ever-bolder manoeuvres. One of the nastiest examples we found was the £239,000 scammed in 2021 from Catriona Oliphant, a city lawyer.[3] Her story brought out the stress and anxiety she was facing at the time, her mother being in hospital for cancer treatment.

This is a common feature of fraud stories. Charlatans seek people who are vulnerable and in a psychologically 'hot state', in which they are experiencing a lot of anxiety. The victim's attention is distracted elsewhere. This means there is 'attention scarcity' for the fraudulent interaction itself.

These frauds are frighteningly sophisticated. We don't think anyone can feel confident that they will always see through them. We

> **Rule 4: Phone a friend, especially when times are taxing**

believe that the best help overall is our Rule 4. Find ways to *slow down* your financial decisions when you are worried and stressed, and consult with a trusted friend. It will make a difference to all your financial decisions – not just instances where fraud is a danger.

We also think that reading the financial news pages in newspapers and other media, provided you don't fall for some of the other stuff being peddled there, is a very good way of keeping on top of the 'arms race' in fraud techniques.

Which? has a dedicated email list for people who want to receive regular alerts about new scams. It's independent, reliable and not annoying; we think it's worth signing up for.

Jonathan writes: The elderly need our help more than ever before

With the rise in the wealth of pensioners, and the increasing use of pension pots rather than annuities, the elderly are a much more tempting target to fraudsters than in previous generations. Added to this is the digital minefield that people of all ages are now forced to navigate. Banking systems — not just self-help access on computers, but call centres — all depend on elaborate security systems. These cannot be overridden by a kindly operator who simply wants to apply common sense. I remember being reduced to tears of impotence when trying to help my father, who was in his final illness at the time, to reset his online password through a call centre. As I was hundreds of miles away at the time, he had to hold his phone to another phone so that the two of us could communicate with the call centre operator simultaneously. The call centre line was faint and crackly, the operator's accent was hard for my father to follow. The whole process took us more than an hour of worry and frustration. An elderly person who is not used to this digital maze is highly vulnerable to fraudsters, who are more than happy to imitate and exploit.

Money remains a highly personal matter. There are plenty of examples of coercion and exploitation by friends and family so we can only tread lightly in trying to broach the subject of whether elder friends and relatives are coping with managing their money. But many could benefit from a relative supporting them.

If the trust they need is there, a lasting power of attorney (LPA) costs a few hundred pounds to register.[4] It will enable you to support financial matters for an elderly person for as long as they want to manage their affairs. Then you can take over complete control if they lose the ability to do so. A financial LPA is very wide-reaching.

A less comprehensive step that an elderly person could take is turning their everyday bank account into a joint one with you. This can help you manage their bills and payments. And by having access to it via an app on your phone, you can see whether any unusual payments have taken place. Be aware, however, that the money in a joint account becomes a joint possession. It's a responsibility to be handled with great delicacy and care. And all the money within the account will be assessed for inheritance tax.

Other helpful approaches that fall short of an LPA include 'third-party mandates'. These enable you to manage some aspects of bank and building society accounts. You can become a third party on the records of utility companies, so that you can query bills and sort out problems.

None of this is a substitute for the most helpful thing you can do with any elderly person still able to manage their money: that's to talk to them regularly about the latest scams. Ask them never to believe anyone who tells them to make a transfer without telling anyone, no matter how convincing the reason sounds. Encourage them to talk to someone they trust about every large monetary transaction. ***Rule 4 – Phone a friend, especially when times are taxing*** – is a powerful tool to help an elderly person to steer clear of scams.

Underclaimed pensions are worth considering if you are helping an elderly person to make the most of their money. Millions of pensioners are not claiming the pension credits they are entitled to.[5] Tens if not hundreds of thousands of women who reached state pension age before 2016 were not paid the top-up they were entitled to as a result of being widowed.[6] Although the state pension is a relatively small amount, and is not very glamorous, it's always a good idea to double-check your friend or relative is not missing out.

Ponzi schemes

Charles Ponzi was a fraudster who operated in the US in the 1920s. Sadly his name is still known because the type of fraud he became infamous for keeps on popping up. It is an old (and constantly new) illustration of the saying 'If it looks too good to be true, it probably is'.

Ponzi schemes offer investors very high rates of return. And they work! But for the first few generations of investors only.

In a Ponzi scheme, instead of your money being genuinely invested and growing, money from new investors is paid out to the first few generations of investors. This satisfies them with their supposed 'market returns'. They will happily talk to friends about these wonderful returns. In this way the scheme grows by word of mouth and for a while everyone is happy. Then it inevitably collapses. And then everyone is extremely unhappy when they see what a house of cards it all was.

Ponzi schemes are not that common in the UK, but we still think there are two useful points you can learn from them. The first is that if anyone is offering you a *guaranteed* return of more than 5 per cent, it's probably a good idea to assume that what they are offering is a scam and possibly a Ponzi scheme. That is, unless you can prove the opposite to the satisfaction of yourself *and* a trusted friend. We stress the word 'guaranteed'. It's perfectly possible to make returns of more than 10 per cent on market investments and for quite a long time. But almost no one legitimate can *guarantee* it.

The second is that there isn't a hard-and-fast division between real Ponzi schemes and what we call 'drifting' Ponzi schemes. It's worth giving two examples to bring this to life.

The first is Bernie Madoff.[7] He was a New York financier who started managing other people's money in the 1960s. There seems little disagreement that he started by making genuine investments on others' behalf. No one quite knows when he stopped investing the money and began to milk new investors to pay out on old investments but at some point the 'drift' took place. The incredible thing is that he was not caught out until 2008. He claimed that he had been practising a Ponzi scheme since the early 1990s, but investigators thought he might have started more than 10 years earlier so he may have succeeded for more than 25 years – very unusual in the history of Ponzi schemes.

Bernie managed to keep the scam secret by keeping returns lower than previous Ponzi schemes (a somewhat credulity-straining 10 per cent rather than an obviously impossible 20 per cent) and varying them a tiny bit each year (he did not offer a guaranteed return). He also kept access to his services fairly exclusive and based on word of mouth; he made them an 'insider secret', something the wealthy love.

Another red flag to watch out for.

The second example we think it's useful for you to know about is the much more recent Dolphin Investments (now known as German Property Group) scandal.[8] The investigation into what happened here is still ongoing so we can't say for sure that this was operating in a Ponzi-like manner. What we do know is that many UK investors put large chunks of their pension savings into Dolphin over the last decade. They were enticed by the magic combination of their investments going to Germany (what a 'safe', 'proper' country!) and in property (what a 'safe' investment!). And as Dolphin claimed it would renovate listed buildings to turn them into apartments, it sounded even more robust, because listed buildings aren't going anywhere anytime soon.

Again, for the first few years investors received spectacular returns. It seems that Dolphin did buy and renovate some buildings. But at some point, the buildings began to be bought but not renovated. Perhaps the final investments were not put into any property at all. The scheme seems to have drifted from something approximately real to something fraudulent. Unfortunately, many people have lost their life savings. Heartbreakingly, some even borrowed to pay a new wave of scammers – who claimed that they would help them get their savings back.

The lesson from Dolphin is that something may have more characteristics of a legitimate investment at the outset than it does a few years in. So if you have a high-return investment, it needs to have your scepticism applied to it at regular intervals.

Regulation by the Financial Conduct Authority

One mistake that the Dolphin investors made was investing in a business that was not regulated by the UK's regulator, the Financial Conduct Authority. In the best scenarios this regulation does mean that some of your capital is protected by the Financial Services Compensation Scheme and that you can appeal to the Financial Ombudsman Service in the case of any dispute. The Dolphin investors did not enjoy this protection.

By and large, FCA regulation is an extremely important safety net, so we don't want to encourage anyone to stop building it into all their investment decisions. In our view, you should check it is in place for every major investment you make. But you should also know that this safety net does have holes.

A recent scandal involved a business called London Capital & Finance (LC&F). Investors put £236 million into this business because (surprise, surprise) it was offering fixed-rate returns of 6.5 per cent or more but they were reassured by the fact that it was authorized by the Financial Conduct Authority. Because of a sleight of hand with the rules, the FCA was regulating LC&F's marketing activity, and not its products.[9] That such a loophole exists will seem crazy to ordinary investors but that is indeed how it was. And when the money went down the drain, the investors found they had no right to call on the compensation scheme.

Banking regulation has a particular wrinkle you should know about. The UK's high street banks are regulated by the FCA and this means that your cash in those banks, up to £85,000 per institution, is protected. But we say 'institution' because, for example, Lloyds also owns Halifax, so if you had £85,000 in each of those bank brands, you would only get £85,000 back under the scheme if Lloyds went bust. So spread your cash across banks if you are holding more than £85,000 of it, but make sure you know who owns the banks. Happily, moneysavingexpert.com site has a tool to help you check. Our workbook will remind you to use it.

Regulated 'sharks'

Unfortunately, regulation may protect you from scammers, but it won't protect you from 'sharks'. We define sharks as people who are engaged in legal and even highly regulated activity, but who are selling financial success stories that aren't evidence-based, or aren't suitable for you. Or both!

We think it's worth examining the main species of sharks, so that you can rapidly swim in the other direction. The general point worth making before we do that is that there is a whole industry whose bread-and-butter depends on it getting a nice slice of your retirement savings. And by far the most attractive model is to take a *regular percentage fee* of what you invest. Because once you are in a percentage arrangement, they get their cut every year until you make a change.

Many people associate long-term investment with uncertainty, worry and indecision so there's a natural psychological tendency for financial investments to double up as *emotional* investments. Moving to another provider may require you to admit that you made a bad (or at least less good) choice. Or that you feel you know better than your adviser. Many people in financial services make a fine living from psychological inertia. It's a bit like the phenomenon of people not watching Netflix but not cancelling their subscription – but on an industrial scale.

Soothsayers

In ancient Rome, when people wanted to know the will of the gods (to help them plan for the future), they consulted somebody known as a haruspex, what we call a soothsayer. These individuals must have had quite remarkable personalities to pull off the method they were expected to practise. First, they would sacrifice a chicken or a sheep. Then, they would look at the gleaming, bloody organs and entrails. According to the look and feel of those organs (rough or shiny? enlarged or shrunken?), they would make divine declarations that gave guidance about the future. Given that this practice survived for centuries, they must have been able to give quite a performance. To our modern minds, this was theatrical, barbaric and (while it may have offered social and emotional benefits) functionally fraudulent.

We have moved on from those days! Or have we?

The reason we bring this up is because we want to drive home the point that short-term predictions about the movements of financial markets might just as well be based on entrails rather than the latest update from Bloomberg News or a complex financial equation. They may be less bloody, but we're not sure they're any more reliable. That is not to say that some of these predictions don't come true. Of course they do; the predictions ultimately boil down to a number going up or down. Given that there are only two possible directions, one of them will happen. As a result, the world is well-supplied with financial forecasters, fund managers and investment consultants whose job it is to pick the best fund managers... and no doubt further consultants whose job it is to pick the best investment consultants! So there is a vast industry of modern-day soothsayers, all trading on their knowledge, connections and intuition.

Daniel Kahneman, the Israeli-American psychologist, won the Nobel Prize in Economic Sciences in 2002 for his work on behavioural economics. Here is his view: 'The reason that intuition cannot be acquired in stockpicking is that there are no regularities in stockpicking to be learned. You develop intuition from successful experience ... With well-functioning markets I do not see intuition having a role in investment.'[10]

Does past performance give *any* clue about future markets?

At this point, you may well question, if Robin and Jonathan are saying that *all* predictions are pointless, what is the purpose of choosing an investment portfolio and asset allocation? If everything is totally random, you might as well focus only on reducing costs. You can invest in anything you want, and buy it and sell it whenever you want, if basing your choices on past evidence is pointless.

That is not *quite* what we are saying! Our view needs three separate points to set it out in full:

- In the very *short* term – we are thinking about predictions on timescales of days, months, even a year or three – success is just as likely to be based on luck as it is on any skill or special knowledge. It's quite sensible to treat short-term movements as if they are random, even if hindsight will reveal rational, underlying causes that people can intelligently comment on.
- Over the *very long* term (and we'll have more to say about this timescale in the next chapter, but we are talking about a period of 100+ years), the performance of different asset classes has reverted to something like an average performance: 'reversion to the mean'. This seems to us a good basis for asset

allocation, and we give you a lot more information about it in the next chapter.

- But just to make things difficult, we live in the medium term! Whether long-term history *predicts* what will happen in the next 20 to 40 years we still can't say. (What about climate change? What about artificial intelligence? What about a conflict between China and the US?) But what we *are* confident of is that basing your decisions on the longest-term performance is a much better guide than any shorter-term view.

The graph below gives a clear visual illustration of that last point.

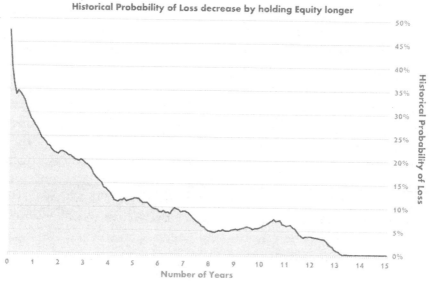

Source: *Pacome Breton, director of investment risk, Nutmeg (a JP Morgan company)*[11]

This is based on mid- and large-company shares from all over the world:

- Over a nearly 50-year period since 1971, people who held these kinds of equities for less than a year had a nearly 50 per cent chance of losing money on them.
- But people who held them for more than 13 years approached an *almost zero* per cent chance of loss.

We stress 'almost zero' — because we know there is quite a difference between that and zero. But it's still a lot better than a 45–50 per cent

> **Rule 3: To dilute your risks, add lots of time**

chance of loss. Moreover, look at the shape of the graph. After people had held shares for more than about five years, their chance of loss continued to dwindle towards zero, but much less steeply than in the first five years. In other words: Rule 3.

The evidence against active management

As you might imagine, given this evidence about the general performance of stock market predictions in the short- and medium-term, the performance of many active managers will fall short. But you might still be surprised by just how badly the evidence stacks up against them. Active managers have access to specialist financial news sources, up-to-the-second data, researchers, personal contacts, journalists, complex algorithms and the like. So this ought to give them an edge, ought it not? Not really. All the other active managers can access the same information! And this probably is yet another aspect of the computer revolution that has tipped the case from active to passive over your lifetime. Computers have not just made it easier to execute passive management, they have also democratized the information sources that active managers used to rely on to give them more of an edge.

We highlight three very strong sources of evidence that this is so.

SPIVA: 73 per cent of active managers underperformed over five years
The SPIVA® Scorecard is run by Dow Jones. SPIVA compares actively managed funds against their appropriate benchmarks on a semiannual basis. It looks at huge numbers of funds managed by active managers in Australia, Canada, Europe, India, Japan, Latin America, South Africa and the US. It takes a very simple approach. Twice a year, it looks at the average performance of a market (the 'benchmark'). Then it looks at whether active funds *buying into that same market* did better. Quite rightly, Dow Jones thinks this is a very fair, like-for-like comparison.

Here are some interesting results as of mid-2021. The full dataset is many times richer and it's worth exploring.

Investing in ...		Percentage of **active funds** that **underperformed** their market benchmark over ...		
		One year	Three years	Five years
Europe	**All companies**	51%*	72%	73%
US	**Large companies**	58%	68%	73%
	Mid-sized companies	76%	49%	59%
	Small companies	78%	55%	67%

*SPIVA gives its percentages right down to basis points; we have rounded up or down to the nearest 1 for ease of reading

Source: SPIVA[12]

The year 2020 was a rollercoaster in global stock markets, because of the pandemic. They plunged by 20–30 per cent, but then (contrary to most people's predictions) recovered completely. Active managers often say their skills, knowledge and foresight come into their own when markets are highly volatile so 2020 was a great year to test that claim.

What you can see in the table above is that the claim is not supported by the evidence. The longer an active fund has been investing, the less likely it has been to outperform the market. Surely the reverse ought to be true! To us this makes any one-year relative 'success' look like luck. In the cell that has given the active managers the best results (top left) it's still approaching odds-on that if you pick an active manager, the index will outperform their picks.

Morningstar: just five out of 54 categories beat the market over 10 years
The second source of evidence is run by Morningstar. Their Active/ Passive barometer tells a very similar story.[13] It surveys 30,000 funds, bundled up into categories to make comparisons fair and easy.

- Of the 54 actively managed categories they monitor, just five categories beat the market over 10 years;
- Most beat the market less than 25 per cent of the time.

Bayes Business School: only 1 per cent of funds outperform on a cost- and risk-adjusted basis in the long run

As we noted in the previous chapter, the high fees active managers require are a strong driver of underperformance. The rest, we think, is because the markets are a zero-sum game. One active manager's success is another one's loss.

'Ah!' someone may say. 'I really do think I can pick an active manager who's one of the good ones. And even in the worst cell in the table above, I have about a one-in-five chance of getting my choice right. Surely that's worth a punt?'

We say: good luck! Now you've seen the global long-term data, we will finish off our attempt to inoculate you by giving you a 10-year view wholly rooted in the UK.

A 2014 paper by Professor David Blake of Bayes Business School, and colleagues Tristan Caulfield of UCL and Christos Ioannidis and Ian Tonks of the University of Bath, looked at 516 UK active funds over that longer, 10-year timescale.[14] According to their analysis, around 99 per cent of all equity mutual fund managers were unable to deliver outperformance from stock selection or market timing.

Somewhat devastatingly, they added a final flourish: 'just 1 per cent of fund managers actually prove to be "stars", being able to

> **Rule 6: Keep investments simple, cheap and automated**

generate superior performance in excess of operating and trading costs. However, they extract all of this for themselves via fees, leaving nothing for investors.' So this is where we bring in Rule 6, our final rule, as an immunization against this type of managers. Simple, cheap and automated is the way to go. Again, we will return to this rule through the rest of the book, and will help you to apply it in our downloadable workbook.

Finally, a word on what SPIVA calls 'persistence'. How many years in a row do active managers display a good track record? SPIVA concludes: 'choosing between active funds on the basis of previous outperformance is a misguided strategy ... there remains a 96.8 per cent chance that a top-quartile fund will not stay in the top quartile for the next four years.'

In other words, there will always be short-term winners by the law of averages but the number of funds that outperform for decades is tiny. The funds that produce stellar returns in the future are unlikely to be those that have done so in the past.

So much for the 'star managers' we'd all like to believe are out there. It is to them that we now turn to – another species of shark with plenty of fees and foibles.

Woodford and friends

Celebrity sells, and faces sell. Over the years, the investment industry has realized that in its crowded, competing jungle of offers, claiming that a named individual has special ability and foresight is a simplification that many consumers will buy into.

Neil Woodford is the most infamous example in the UK, but he certainly won't be the last. He was the most celebrated 'star manager' for more than 20 years, yet his name is now inextricably linked with financial failure. Neil began his star career in 1998 at Invesco Perpetual. He ran actively-managed funds that grew to £25 billion of assets.[15] He began to get a name as an exceptional soothsayer by avoiding the worst excesses of the dot com bubble and then the 2008 financial crisis. Whether this was luck or judgement, it was soon to run out – but he didn't know it.

In 2014 he left Invesco to set up his own investment vehicle. Money flooded into it, because he was *the* star manager of his generation. Investors thought he could do little wrong. Very shortly, he was managing more than £10 billion of other people's money. But he had lost his Midas touch. By 2019, his fund had halved in value, losing billions.[16] It eventually emerged that it held less than 20 per cent of assets in FTSE 100 companies (compared to more than 50 per cent when it was created). Instead it had migrated 20 per cent of the assets into companies that could not easily be bought and sold.[17] This was not what investors believed they had bought into. They thought they had put money into a liquid fund based on fairly mainstream businesses and could draw it out at any time.

Suddenly, as the bad news about the Woodford fund began to multiply, too many people wanted out. But because much of it was invested in companies that are not quick or easy to sell, there wasn't enough cash to pay them. The fund had to be suspended, with all investors' money frozen inside it until the situation improved.

It didn't. By the time it was eventually unlocked, investors were receiving between 46p and 59p in the pound back on their stake in it – instead of the stellar return Woodford's 30-year reputation had led them to expect.[18]

And emblematically of all that is bad about the investment industry, for a while even after the crisis, Woodford and his fund continued to take multi-million-pound management fees as if nothing had changed.[19] And the investment platform Hargreaves Lansdown kept his fund on its 'best buy' list right up to the day of the fund's suspension.

Lawsuits resulted.

Woodford's equity fund was regulated by the FCA under normal rules. And this is a good reminder that the FCA's regulation is never intended to protect you against losing capital you hold in bad investments. It's meant to protect you against rule-breaking and fraudulent practices.

Some people say that Woodford broke rules, others that the FCA's rules were too lax. Whether either of those arguments wins out in the parade of post-mortems won't change the point: no regulatory rules are perfect, no regulator is perfect and you can lose lots of money on mainstream, regulated investments, having also paid star manager fees, as these investors did to Neil Woodford.

Woodford won't be the last. Names and faces are easy to remember and businesses find it easy to weave stories around them. Woodford was a media darling. Some of the journalists slating him now waxed lyrical about him a few years ago. People think they're being smart by investing in funds that are recommended in investment magazines, or the weekend money pages but it's a risky stream of unregulated opinion. There's no accountability when things go wrong.

The key takeaway from this sorry saga is that investing for the long term in a broadly diversified portfolio has a greater chance of success than putting your trust in soothsayers.

Closet trackers

Closet index tracking is the very dubious (but sadly widespread) practice of charging active management fees for funds that essentially hug an index. Fund managers the world over have been getting away with it for years.

In 2018 the Financial Conduct Authority revealed that a number of asset managers had been forced to pay back £34 million to investors overcharged by closet index funds.

'By the end of last year, we'd reviewed 84 potential closet tracker funds,' said the FCA's Director of Supervision for Investment, Megan Butler.[20] 'In 64 funds we've required the manager to make it clearer to consumers how constrained they are. We found the other 20 were adequately describing how they were being managed. Overall, £34m in compensation has been paid to consumers.'

But £34 million was a tiny drop in the ocean. The FCA's market report into the asset management sector stated that in 2017 there was £109 billion in partly active funds charging fully active fees. Fund managers do this because it's a way of guaranteeing a steady fee income without doing much work or incurring much expense. By definition, closet index funds will always underperform the market, but never so drastically that investors take their money out.

Robin is involved in the True and Fair Campaign which is pressing, among other things, for the eradication of closet trackers. But the FCA stubbornly refuses to make this species of shark extinct.

Are you paying fees into one of these funds?

'This time it's different'

Beware anyone who says this. It's the most dangerous phrase in the English language for investors. One day it may be true. But anyone who says they know *when* is fooling themselves or trying to fool you.

In the next chapter we will look at the historical rates of return from different asset classes – looking back as much as 120 years. If you had relied on the historical rates for the first 40 years, and bought widely, then held for the second 40, you would have done well. And if you had relied in the same way on the historical rates from the first 80, you would also have done well so it's entirely possible your investing lifetime will follow the same pattern – we certainly haven't found a better planning assumption. However, in the meantime you will encounter people who tell you that is old-hat thinking: 'This time it's different.'

Hindsight is a wonderful thing, so let's look at some previous bubbles where that phrase will have been used many times.

Tulips and mangoes

In February 1637, the price of flower seeds and bulbs in Holland plummeted (by 40 per cent on a year-on-year basis). But the price of *tulip* bulbs dropped much more spectacularly – by 99.999 per cent.[21] Contrary to popular history, this fantastic crash in the price of tulips did not affect a wide section of Dutch society. Although the records are very fragmentary, it seems that a minority of rich merchants and nobles lost money. The collapse mostly involved contracts that were promises to pay, rather than full prices already paid. The Dutch government stepped in and created an arrangement that enabled people to release themselves from some of these promises at a lesser cost.

So the tulip bubble was less colourful than how history has depicted it. But at the heart of it there was indeed a strange social mania, and that is why it has entered stock market history as the first recorded 'market bubble'. According to contemporary records, at peak, a single bulb from a prized tulip variety, the 'Viceroy', was trading at a cost of *eight years' wages* for an ordinary labourer. At some point, people believed this made sense! Everyone looks back on this and finds it hard not to conclude that the market had completely lost touch with reality, then the only thing driving the final price rises was a manic fear of missing out (FOMO).

That particular bubble settled into myth and memory, but new bubbles keep on popping up. Almost exactly 360 years later, in the online magazine *Wired*, the writer Kevin Kelly set out what he called 'New Rules for the New Economy'. These were his reflections on the new companies and markets emerging from the fledgling internet. This article is a classic of the genre 'this time it's different.'

More than one phrase comes back to haunt him, but our favourite is: 'In the past, an innovation's momentum indicated significance. Now, in the network environment, significance precedes momentum.'[22]

This was not very clear or elegant, but it was an indirect way of confirming what many dot com businesses believed in 1997. They thought it was vital to grow fast, but not particularly important to worry about having far too few customers to be profitable. This was a fundamental belief of the boom. Companies aggressively bought market share while racking up huge losses. They thought of it as a land grab: if they could grab enough land (customers) in cyberspace, they would soon become winners.

In 1997 the boom was beginning to rise ever more sharply. FOMO peaked first, and then the boom itself peaked on 10 March 2000, after which markets cratered. By October 2002 the Nasdaq index (the bellwether of the technology stock market) had lost 78 per cent of its value.[23] We, the authors, both lived through this boom and there are many astonishing stories that we heard about crazy companies and demented decisions. One favourite was the UK business clickmango.com, an online health food store. It hired the actress Joanna Lumley as its public face and advertised on television, securing £3 million of venture capital in just eight days. In 2000, it was promising £23 million of annual sales by 2003 and a £100 million market capitalization shortly after. But behind all this brouhaha, it was pulling in about £2,000 a week – about as much as a successful corner shop.[24]

Needless to say, when the peak passed, Clickmango soon became a distant memory and the £3 million might just as profitably have been tossed into the Thames. However, as *Wired* later pointed out, virtually all the most notorious failed dot com ideas became successful businesses. None benefited their original investors. New, more rational business owners patiently turned similar ideas into a profitable reality.

Buying health foods online today is perfectly normal and companies make money out of it. And look at Amazon. It was mocked in the dot com boom for continually losing money, lost 90 per cent of its value in the crash and continued to make losses for many years after. At one point it was amusingly described as a charity that enabled hedge fund managers to donate money – so that the middle classes could buy more stuff to crowd their homes. But who's laughing now? Amazon is now so large and profitable a business that some people are asking whether it should be broken up ... as a monopoly!

The biggest problem with the dot com boom was not that the ideas being invested in were intrinsically bad (although a few were, of course). It was that the investment flooded in before there were enough consumers online to use them and good enough broadband infrastructure for habits to change. Something different was indeed happening. But (and this is important) ... slowly! And it was not something radically different, not an endless 'flywheel' of ever-increasing profits ... just somewhat different. Above all, it was not different at the *'this time'* when everyone thought it was.

The lesson for us is that the biggest risk of getting caught up in a bubble is believing the sharks and soothsayers who tell you they understand not just the *difference*, but *how to exploit the timing*. And the second biggest risk is succumbing to fear of missing out *at a level that threatens your financial existence*. If either of us had put 1 per cent of our net wealth into the Nasdaq on 9 March 2000 and stuck with it, by today, we would have made perfectly good money out of it. And just as importantly, on the day disaster began, 10 March 2000, we would not have been so panicked that we would have felt obliged to sell it all.

So in our view, slow and steady wins the race. It does make sense to track long-term trends. If something appears genuinely new, is nowhere in your portfolio and it hasn't disappeared after seven or eight years, you may want to dip your toes in it. But do so at a level that you can afford to lose. Half a per cent or 1 per cent of your wealth is not a bad rule of thumb. And if you follow Rule 2, there's a fair chance you will have bought into it already. We think that the best way to invest is very, very widely indeed. In the next chapter we will encourage you to invest in a range of asset classes. This means that you will have a tiny slice of lots of what's happening in many markets.

Rule 2: Take a slice of everyone's business

During your investing lifetime a company, or multiple companies, may create a commercial form of generalized artificial intelligence. If they can, this would substitute parts of human labour in a wide variety of fields. Because its application would be so widespread and valuable, and the cost of capital and sales would be so low, the market value of such a company would likely make Google, Apple or Amazon look like chump change. This could change our lives considerably and if so, it will change markets and economies.

If you invest in very wide (worldwide) indexes of companies and you invest in micro and small companies, not just established ones, the chances are that if that company comes into existence, you will own a slice of it from its very early years. Certainly, with hindsight you will wish you had bought a bigger slice but think of the alternative: endlessly attempting to spot that needle of a world-beating technology company in the haystack of the worldwide stock market!

Beware investment 'themes'

This subject of spotting winners takes us to a final and very subtle species of shark (before we turn the mirror on ourselves): those who peddle investment 'themes'.

Pick up any investment magazine or the money section of a Sunday newspaper and you'll see what we mean. Robotics, artificial intelligence, infrastructure, healthcare and plant-based food are some of today's 'hot' themes. It's anyone's guess what subjects fund industry marketers will be writing about in a few years' time.

The reason why investment themes, and thematic funds in particular, are so popular is that they come with a ready-made narrative. As we have seen, investors love a good story. They are far more likely to be swayed by a compelling narrative than by data and evidence. Unfortunately, what makes for a good press release rarely makes for a good investment. The main problem is this: fund management companies know that, despite all the warnings that they shouldn't, both retail and institutional investors (and indeed many financial advisers and investment consultants) tend to choose funds primarily on the basis of recent performance so, naturally, most new product launches are in sectors that have seen strong returns in the last few years. But when you take a longer-term view, the picture is very different. Research by *Morningstar* in 2021 showed that thematic funds have trailed the overall equity market by about four percentage points per year over a trailing 10-year period.[25]

Morningstar also revealed that thematic funds tend to come with higher risk. They typically invest in holdings that are significantly smaller, pricier and less profitable than the average stock. All of these traits are associated with higher volatility. Even for investors who can tolerate that extra volatility, however, *Morningstar* found the returns delivered by thematic funds over the past 10 years have generally not been high enough to compensate for the additional risk.

But it gets worse. Survivorship rates for thematic funds are pretty dreadful. Because most funds that cease to exist had poor performance records, their demise artificially boosts the average performance of the funds that did survive.

Robin writes: Private equity, or how to enrich millionaire asset managers

There are some phrases financial professionals use that should raise a red flag for most consumers. One of them is 'alternative investments'. As we will explain in the next chapter, most savers and investors should simplify their focus to three asset classes: equities, bonds and cash. The term 'alternative investments' covers a multitude of other unsuitable options.

The current fad in alternative investments is private equity (PE). PE is a route to investing in companies not listed on the stock market. Historically, private equity has been confined to the institutional investing space, but asset managers are keen to target so-called 'retail' investors (industry-speak for you and me). Why is the PE industry so determined to sell everyone its wares? As Oxford finance professor Ludovic Phalippou has shown, PE funds generate huge fees for their managers while delivering largely mediocre performance.[26] He also shows how much easier it is for PE to disguise the value (or lack of value) provided, compared to public market funds.

A claim that's often made by PE advocates is that it's a useful diversifier but research suggests otherwise. When public equities fall in value, private companies tend to do the same. The only difference is that while we can clearly see prices falling in public markets, the ups and downs in private equity are much murkier.

Hedge funds are another alternative investment... to avoid! As the name suggests, they're supposed to provide a hedge (in effect, a bet) against falling equity markets but the data show that most of them don't. Indeed, because of the huge fees they charge, the vast majority will underperform a low-cost global equity fund in the long run.

Whenever you hear about hedge funds that have been on a spectacular winning streak, remember: there are bound to be short-term winners by the law of averages. Why, then, do so many people continue to invest in private equity and hedge funds? The reason may be largely behavioural. Professor Meir Statman from Santa Clara University has explained how, for some people, expensive investments express parts of our identity. They invest in them for the same reason they wear a Rolex watch or carry a Gucci bag.[27]

Of course, wise investors won't mix up their portfolio with a status symbol. As the author William Bernstein put it in *The Four Pillars of Investing*: 'You're not going to impress the crowd at your country club by telling them you own shares of an index fund. Let them laugh; the joke's on them.'[28]

A point of care about Rule 6

We believe that the principles of investing widely (Rule 2) and keeping costs low (Rule 6) will stand the test of time for *any*

Rule 6: Keep investments simple, cheap and automated

market environment. As will Rule 3 (taking a long-term view of risk). We also strongly recommend that for Rule 6, you take the evidence of history and basic maths as your guide and focus on the simplicity and automation of passive investments. This is not just for their low costs, but also for their reliable track record compared to active investments.

However, we are encouraging you to invest over a very long period of time and this might be 40 or 50 years for some people. Over such a long period the merits of the passive approach *might* change. We would not want to be yet another voice saying 'but this time it really is different!' So we wouldn't be doing our duty if we didn't discuss with you the implications of the overall proportions of passive and active investing in the stock markets.

As long as active investing is significant enough to move prices in the marketplace, and as long as its fees stay materially higher than passive investing, we believe that passive investing will offer all the advantages that we have set out above. But imagine this thought experiment: what if all active investors exited the marketplace and the only investment taking place was passive, automated and index-based?

It's currently highly hypothetical but the implications are worth a digression.

Active investors scrutinize companies' performance. They have the ultimate sanction of selling shares – walking away – from a company that has adopted a bad strategy, unethical business practices or anything else that should materially alter its worth.

The fund managers that run passive investment funds, although they may own shares in the same company, cannot do that. They can only follow their index's rules. They are obliged to buy and sell the company's shares only in proportion to its presence and value in the marketplace. Yes, they will sell when their fund-holders want to realize gains but they must also buy when their fund-holders have more money that they want to invest. None of this is directly driven by scrutiny of the company's performance. In that sense, they are owners without an exit. So in a passively dominated marketplace, capitalism would cease to scrutinize company performance and punish or reward it through share prices.

Of course, other aspects of capitalism would function like they do today. Consumers and employees would vote with their feet. Company managers would devise strategies for new products and to compete in new markets. Regulators would reshape markets. But share prices might not reflect this as closely as they do today.

This situation could not possibly stay static. In this hypothetical scenario, active managers would come back into business because at that point, it would be much easier than it is today to spot the gaps between the real value of companies and their share prices. And of course, capitalism loves to exploit such a gap.

But how likely is this hypothetical situation?

If a tipping point will ever be reached, it is certainly very distant right now.

At the moment, estimates of the proportion of the market under passive management vary widely. We have seen estimates that range from one-sixth of the total marketplace to one-third of some of the marketplaces for large companies. But it's not just about what is owned; trading *frequency* matters. It drives trading volume – and therefore how prices change. Broad, market-cap-weighted index funds tend to have much lower turnover than their actively managed counterparts so their share of trading volume is considerably lower than their share of assets. In a 2019 study, Vanguard estimated that stock index funds account for less than 5 per cent of trading volume on US exchanges.[29]

We think that an appetite for active management will continue to be driven by everyday investors and even more by family ownership of businesses, by billionaires and the super-rich. These people can very comfortably pay high fees for what they think will be remarkably high returns. And provided there is always a dynamic between active and passive management in this way, passive management will be by far the better bet.

Our hypothetical scenario might be analogous to saying: 'What would happen to the value of all the insurance companies if all the houses in the world were burned down by arsonists on the same night?' Intellectually intriguing, but hardly important for practical purposes. But over a very long investing lifetime, there *might* be a tipping point well short of total domination by passive investment. The evidence *could* change. Or governments might foresee the difficulties that would arise from a tipping point and legislate accordingly.

We think it is worthwhile to acquire the habit of checking in with the SPIVA index every couple of years to see how passive versus active is faring. We hope that long after you've got all the use you can out of this book, you'll still be in the habit of following the evidence.

Now take action

Our workbook will help you to:

- Health-check your digital security;
- Check that your investments are regulated by the FCA;
- Check the ownership of multiple bank accounts;
- Check that you are not paying high fees for closet tracker funds;
- Sign up to the scam alerts email sent out by *Which?*

6

Take the Right Risks

In Chapter 4 (*Capture Market Returns*, see pages 67–86), we set out the basic principles of investing and why we think passive investing gives you the best long-term prospects. In this chapter, we're going to tell you *how* to do it: how to design a portfolio that has the right mix of assets for your financial future. And that means taking the right mix of risks. Because each asset class has its different level of growth – and risk. As you blend them, you balance your growth and risk.

One way of designing this risk mix is to get it done by a professional who understands you – and can help you stay disciplined. We have more to say about choosing an adviser in Chapter 9 (*Find a First-Rate Adviser*, see pages 202–28), but here we set out the practical principles that will be needed to capture market returns. Whether you design your portfolio yourself, or act on the recommendations of an adviser, we think you will always need to understand these principles.

There's no getting away from it – this is the longest chapter in our book. It covers important principles about investing, principles that many people find mysterious or overwhelming. We want to make managing risk understandable and as a result, less daunting. We hope that by the time you've finished this chapter, you'll be much more confident in shaping a mix of investments and blending their risks.

To start with, we'll look at the 'race' between income, fees, inflation and growth. This will help you understand how much you might need your portfolio to grow. Then we'll look at the long-term historical growth records for different asset classes. This will help you understand how much you can 'safely' withdraw. We'll also think about the role of cash when there is a stock market crash. After that, we'll look at some classic 'mixes' of asset classes. This will help you understand how to raise or lower the level of risk by mixing asset classes.

Finally, we need to demystify the actual financial products you'll need to use. There is a range of different financial products that you can use to hold your simple portfolio, including, of course, a pension. We'll explain all these. We'll give a 'buyer's guide' to some of the lowest-fee providers. Many will automatically blend your investments into a portfolio that matches your appetite for risk.

Going up the mountain and coming down it

In Chapter 3 (*Manage Your Money*, see pages 42–66), we started the analogy of the pensions 'mountain' that you have to climb. At your chosen resting place on the mountain is a pension pot. It needs to be enough to fund the retirement you want, at the income level that matches your lifestyle. If you'll forgive us for extending that metaphor a little, we want to talk about going up the mountain, then coming down it …

Going up the mountain is what pensions experts call 'accumulation'. In simple language, it means investing *before* withdrawing any money. Indeed, the way the law works is that if your money goes into a pension product, you're not *allowed* to withdraw it until age 55 (57 from 2028 onwards). The earlier you start accumulating, the more risks you can take, because time will smooth them out.

Going down the mountain is what the experts call 'decumulation'. This ugly word quite simply means spending your pension. The mountain metaphor is quite helpful here, because more accidents happen when people come down mountains than when they go up them.[1] It can be quite psychologically daunting when you realize that your pension pot is never going to increase again, only decrease. Should you spend too fast, or find that your remaining assets are growing too slowly, that's when accidents will happen. This is why we are going to start our explanation of the asset mix by focusing on the challenges that decumulation will bring. What should you be worrying about when you start to go down the mountain

The principles of growth and taking income
Scenario 1

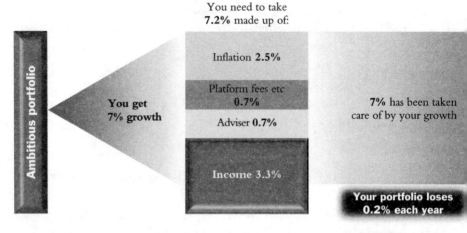

You need to take
7.2% made up of:

Ambitious portfolio

You get
7% growth

Inflation **2.5%**

Platform fees etc
0.7%

Adviser **0.7%**

Income 3.3%

7% has been taken
care of by your growth

**Your portfolio loses
0.2% each year**

**... so it won't run
out for 500 years**

(decumulate your pension)? Because that, in our view, is a helpful way to understand the need for the right mix in your portfolio.

As we'll explain later in this chapter, investment strategies for accumulation and decumulation used to be very different. Most people used to spend all their pension pot on an annuity as soon as they retired. Since 2015, all this has changed but you will still find a lot of advisers recommending a more cautious approach to investment after you have retired. For the reasons you'll see us set out in the rest of this chapter, we're not sure that's optimal any more.

Growth should ideally outpace what you spend

What if the capital you had in investments at the beginning of your retirement grew every year, to become even larger at the end? In this scenario, you would have indeed spent some of the growth that your portfolio of investments gave you annually but because growth outpaced your ability to spend, it kept on growing larger and larger. When you died, there would be a large inheritance for someone else.

The principles of growth and taking income
Scenario 2

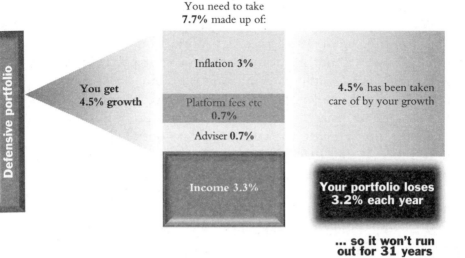

You need to take
7.7% made up of:

Inflation **3%**

You get
4.5% growth

Platform fees etc
0.7%

Adviser **0.7%**

Income **3.3%**

Defensive portfolio

4.5% has been taken
care of by your growth

**Your portfolio loses
3.2% each year**

**... so it won't run
out for 31 years**

For most people this will be simply too hard to achieve. Either they would need to start with a fabulous sum that is much more than enough to meet their needs or they would need to enjoy eye-popping growth for decade after decade. Most people should probably ask themselves whether the scenario we've set out would be a desirable outcome anyway. Sure, it's good to leave money to your partner, children, relatives, friends or charity. But if, when you die, you leave more than you had saved at the very outset of your retirement years, have you truly used them to your best advantage? Think back to the themes of Chapter 1 (*Your Money or Your Life?*, see pages 13–26).

A scenario that is probably more realistic, and indeed may be more optimal, is that your retirement spending gradually eats away at your investment portfolio, but with a comfortable margin of error. You never run out of money, but you do end up with a lot less money than you started with. The graphics above, using some simplified examples, give an idea of how this might work.

Looking at scenario 1, let's say you invest in an ambitious portfolio and over your retirement you get an average growth of 7 per cent. But let's say you will actually need to 'spend' 7.2 per cent each year. This is made up of average inflation, average platform and fund fees, average money manager fees and withdrawing an income of 3.3 per cent. (We'll come back to this magic 3.3 per cent figure later.)

We say 'spend' because the 2.5 per cent for inflation never comes out of your portfolio. It is a necessary subtraction from the growth rate because without it, the real value of your portfolio will be shrinking. (As we said before, inflation is insidious because it is an invisible cost that many people forget.) However, the remaining percentages are what you withdraw to spend. So in this scenario, each year after growth, you take a tiny bite out of your portfolio in real terms – less than a quarter of 1 per cent. Your portfolio is being reduced in size each year, but *extremely* slowly. In fact, if you take 0.2 per cent each year, it will last 500 years. So you will be very safe.

What's not to like? We're afraid that if it were that simple, no one would have any problems. And there are many … So here are all the ifs and buts you need to consider:

- Growth will not be the same each year. Some years, it will be negative, others it may be 10 per cent. So whatever asset allocation you choose, there will be significant highs and lows. And you might lose your nerve and sell at the wrong time.
- In the next part of this chapter, we'll look at the historical rates of return and you'll see that consistent 7 per cent growth is very hard to achieve. It requires a highly ambitious risk-taking approach. If you want to be more cautious in your investments, or about your prospects, you will probably need to plan for something like 4 or 5 per cent growth. It might not sound as if that will make a huge difference – but it will.
- No one knows what inflation will be. For 30 years or more, it ran low in developed countries, then it shot up. In 2022, it hit 50-year highs. So it could be significantly higher than 2.5 per cent in the future. (This would probably boost growth a bit more too, but no one can be sure of that.) In fact, the average rate of inflation in the UK since 1900 has been 3.6 per cent.[2]

- And of course you don't
know how long you will live
(although 500 years gives
a very comfortable margin

Rule 5: Only focus on what you can control

of error!). So there are an awful lot of factors you can't
control. But there are three things you *can* control: your asset
allocation, how much you take as your income, and the fees
and adviser charges you pay. We hope this helps to underline
the importance of Rule 5.

Now look at scenario 2. Inflation is up to 3 per cent, your average
growth down to a more realistic 4.5 per cent but your other needs
stay the same. Growth will therefore supply a much smaller slice of
what you need. However, even though your portfolio will decline
by 3.2 per cent each year as a result, it will still last a good while:
31 years. For some people, retiring at 67, seeing them through to 98
will be just fine. If they live until they are 90, they won't run out of
money and there will be a good amount left in their pot.

The 'safe' withdrawal rate

Why have we included a figure of 3.3 per cent as the amount you
will be able to withdraw as income? If growth happened to be 10
per cent in a particular year, why wouldn't you just knock off the
2.5 per cent for inflation, then the fees and after that you could
withdraw as income whatever is left over from your 10 per cent?

The reason is that the scenarios above are based on averages. In
reality, returns will go from positive to negative – and back again –
over the period in which you are drawing down your income. So you
need 'fat' years to fund your 'lean' years. It might make intuitive sense
to take all the growth you can each year, leaving capital untouched,
but the evidence shows that you will very likely run out of money
too early if you do.

One of the single most important pieces of research in the history
of retirement turned this into a rule. It was set out in a 2000 paper
by William P. Bengen called 'Determining Withdrawal Rates Using
Historical Data'.[3] William modelled what could have happened to

people who retired every year since 1926 if they had followed a simple rule. He asked how much they could have withdrawn from their initial portfolio, adjusting the same amount for inflation each year, without running out of money. All the while, he expected them to follow the principle that the lean years would need to be funded by the fat years. His lean years helpfully included the 1929 Wall Street Crash, the worst fall in the history of the stock market. Each time, he ran their retirement clock for 30 years.

After running his different scenarios, he concluded that the answer was 'about 4 per cent' and this has become very famous as his '4 per cent rule'. He also used the words 'safe withdrawal' so it has become known as the *safe withdrawal rate*, or sometimes 'SAFEMAX'.

We use the words 'safe' in scare quotes because we do want to keep on emphasizing that 'safety' is probabilistic and relative, not absolute and guaranteed. But what he developed was indeed an extremely helpful rule of thumb. However, Bengen's rule was based on US stock market data. As we will see below, the UK stock market tends to grow more slowly.

Unless you make all your investments outside the UK, you'll always need to ask about sources of data and think about that difference. Fortunately, some further authors came to the rescue and did similar work for UK stock market history. Wade Pfau asked: 'Does the 4 per cent rule work around the world?'[4] He came up with a figure of 3.36 per cent based on UK market returns. (He also said 4 per cent was now a shade too optimistic for people in the US.)

For caution and simplicity, we have rounded his UK rule down to 3.3 per cent. It's very important to be clear what the rule means. Both the 4 per cent rule and the 3.3 per cent rule depend on *what your portfolio is worth at the start of your retirement*. They say: if your year 0 pot is worth £1,000,000, then in year 1 you can take 4 per cent (US) or 3.3 per cent (UK) out – so, £33,000. But let's say your portfolio has increased to £1,200,000 the following year, because of spectacular growth. Pfau's rule says you should now only increase your £33,000 *by inflation*. He *doesn't* say that you can now take 3.3 per cent of £1,200,000 and raise your retirement income to £39,600 in one year. As much as possible of the extra £200,000 in your portfolio from this 'fat' year will be needed for future 'lean' years.

(Pfau also assumes that you will have at least 60 per cent equities in your portfolio. We'll come back to this important question of blend later in this chapter.)

So as you can see, the rule is a bit of a straitjacket and too linear for normal life. What your portfolio is worth on the day you retire becomes a sacred amount. You apply the rule to it on that day and that creates a static income for the rest of your life – it's a bit like funding your own annuity.

Virtually nobody's life works this way. Most people will end up spending less in the later years of their retirement. Most people, unless they retire at 67 or so, will get a state pension earlier or later than the day they retire. Both of these factors mean you will need to vary the annual income you require. And of course, virtually anyone would look at their investments and try to work out how to economize if their pension pot was shrinking too fast. The rule doesn't try to model any of this. We should also say that the rule has come in for plenty of criticism about whether the evidence still fully justifies using such high numbers. Many people believe we are now entering a low-growth period where either 4 or 3.3 per cent would be over-optimistic. We will come back to this later.

The rule also does not account for fees and this casts a further interesting light on our message about keeping fees low. If, on top of 3.3 per cent, your fees are adding up to around 0.7 per cent, they are nibbling away at your margin of error, but you still have about a 90 per cent chance of not running out of money. However, if your fees are topping 1 per cent, there is no way you can count on a margin of error to pay for them. You are in the danger zone for running out of money and will have to reduce your income below 3.3 per cent accordingly. It's yet another piece of strong evidence to show that the cost of fees really can make all the difference between a successful retirement and a busted one. Unless you are in the happy position of having far more money saved up than you need, we think the best way of digesting all this is to adopt the following principles:

- When I retire, I need the largest level of risk in my portfolio that I can stomach, to give the highest possible level of growth.

- In the UK, I should use 3.3 per cent of the value of my portfolio at retirement as a ceiling for my expectations about what I will be able to withdraw as regular income. If I take a little bit more out than that in the early years, what I take in the later years should balance out to an average of 3.3 per cent.
- If my fees are above 0.7 per cent, or I've put less than 60 per cent equities in my portfolio, I should withdraw even less than 3.3 per cent for myself.
- For the first half of my retirement, I will need to make sure the fat years are left well alone, to fund future lean years.
- I will need to keep it all under review, to see what happens to my portfolio in reality, and adjust course if I need to.

With all the warnings above about the limitations of 3.3 per cent, it's now time to use the powerful maths it introduces. It powers a crude (but useful) formula to calculate the pot you need for your retirement. You divide your desired pre-tax income by 0.033. That will give you the pension pot size required to generate it. So, if you want to have a pre-tax income of £35,000 a year:

$$£35,000 \div 0.033 = £1,060,000 \text{ pension pot}$$

This is crude because it doesn't take account of changes to your income from the state pension and it doesn't take full account of taxes and fees (it crudely simplifies by expecting tax-free withdrawals to roughly balance out fees). But it is quick and simple, and so it's not a bad way to double-check your place on the 'pensions mountain' we introduced in Chapter 3 (*Manage Your Money*, see pages 42–66). We will help you to apply it in a more considered way in the workbook.

So what growth can I expect?

Now we turn to the actual history of what you can reasonably expect from different asset classes, whether you are accumulating or decumulating. Elroy Dimson, Paul Marsh and Mike Staunton are experts in market history (starting with their 2002 work *Triumph of the Optimists: 101 Years of Global Investment Returns*). Their long-term data is updated in frequent reports. This is what the 2022 report told us.[5]

Historical rates of return 1900–2021			
Asset class	Nominal (pre-inflation) rate	Inflation rate	Real (post-inflation) rate
US			
Equities	9.6%		6.7%
Long-term government bonds	4.9%	2.9%	2.0%
Treasury bills	3.6%		0.7%
UK			
Equities	9.0%		5.4%
Long-term government bonds	5.4%	3.6%	1.8%
Treasury bills	4.6%		1.0%

Source: copyright © 2022 Elroy Dimson, Paul Marsh and Mike Staunton, used with permission

As we have noted in the previous chapter, we think that because figures like these reflect what has happened over a very long time, they are the least worst guide you have to the future. They have included two world wars, the Wall Street Crash and the consumer boom of the 1950s and 60s. They have also included the stagflation of the 1970s and the computer boom since the 1980s, as well as two pandemics – the flu pandemic after World War I and that of 2020. But of course they don't guarantee the future. As the investment research expert Larry Swedroe says, 'Never treat the likely as certain'. And although they are very useful figures, the frame in which they have been selected is very important so we want to spend just a few moments looking outside that frame and at other viewpoints.

The first thing to point out is that we ourselves have picked out just two countries – from the many covered in Dimson, Marsh and Staunton's report – the US and the UK. Look at other countries' markets from that same report and you'll get different results for the same period. And here we underline the point made above, that the real returns from the UK record are distinctly lower for equities than the US. So, already, you have to choose a country or countries as an anchor point for your assumptions.

But the time frame matters too, as well as the geography. In 2019, Aizhan Anarkulovaa, Scott Cederburga and Michael S. O'Doherty published a very interesting paper called 'Stocks for the long run? Evidence from a broad sample of developed markets'.[6] This looked at the return on equities only, but for the longest possible continuous time periods and over a very wide range of markets. Some of these market records went back to 1841. Perhaps going back a further 60 years is better? Maybe. Remember, that means including the stock market record for a time before there were cars, widespread railways, electricity, photography or the germ theory of medicine. And for decades and decades when insider trading was acceptable business practice.

The good news is that the real average return across all these markets and time periods was high. The average person who bought a randomly distributed $100,000 investment and held it for any random 30-year period could expect to get $738,000 back. But this is an average. Another way of looking at the data is that about 12 per cent of these hypothetical investors did not get back their entire $100,000 even after 30 years. The model just happened to put them in the wrong 30-year period and the wrong 'basket' of markets. And these were investments only in equities. It's the asset class that people say 'always comes right' in the long term.

The authors make some interesting points about 'survivorship bias'. They cite the example of the Czechoslovakian stock exchange, which thrived before World War II. When the country became communist in 1945, its stock market was nationalized. Investors didn't just suffer a 20 or 30 per cent loss — they lost everything. Is this catastrophe of total loss so unusual that it should be expunged from the averages they put together, or an important part of the jigsaw? (They included it.) So frames, choices and biases inform all such headline numbers. But that said, let's look at some other asset classes and their long-term rates of return.

We have sorted this table by real rate of return (i.e. after adjustments for inflation) so that you can see which asset classes have returned the most.

Asset class (NB – all data from US unless otherwise noted)	Nominal (pre-inflation) rate	Real (post-inflation) rate of return	How far back and source	Our commentary
Micro-cap equities	14.8%	**10.8%**	1972; Portfolio Visualizer[7]	**Micro-** and **small-cap**. This means tiny and small companies, based on their market capitalization (essentially, the purchase price of the company if you were to buy it). A very large company is likely, although not certain, to grow less quickly than a small company, because it may well have claimed most of its possible customers already. The smaller the company, the bigger its *potential* marketplace. Therefore, it seems likely (and the figures bear this out) that the smaller the company you invest in, the higher your average rate of return.
Medium-cap 'value' equities	14.1%	**10.1%**	1972; Portfolio Visualizer	A 'value' company is one that is trading at a lower price than its actual value. The 'actual value' is usually calculated on a reasonably objective measure. This is quite technical. But trying to put it as simply as possible, you calculate the value of a company's **assets** (assets minus debts and liabilities), and divide it by the value the **market** assigns to it (share price x number of shares).

Asset class (NB – all data from US unless otherwise noted)	Nominal (pre-inflation) rate	Real (post-inflation) rate of return	How far back and source	Our commentary
				If the ratio you get from this calculation is below 1, the stock is considered to be overvalued. If the ratio is greater than 1, the stock is considered undervalued. For completeness, we should tell you that there are other ways of arriving at this conclusion, some of them a little bit too subjective for our tastes.
Small-cap equities	13.3%	**9.2%**	1972; Portfolio Visualizer	*(See comments on micro-caps above.)*
Large-cap equities	11.7%	**7.6%**	1972; Portfolio Visualizer	These are very large, often multinational, businesses.
Emerging market equities	9.3%	**5.2%**	1995; Portfolio Visualizer	These are companies outside the traditional stockpicking grounds of Europe, the US, Canada, Japan, Australia and the like. At various times they might include, Brazil, South Korea, Israel and so on.
Gold	7.9%	**3.7%**	1970; A Wealth of Common Sense[8]	
UK long-term government bonds	5.4%	**1.8%**	1900, Dimson, Marsh & Staunton[9]	
Property	4.2%	**1.2%**	1928; Mindfully Investing[10]	

Asset class (NB – all data from US unless otherwise noted)	Nominal (pre-inflation) rate	Real (post-inflation) rate of return	How far back and source	Our commentary
US Treasury bills	3.6%	**0.7%**	1900, Dimson, Marsh and Staunton	
Cash	4.6%	**0.5%**	1972; Portfolio Visualizer	
Commodities	−0.2%	**−4.3%**	2007; Portfolio Visualizer	This means anything from oil to food – physical items that people need. We're not sure how much faith you should put in any track record going back less than 15 years but broader and longer research shows that commodities have been very volatile. They have been surprisingly ineffective at balancing risk in portfolios.[11] This seems very odd given everyone needs them.

Sources: multiple, see endnotes

So what?

Well, the first thing we want you to see at the top of the table is that over the long run, quite high real rates of return are possible. This is almost all US data, so you would need to dampen it down a bit for the UK, but even so you can see that, with reinvestment over a long period of time, these high rates would deliver substantial wealth.

By contrast, you may be surprised by the low long-term rates of return on gold (given the myth and glamour surrounding it) – and on property. (Robin has more to say about the UK's love of property as an investment in the next chapter.) But that brings us to another important point about this table: it covers more than just investing in companies. Gold, property and commodities are not companies, although there are ways of investing in companies that make money from them. Cash and government bonds are not companies either. If you look carefully at the table above, the long-term conclusion must be that investing in equities (companies) grows your money most. Although other ways of growing your money do exist, they give you lower rates of return.

We didn't want to make the table a fog of numbers, so we excluded data about the volatility of each asset class. That's a bit naughty, because this chapter's theme is all about risk. But you can rest assured that the higher the return, the more it will swing from high to low. For example, in the historical series of returns for US micro-caps, the biggest gain in one year was +80 per cent and the biggest loss in any one year was -40 per cent!

Remember, this is not the performance of individual companies, but stunning swings of a whole market. So, for example, if you invest in micro caps your investment will undergo simply enormous ups and downs. If you choose this, you will need to be sure you can deal with your mood swings if a big chunk of your portfolio goes down by 40 per cent.

The only free lunch in investing

Diversification has been described by Nobel laureate Harry Markowitz as 'the only free lunch in investing'. Diversified investors

Rule 2: Take a slice of everyone's business

will not hang their hopes on one asset class, or one sector, or one country, or one stock. They'll spread their exposure across and within stocks and bonds, across different markets, industries and currencies.

Diversification increases the reliability and predictability of returns. When Robin interviewed the Nobel Memorial Prize winner William Sharpe, he asked for Sharpe's golden rules (noting he had won a prize for 'pioneering work in the theory of financial economics'). He gave Robin this reply: 'The three most important things are diversify, diversify, diversify'.

(Sharpe then added, 'And then I'll give you three more: "keep costs low, keep costs low, keep costs low." You'll notice that our six rules take you a bit further than Sharpe wanted to go, but his two golden rules are echoed by two of ours.)

Keep the importance of diversification in mind throughout the rest of this chapter and as you use our workbook. We have more to say about diversification in Chapter 7 (*Manage Your Mix*, see pages 152–86) as well.

Classic asset allocation mixes

We hope you can see now that diverse asset allocation is not only a critical tool, but one of the few that is under your control,

> **Rule 5: Only focus on what you can control**

reminding us of Rule 5. Stock selection and tactical market timing may have an influence, but as we saw in the last chapter, this supposed skill is almost indistinguishable from luck.

The overwhelming driver of your portfolio's growth is asset allocation.

Growth or defence?

Looking at the table in the previous section, pages 125–7, it is obvious that some assets are likely to lead to higher growth over the long term. So why wouldn't you just pile into those and ignore the asset classes towards the bottom of the table? The reason is that the lower-growth asset classes are what is known as 'defensive' assets. Because cash, bills and bonds attract low, but fixed, interest rates, they tend to hold their value when the stock market goes haywire. So a typical portfolio will hold both categories of assets, growth assets and defensive assets. There are endless, raging debates about what the best balance is between the two.

When people had to buy annuities for their pensions, life was much simpler. The theory was you should have a portfolio clearly oriented towards ambitious growth, up until five to 10 years before the retirement date, then your portfolio would gradually switch towards defensive assets.

Investors' biggest fear was that they would suffer a large stock market loss shortly before they needed to buy their annuity. If so, they would suffer a permanent loss of income as a result. Defensive assets were a way they could trade off the prospect of growth for maintaining value. If you do want to buy an annuity (and it's still an option), this is a good plan. If you don't, your investment period is open-ended and the choices are not so clear.

A classic cautious, defensive portfolio could look like this.

A defensive portfolio

A classic 'defensive' portfolio *targeting long-term pre-inflation growth of around* **6%** *anticipating ups and downs of as much as 10%*			
Proportion of your portfolio	Asset category	Sample asset types	Comments
70%	**Government bonds**	UK gilts	These have low, but pretty secure, fixed rates of growth. However, they can risk being so low that they don't outpace inflation.
30%	**Large and medium-cap equities**	UK large-cap Developed world large-cap Mid-cap	For all the reasons we've given above, these are higher-growth, but more volatile.

So who is this portfolio good for? If it achieves its goal, it will barely outpace inflation and fees. As soon as you start drawing an income, the chances are that you will always be eating into your capital.

It would be good for those close to buying an annuity.

It would also be good for people who already have enough money in their retirement portfolio to fund their full retirement and simply hope to maintain the real-terms value of remaining assets while they run it down.

And it might be helpful for people who know that they are of a cautious disposition and wouldn't be able to live with the highs and lows of big risks. However, even this kind of portfolio could drop significantly in any year. Over a long investing period you would probably experience a single-year drop of nearly 10 per cent.

We should also note that the 4 per cent/3.3 per cent rule rested on research into what would have happened to portfolios with more than 60 per cent equities. This portfolio contains far less so it sets you outside those rules. If you use this kind of portfolio, you will probably have to take an even more cautious approach than drawing down 3.3 per cent adjusted for inflation each year.

Risk ratings and portfolio pickers

As soon as you come into contact with a financial adviser, they will assess your attitude to risk. This is entirely sensible. Their job is to work out how to invest in line with not only your aspirations, but your habits and attitudes.

These days their risk tolerance questionnaires (RTQs) are usually online and can be quite elaborate. The questionnaire will assign you to a risk rating from ultra-cautious to ultra-carefree, usually on a scale of 1 to 10, but in some cases 1 to 5, and in other cases, words rather than numbers.

That's fine. It's after that when the problems begin to pile up. A sensible principle has been fractured into a wide variety of 'in-house' approaches with overlapping, but slightly differentiated, common language. If you bounce from one adviser to another, you'll find they use the same 'risk words' to mean slightly different things. Then the problems begin to increase as the risk ratings are turned into portfolio design. A study of 'Risk Tolerance, Return Expectations, and Other Factors Impacting Investment Decisions' by Sam Sivarajan and Oscar De Bruijn showed that advisers would give quite widely varying portfolio designs in response to the same risk tolerance questionnaires. What drove the designs was more their prior beliefs about investing styles.[12] Again, we think that the principle that your risk appetite should help build your portfolio is entirely sensible. What we find difficult to navigate is spurious precision: allegedly giving a clear-cut differentiation between a portfolio responding to risk level 8 out of 10 and one responding to 7 out of 10.

We also guarantee that if you show any adviser the 'cautious' portfolio above, their nose will wrinkle. They will immediately begin to quibble about a particular asset class or a percentage. That is not to say that they are wrong, nor that they don't have considerable expertise. They have much more than we do. But it does mean that you are buying into fallible human judgement, not robotic precision! We'll have more to say about picking the best adviser you can in Chapter 9 (*Find a First-Rate Adviser*, see pages 202–28).

The investment author Larry Swedroe summarizes the evidence thus:

> Advisers need to do a better job of understanding their clients' susceptibility to various behavioral biases. Investors are best served when advisers identify their clients' overconfidence, anchoring tendency, propensity for maximising versus satisficing, susceptibility to recency bias and herd behavior. With that said, since advisers are also humans, they are likely to be affected by the same behavioral biases, notwithstanding their training and experience. The typical RTQ does not address these issues.[13]

For what it's worth, the portfolio above very roughly corresponds to three out of 10 on the risk scale. If you've followed our explanations so far, it won't take much imagination to see which asset classes you should dial up or down to make it more cautious, or more ambitious. To balance it out, we now present a representative portfolio towards the upper end of the scale. Let's say (with no spurious accuracy) – very roughly, 7.

An ambitious portfolio

A classic 'ambitious' portfolio targeting long-term pre-inflation growth of around **9%** anticipating ups and downs of as much as 20%			
Proportion of your portfolio	Asset category	Sample asset types	Comments
30%	**Micro- and Small-Cap equities**	*UK Small-Cap equity* *US Small-Cap equity*	These are likely to offer the highest rates of growth. The fees are likely to be higher than 0.5 per cent.
50%	**Large- and Medium-Cap equities**	*Global Large-Cap growth equity* *UK Large-Cap equity*	To make it simpler, you can just buy into a global fund of Large- or Mixed-Cap equities.

A classic 'ambitious' portfolio targeting long-term pre-inflation growth of around **9%** anticipating ups and downs of as much as 20%			
Proportion of your portfolio	Asset category	Sample asset types	Comments
20%	**Government bonds**	*UK gilts*	These are low interest bearing, conservative assets – the only truly conservative asset class in the portfolio.

We need to take a brief detour into pessimism here, which helps explain some of the thinking behind this portfolio. Although not all agree, many eminent academics (notably Dimson, Marsh and Staunton) are predicting lower returns in the future than investors have enjoyed in the past.[14] They reason that the returns on bonds have been low for a long time and show no signs of rising. They argue that the 'risk premium' future investors will get by investing in equities has a ceiling. They argue history shows that this is linked to the returns on bonds. In their view, a 'balanced' portfolio of 70 per cent equities and 30 per cent bonds will yield an after-inflation rate of return ('real return') of just 2 per cent.

The ambitious portfolio we have set out above therefore contains only 20 per cent bonds. If we calculate its pre-inflation (nominal) rate of return based on the longest historical averages we can find, the *nominal* rate is high – 12 per cent. But let's dampen that down, assuming that Dimson, Marsh and Staunton are right. Even after that, it's still plausible that this portfolio could give a 9–10 per cent pre-inflation rate of return and therefore a respectable after-inflation rate of return. So who is this portfolio good for? In our view, you would select this type of portfolio for one of two reasons:

- You have a 'medium-towards-high' risk appetite. If the stock market falls by 20 or even 30 per cent in one year, you'll not be too upset. You will know that next year it will probably rise and in six or seven years' time, it will almost certainly have recovered.

- Your financial situation is such that you can't live with a lower rate of long-term growth.

This second point is fine if it combines well with the first. However, if you are risk-averse *and* all the same need higher growth, that's the most uncomfortable combination possible. To compound it, that's probably the scenario with the strongest case for handing over your money management to an adviser. This is because they won't have the same strong emotions as you about the money they are managing and are more likely to make rational and consistent decisions. But unfortunately, as their additional adviser's fee will always claim a substantial fraction of your growth, it will then further ratchet up your need for growth.

Cash for a crash

There is an approach to investing that can help you to deal with the psychology of loss and we recommend it. However, we recognize its ideal form may not be feasible for everyone. This is the use of cash as 'self-insurance' against a stock market crash.

If the stock market falls – let's say, a dramatic fall of 40 per cent – the historical evidence shows it is likely to recover eventually. How long will that take? Unfortunately, nobody knows, despite innumerable articles and books trying to dissect what happened in different markets and average out the different cycles. Some recoveries took four to six years, others took as long as 13. There is still a debate about whether the Wall Street Crash cycle took 25 years for full recovery. (Some people say it took only four-and-a-half.)[15] However, another way of looking at the problem is: how long could you stop worrying about it?

One decent answer is that when you retire, you should hold enough money in cash or bonds, alongside your lower-risk stocks, to cover several years of your retirement spending.

The crash begins. The next day, you stop withdrawing any money from your equity investments and you simply switch to living off your cash for several years. During that time, you would have to be incredibly unlucky for equities not to begin their climb back towards a new peak. Sure, they may not have fully recovered but it does mean you won't sell any of them at their lowest value.

This protects you from something called 'sequence of returns risk' – a nasty, vicious circle that can happen with retirement spending. Suppose your equities fall in value. If you are still drawing money down by selling them, you then have to sell more equities to maintain the same income. This digs you into an ever-deeper hole, because the equities you have left over need to rise in value *even more* to make up the difference in future. If you *can* switch to cash, you can sidestep that return risk. You just leave your market-based assets to regrow. This is good financial planning and clearly it can also give you peace of mind.

Now, in the ideal scenario, you would have a nice 'ambitious' pension portfolio reflecting the kind of asset mix we have

Rule 3: To dilute your risks, add lots of time

suggested above. And *outside* your pension product, you would also have three to five years of spending in cash. You would invest most of that cash in higher interest-bearing accounts. That would lock it out of your reach for a year or two, but it would still be accessible when you need it. When a crash happened, you would ignore your portfolio for a couple of years and sit it out – reflecting from time to time on your new best friend, Rule 3.

Most people's finances will not get close to this blissful state. And even if yours can, it's important to remember that you can have too much cash. If it is being eaten away by inflation, because it is invested in accounts that offer sub-par rates of interest, that's a problem too – especially if you never need to call on it in a crash.

If you can't arrange things with substantial cash *outside* your portfolio, the next best thing is to make sure that the proportion of bonds and gilts in your portfolio always covers three to five years of spending. Bonds and gilts are a lot like cash – they are low-interest and pretty secure – but they are less liquid.

There is a chance that in a crash, some *corporate* bonds might suffer alongside equities, or the market for re-selling them could weaken. So you might not escape the impact quite as cleanly if you are invested in corporate bonds, as you would with government bonds. For this reason, we have only put government bonds in our illustrative portfolios.

The asset allocation spectrum

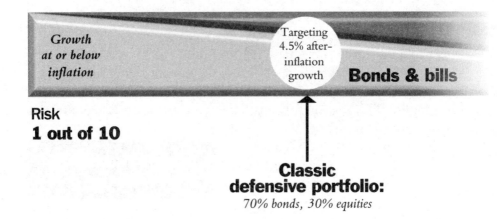

Growth at or below inflation

Targeting 4.5% after-inflation growth

Bonds & bills

Risk
1 out of 10

Classic defensive portfolio:
70% bonds, 30% equities

More bonds, bills and cash

Almost no ups and downs

If you are withdrawing 3.3 per cent a year then five years of bonds amounts to about 16 per cent of your portfolio in this asset class – which, by no coincidence, is close to the amount in the ambitious portfolio above.

What is your reaction?

Now you have seen our take on a defensive and an ambitious portfolio, you have seen two ends of a spectrum. Neither is the extreme end, but it's not hard to see how you could dial the risk up or down.

At the extreme of caution, you could invest only in bonds and cash. At the extreme end of ambition, you could invest only in medium- and small-company stocks. And in the middle, you could approach a 50/50 mix of equities and bonds.

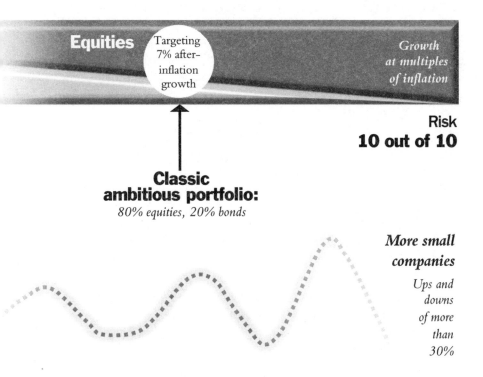

Equities Targeting 7% after-inflation growth

Growth at multiples of inflation

Risk
10 out of 10

Classic ambitious portfolio:
80% equities, 20% bonds

More small companies

Ups and downs of more than 30%

Your instinctive reaction to each of our examples will be a first step to help you to work out what is the right portfolio approach for you. We have a whole worksheet in our workbook to help you think it through. And it points you to a free online tool that can help you experiment.

You will also need to consider whether you want to be more risk-taking in the early years of accumulation. Then, more

Rule 6: **Keep investments simple, cheap and automated**

risk-averse when you move to drawing down your money. You will find that there is plenty of easily accessible information on the internet about other people's portfolios. You can simply copy others for inspiration. For example, the Forbes article '6 Expert Investment Portfolios You Can Implement Today'.[16] It gives portfolios advocated by six experts, all of which could be implemented using the 'simple, cheap and automated' mantra we're setting out in Rule 6.

However, it's one thing to design portfolios in your head. In the real world, you have to engage with financial services firms to implement your wishes. So in the remainder of this chapter we get down to the nuts and bolts details about financial products that buy real investments to put your principles to work. Yes, it's time to grapple with the financial services industry.

Jonathan writes: Getting to know the City of London

My work at the Money Advice Service gave me an opportunity to get to know some of the 'great and the good' from the City of London, understand how it works and see what makes it tick. Whatever you think of 'the City', this insight was a privilege. Not many people get the chance to weave in and out of the offices of so many firms – and of their critics.

London is one of the most celebrated and lambasted financial services centres in the world. It has simultaneous reputations for buccaneering risk-taking, with no thought for collateral damage ... and a hide-bound regulatory regime, layered on top of an old-boy network and creaking centuries-old traditions. Being entertained at a financial services industry dinner in the lavish Guildhall, which was built on top of the Roman amphitheatre, certainly brought all this together in one vision ... not least because of the many pink-faced men of my own age and colour speaking very loudly to each other. However, there are more and more women in positions of influence (I met some inspiring individuals) and they are bringing fresh air into the stuffier institutions. There is also a vibrant financial technology ('fintech') industry that has given a shake-up and a wake-up to the bigger, older and fatter banks. As we've said earlier in this book, this fintech industry is creating a golden age of free or very cheap innovations for UK consumers. And in my view, looking at the last decade or so, although the regulator is always pilloried for rip-offs that slip through the cracks in its supervision (or gaps in the regulatory rules themselves), UK consumers have been, on average, decently protected from widespread problems. We also have a fair degree of recourse when something objectively wrong takes place.

My focus was on consumer education. The fundamental issue, as I see it, is that financial services products are intrinsically complex. Yet most of us are too bored or scared by these products to correct this imbalance: the mismatch between the firms, who know everything, and consumers, who know too little. The worst firms exploit this 'information asymmetry' to cream off profits; the best firms do their utmost to simplify the products themselves, the information that explains them. And they are transparent about fees.

It's been our aim that by reading this book you will have sufficient understanding of the basic principles and rules of investment and pension products so you'll know the key questions you need to ask about them. We've also given some 'buyer's guides' dotted throughout the book. Necessarily, these guides simplify and they are definitely *not* reviewing everything that's out there. You'll need to look around to find out what's right for you. They are intended, however, to help you to see what the *better* products are likely to look like in terms of fees and service model.

The City of London is very old, yet always changing. So over your investing lifetime, keep your eyes wide open ... for better and better savings and investment products.

How to accumulate a pension with the right risk mix for you

You may have noticed that our language so far in this book has been a little imprecise; we have talked about pensions, your pension pot, savings and portfolios. This was deliberate: they can all overlap. Now's the time for us to be more precise and home in on how they fit with the financial products available to you. Because the only way you can build the right portfolio for you, with a suitable blend of risks, is by using the best financial product to help you do so.

Retirement and product language is, we regret, horribly confusing. The diagram below will help us to clear a few things up.

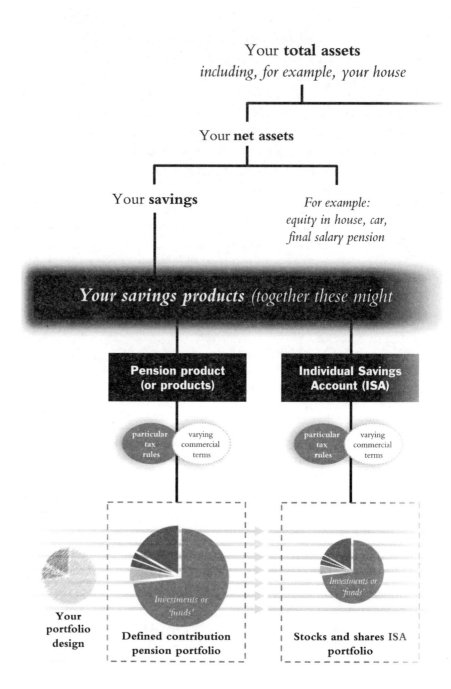

Your **total assets**
including, for example, your house

Your **net assets**

Your **savings**

*For example:
equity in house, car,
final salary pension*

Your savings products (together these might

**Pension product
(or products)**

**Individual Savings
Account (ISA)**

particular
tax
rules

varying
commercial
terms

particular
tax
rules

varying
commercial
terms

*Investments or
'funds'*

*Investments or
'funds'*

Your
portfolio
design

**Defined contribution
pension portfolio**

**Stocks and shares ISA
portfolio**

The language of financial products

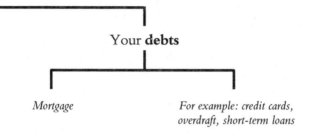

Your **debts**

Mortgage   For example: credit cards,
                            overdraft, short-term loans

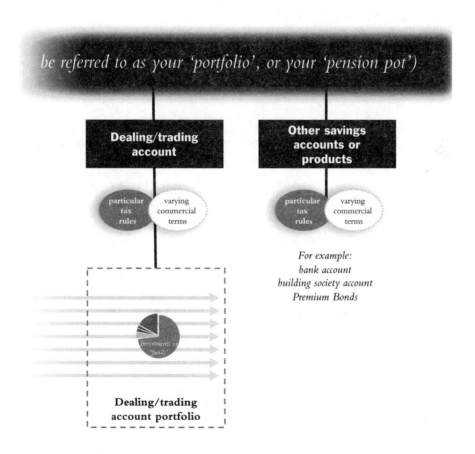

be referred to as your 'portfolio', or your 'pension pot')

Dealing/trading account   **Other savings accounts or products**

particular tax rules   varying commercial terms   particular tax rules   varying commercial terms

                                            For example:
                                            bank account
                                            building society account
                                            Premium Bonds

Investment or 'funds'

Dealing/trading account portfolio

Your **assets** are everything you own. Your **net assets** are everything you own minus your debts – for example, if you have a mortgage on a house. Typically, a good deal of your net assets will not be savings. For example, if you have a final salary pension, or you have equity in a house, these would count as part of your assets. But they can't be sold quickly or easily.

The real focus of this book is on what you do with your **savings** assets.

What makes life complicated is that there are lots of different **savings products** to help you. (We have only schematized the main ones here.) Whether a product is right and attractive for you depends mainly on two things: its tax rules and the commercial terms the provider offers you – both shape the benefits you can get from it.

The commercial terms might include rates of return, fees and the speed at which you can turn all or part of the product into cash. As for tax rules, we are going to say a lot more about these in the next chapter. We warned you right at the start of this book that tax rules are not simple. The best we can do is give you coping strategies to deal with their complexity! But they make an enormous difference to what income you can get from your products and when. Unfortunately, you may have to make more choices about tax rules during your retirement than you did during your working life.

So, there are different savings products. The main savings products we want to draw to your attention here are:

1 You will need a **pension product**. These are formally known as defined contribution (DC) pensions. A DC pension product allows you to invest for a retirement income under specific tax rules. Essentially, you get a tax subsidy when you pay in, but when you draw out, you pay income tax. Unfortunately, the informal/sales language around DC pension products is especially tricky:
   • A lot of pension companies call these products '**funds**', but some enable you to buy, within their product, investments formally titled 'funds'. So the word 'fund' ends up being used for rather similar things, all subtly different.

- Most people and many advisers will informally call this a '**pension pot**'. For a lot of people it will be the only pot they have. But some people will have multiple pensions, or other savings that are going to make a significant contribution to their retirement income. If so, they may be better off thinking of their pension pot as the sum of all their savings. In our workbook, we use this language.

2 You will benefit from putting money into a **stocks and shares ISA**. This is tax-free, during your lifetime. (If you are under 40, and investing for the long term, take the version of it that is available to you with extra tax subsidies – the Lifetime ISA.)

3 If you have still more money you can invest, you can put it in a dealing (or trading) account. It can also be known as a **General Investment Account (GIA)** – a taxable method of investing in stocks and shares. It's just like the first two products, but without any tax privileges. You can take money out of it at any time. This is different from a pension product, which is 'locked' until you are aged 55 (57 from 2028).

4 You will need a **cash savings product**. You would use this to store emergency cash – for example, if you are 'self-insuring' against a stock market crash, as we covered in the previous section. Interest from these is usually taxable but there are generous tax thresholds so you would have to have a lot of cash invested to start to pay tax. (And gains from Premium Bonds, one of the cash products we think is quite useful, are not taxable.)

Now back to portfolio design and Rule 6's stress on **keeping it simple**. The products set out in points 1–3 above all enable you to invest in stocks, shares and bonds so you can apply the same portfolio design to all of them. And we recommend this as the simplest and easiest approach.

We suggest you think through a single portfolio approach. Then, within your pension fund, your stocks and shares ISA and your dealing account, you buy investments that most closely match your chosen approach.

Ideally, you would buy exactly the same investments and have exactly the same charges within each of your products. (Because you would be using different products, you would need to access your savings and growth under different tax rules.)

With some providers, this can't be done – they don't offer all these types of products, or if they do, they don't offer the same investments within each of them. But this is changing. Interactive Investor make it particularly simple to buy the same investments within different products such as pensions and ISAs. More and more providers are joining this race.

If you don't use one such provider, you can buy from the same asset classes within each of your different products. You

> **Rule 6: Keep investments simple, cheap and automated**

would be applying your portfolio design principles, rather than exactly duplicating investments. However, there's growing help available that can automate the application of your particular risk appetite to a portfolio. In the first category of products, pension products, there are now commercial providers that do a lot of the portfolio work for you so we'll look at these now to help you implement Rule 6.

They enable you to buy according to your portfolio design principles – then more or less leave them alone. What could be more simple and automated than that?

'Investment pathways' and other managed approaches

There are now many pension providers who will automatically manage a portfolio of largely passive investments according to a predetermined plan. The plan follows principles about different asset allocations for different stages of your life. Other providers will turn your risk appetite into a portfolio mix that they then keep constant over time. There are far too many for us to cover comprehensively. Here, we're going to delve into just four providers to give a sense of what is out there.

MoneyHelper offers a tool that enables you to contrast and compare several of these products at once, but they don't claim that their tool covers the whole of the market.[17] As far as we know – annoyingly – there is no single, definitive online contrast-and-compare tool.

You should be aware that our commentary on these products is our own understanding of them, based only on their published information. We may misunderstand things they have stated, or things may change that will make our commentary out of date, so please use our commentary as a way of thinking about what you can now look out for in the marketplace rather than as a recommendation or evaluation of the best of the best.

You will remember from Chapter 5 (*Capture Market Returns*, see pages 87–113) that there are four layers of fees that you might have to pay: platform fees, product fees, transaction fees and money manager/adviser fees. As best we can, we comment on them here. None of the products below requires you to pay an adviser fee. Indeed, the key advantage of these products is you might feel confident enough to invest in them *without* needing a money manager to watch over them. They are designed to stand in for a fair portion of what a personal money manager would do.

Nest Pensions

At the same time as auto-enrolment was brought into law, the UK government set up a publicly owned pension provider. If employers don't want to work with a commercial pension provider, Nest Pensions is the default 'public' option. (This has nothing to do with civil service pensions, which are completely separate from Nest.)

This gives Nest an interesting place in the market. They are managing the private pensions of more than eight million people in the UK. However, you can't open a pension with them unless your employer chooses them so they are not an open-market, commercial provider. But because so many people are with Nest, and also because they are a very good option, we will cover them here.

The big advantages of Nest are that they have *very* low fees. They charge 0.30 per cent per year – or 30 basis points – as the 'platform fee', with no product or transaction fees whatsoever. To our knowledge, this is as low as it gets. They also have good products and a good track record for their first decade or so of existence.

Nest's disadvantages are that not everyone can join them, they charge a one-off fee on each slice of money you put *in*, and above all, you can only ever invest in one of their products at a time so you have to choose the Nest pension investment product that is best for you. Nest will put all the money you hold into that one product.

But you can switch all your money in Nest from product to product. This means you could use the Nest products that are best for you at different times in your life. They have multiple products and they are all pretty good. Out of the six or seven on offer, we only cover two here.

The first is the [Year] retirement fund.[18] The name is extremely unwieldy, but lots of other things about it are better. Nest name it by the year you plan to retire. They manage your pension investments through several phases up, working towards that date:

- for the first five years Nest aim to encourage you to hold to a savings habit by avoiding sharp falls in value;
- they then go through a long phase of seeking higher growth, with more volatility;
- finally, for the 10 years before your retirement, they slow down, with more of a focus on maintaining the value of your money.

Each fund has a slightly different performance, but at the time of writing none of the long-range funds (2030–60) had a return history *after management charges* of less than 7 per cent growth each year. We find very little to dislike about this.

The second product of interest is Nest's Guided Retirement Fund. Only available to people between the ages of 60 and 70, it has three components:

- its *wallet*, which holds short-term money for your income each year;
- its *safe*, which holds very low-risk assets that are held in case of a market crash;

- and a *vault*. The vault is slightly more complicated as it has a dual purpose. It aims to grow your money for use in the years up to age 85 and to set aside a good amount to allow you to buy a lifetime annuity from age 85. And so far, it's working: the vault performance *after charges* is more than 14 per cent growth each year.

You can transfer your pension funds from another provider into Nest for no charge. This creates a great wheeze if you have a significant pot elsewhere. If you have a pot elsewhere already, you could:

- briefly work for an employer that uses Nest;
- accumulate £1 into Nest through the employer's auto-enrolment arrangement;
- quit your job;
- then transfer your larger pension pot in and enjoy Nest's low-fees arrangement for the next 40 or 50 years.

That might sound a bit extreme but if you are job-hunting, it's worth asking a prospective employer if they use Nest.

Vanguard target retirement funds

John Bogle, who founded Vanguard in the mid-1970s, more or less invented passive investing – so now is the time to pay tribute to him here. Not only did he come up with an enormously powerful concept to help everyday investors, but he founded a not-for-profit business to help them make the most of it. As a result, Vanguard is a simply enormous mutual organization with a very long track record, clear and easy-to-use products and low, simple fees. Given everything else you've read so far, you would expect us to view them with great enthusiasm, and we do.

Their target retirement funds charge 0.15 per cent as a platform fee and about 0.24 per cent as a product fee. Vanguard do not charge transaction fees. Their fees vary a little according to how much you have invested but overall, they are highly competitive with Nest.

Like the Nest year-dated retirement funds above, Vanguard gradually alter your balance between stocks and bonds, according to how close you are to retirement.

If we take their retirement date 2040 fund as an example, right now it would be 80 per cent stocks, 20 per cent bonds. As you approach retirement, you would approach a 50 per cent stocks/ bonds split. Before fees, the average performance of this product has been 10.5 per cent growth a year.

Vanguard also offer what they call 'LifeStrategy' funds. To us, the name seems ill-suited – it implies change, but the investment approach it applies is in fact static. You choose your risk appetite and the fund continuously invests according to this. For example, they have LifeStrategy 80, a fund with 80 per cent equities, 20 per cent bonds. This is a close match to our 'ambitious' portfolio above. Vanguard's platform fee is 0.15 per cent but the product fee is a shade lower – 0.22 per cent. Although this is not a pathway product, because it doesn't change over time, what Vanguard will do is continually rebalance the portfolio to make sure that it matches your risk appetite. (We explain more about rebalancing in the next chapter so take note now that you can get somebody to do it for you, and for a very low fee.)

Robo-advisers, and the best of the rest

Nutmeg are known as a 'robo-adviser'. We have much more to say about the 'advice' side of robo-advisers in Chapter 9 (*Find a First-Rate Adviser*, see pages 214–16). Here, we focus on the products you can access through robo-advisers.

This ugly (and not very helpful) term means (broadly) that they ask you to answer a risk appetite questionnaire. They can then offer you a pension product with a portfolio that matches that appetite. So, for example, if you stated that you identify with 4 out of 5 on the risk scale (so quite adventurous), Nutmeg could offer you a product that roughly reflects our 'ambitious' portfolio above. Their fee structure is more complicated than the other providers above but for example, to invest £300,000 in a fixed allocation pension, they quote a total annual fee of 0.51 per cent.

Nutmeg have lots of other products, including an actively managed pension product, ISAs and trading accounts, so they are part of a growing number of providers, alongside Interactive Investor, that can enable you to buy the same investment products (following your overall portfolio choices) in a pension, a stocks and shares ISA and a trading account.

We have commented on these four providers to give a flavour of what's out there in the marketplace but there are lots of other good providers. We recommend you look into Aviva, Interactive Investor and Scottish Widows as some of the lowest-cost providers in the marketplace. The next tier of cost would take you to PensionBee, Fidelity, Standard Life and Legal and General. Of those shown within the comparison tool on the MoneyHelper website, Hargreaves Lansdown is, at the time of writing, the most expensive.

If you have multiple pensions, we recommend you consolidate them into one provider. This will make managing them and understanding growth as simple as possible. PensionBee specialize in making this simple for you, including tracking down the details for past pensions. But it's getting easier and easier to do it yourself.

By about the middle of this decade, the UK government plans to have created a Pensions Dashboard that will bring together in a single view all the pensions you have. This will be helpful, but as far as we know, it will just be a window on the different pensions you have – it won't allow you to change your investments or consolidate them. So, combining DC pensions in a single product is a very sensible route to take. However, it's only worth doing if you equal or lower your fees in the process. And it's never worth transferring away from a pension that your employer will contribute to, if transferring cuts off the flow of future employer contributions.

So to summarize

This has been quite a dense chapter, covering a lot of ground. We have gone into a good deal of practical detail about how to implement choices and decisions but remember that our big theme is that you can't avoid risk, so you need to take the risks that are right for you. And by diversifying your portfolio, the ups and downs of your high-risk, high-growth assets will be smoothed out by the slow-burning returns from bonds and gilts.

We sum up as follows:

- At all times inflation will take value out of your pension pot, as will fees. When you start to decumulate, you will also start to withdraw income. So when you are 'coming down the mountain' your pot will need to grow nearly as fast as those three factors are reducing it. For that to happen, you will have little choice but to take a fair degree of risk.
- When you retire, withdrawing 3.3 per cent income is a (rather inflexible) rule of thumb. But when tested against the UK's historical stock market performance and 60 per cent equities, it reduced risk to close to zero.
- Spreading your risk also reduces it. The more you invest across a very wide range of companies, the higher the growth you are likely to get.
- The smaller the company, the higher the likely growth. But the higher the growth, the higher the volatility.
- The higher the volatility, the more you need to take a long-term view of risk, so early in accumulation is the best time to take the biggest risks.
- Whether you design your own accumulation portfolio, get an adviser to do it or buy an 'off the shelf' arrangement from a pension provider, you'll need to work out how much you want to keep in low-growth bonds to protect you against the risk of a crash. Analysing your reactions to our 'defensive' and 'ambitious' sample portfolio designs will help you to start this thought process.
- When you begin to decumulate, keep 'cash for a crash' if you possibly can. Ideally, it should be a couple of years, or more, of your retirement income.
- It's getting easier and easier to design and buy your own portfolio. If you do, for simplicity, we would recommend buying the same mix of assets in a pension, an ISA and a trading account. Preferably the exact same investments, if your provider makes that possible. That way, you will always be clear about the risk mix you have in play.

- But the simple and cheap way to implement Rule 6 is to use pre-designed portfolios and passive pensions based on

Rule 6: Keep investments simple, cheap and automated

automated investment pathways. Some of these offer among the lowest fees in the marketplace.

Now take action

Our workbook will help you to:

- Consider your risk appetite and whether you want it to change between when you 'go up the mountain' and come down it;
- Quantify your cash 'safety net' options;
- Create a shortlist of low-fee providers that can offer the investments you want to generate your chosen risk mix.

7

Manage Your Mix

Our Rule 6 recommends you keep your investments simple, cheap and automated. And the less you fiddle with them, the more likely you are to get long-term returns. However, that doesn't mean you can leave them alone completely. This chapter is about things you will need to do every so often. They will make sure you are still getting the best out of your investing and applying Rule 1.

Here, we are striking a delicate balance as we don't want to turn you into someone who repeatedly and anxiously tweaks your portfolio. We want to establish a mental 'dashboard' that you can look at once or twice a year and reflect on before you take action.

> **Rule 1: Have a purpose, a plan and a method**

We think that you should regularly look at these eight issues across your portfolio:

1 Being aware of the **taxes** that you will have to pay and how the withdrawal choices you make will increase or decrease these.
2 Check, and **change providers**, if you find you can get better deals and fees.
3 Checking that the way your money is being invested, and your taxes are being spent, lines up with your **values and goals**.
4 **Rebalancing** your portfolio between different asset classes. Happily, this can be almost completely automated, as we've set out in the last chapter.

5 Checking your exposure to different **geographies and sectors**. We'll also look at the question of how much of your investing should be in foreign countries. Both are tricky.

6 Making sure you claim the **maximum state pension** and any credits that might apply.

7 Keeping **social care costs** in your line of sight.

8 Considering buying a **later-life annuity** at age 75 and again at 85.

These eight points should be on your mental 'dashboard' throughout your investing career, the first and final ones mostly during decumulation. The middle six you'll need to look at regularly throughout. If you have an adviser managing all your money, we would expect them to provide you with significant and valuable support for all of these areas.

Managing the tax mix

Taxes are the subscription we pay to be members of a civilized society. So:

- Neither of us is in favour of tax *evasion* – that is, illegal ways of paying less tax than the law requires you to pay.
- Nor are we in favour of tax *avoidance,* which means, as the UK government puts it, 'bending the rules of the tax system to gain a tax advantage that Parliament never intended. It often involves contrived, artificial transactions that serve little or no purpose other than to produce this advantage.'[1] This rarely ends well.

Tax *planning* means reducing the amount of tax you pay within the spirit and the letter of what the law allows. It is perfectly legal. For many people, tax planning during their working lives is irrelevant, because they earn mostly income that is taxed at source. They have next to no choices to make. However, when you stop working, the tax rules become more complicated. The more different products you have, the more choices you will have. Some choices will mean you pay tax that you don't need to pay.

We think that prudent tax planning will be both necessary and desirable during your retirement. Again, even if you are accumulating, and those taxes are a long way off, it's probably worth understanding them now. They will affect choices you make outside your pension products.

The consequences of tax mistakes and the need for advice
If you think about it, the consequences of bad investment decisions and bad tax decisions are very different. If you make bad investment decisions, especially if you are applying the investment approach we have set out so far, you will be able to see the consequences unfold gradually. And those consequences will be quite gradual in their results. Essentially, your portfolio, or parts of it, will decline in value, in front of your eyes.

If you make bad tax decisions (because you didn't know about a tax, or thought you understood the rules and in fact you had not) the consequences may not be visible for many years. And then they may come to you all of a sudden in unplanned-for demands. These could be large. HMRC can investigate your affairs quite a way back – six years for careless tax returns and four years for innocent errors. (It's 20 years for deliberate evasion.)

Some tax rules are much more complicated and difficult to understand than our simple rules of investment, so we think there's

> **Rule 4: Phone a friend, especially when times are taxing**

a very strong case for saying that the most important use of an adviser is not for investment support, but for tax planning. Anyway, we'll come back to that theme in Chapter 9 (*Find a First-Rate Adviser*, see pages 202–28).

We hope this also helps to underline a health warning about the next section. Although we are going to give a thumbnail sketch of the tax situation people currently face in retirement, it is constantly changing. And we are simplifying it, to make it as understandable as possible.

We published this book just before an annual budget. There have been many years of rumours of major changes to pension taxes, but by and large, chancellors have only tweaked them. So we do recommend

you take a look at www.evidenceinvestor.com/corrections to check
for any updates about big changes in the system.

And by the time you retire, you certainly *will* need to dig deeper for
your own circumstances. The best way to think about this tax section
is that it is designed to help you orientate yourself in a landscape,
rather than to give you the precise height of each mountain, or the
depth of each valley.

The main taxes you'll face in retirement

The tax graphic that follows reflects the graphic we showed you in
the last chapter (pages 140–1). It now looks at the basic tax principles
for each of the main financial products we covered.[2]

Some taxes are age-specific. A pension product is the most
important example. You can't withdraw funds until you are 55 now
(57 from 2028), and when you do, taxes apply. (There is an early
access exception for people who are very ill, or in other unusual
circumstances.)

National Insurance contributions are more complex. You don't
pay them at all if you are not working. And you don't pay them after
state pension age, even if you are. However, there is probably now
the potential for more confusion about this with the introduction
of a Health and Social Care levy. This will come into effect fully
in 2023, to pay for the NHS and social care (although at the time
of going to press it is subject to debate in the Conservative Party
leadership election). It is levied in exactly the same way as National
Insurance. But it has a different 'brand name' – to confuse or inspire
voters, depending on your point of view. And …

- For as long as you are employed, you will pay the levy
  (currently set at 1.25 per cent).
- Until state pension age, you will pay National Insurance
  contributions as well.
- If you continue working beyond the state pension age,
  National Insurance contributions drop away, but the 1.25 per
  cent levy will continue to be payable as long as you work.
- A similar 1.25 per cent levy is also payable on dividend
  income (see below) that you earn above the tax threshold.
  This applies at all times, whether you are in work or not.

How savings products are taxed

	DC pension	Stocks and shares ISA
Income tax	Yes, taxed as if you were earning, but 25 per cent comes tax-free, up to the value of the lifetime allowance (see below).	No
National Insurance	No	No
Health and social care levy*	No	No
Capital Gains tax	No	No
Tax on dividends	No	No
Inheritance tax	No, a pension is outside the scope of the tax. Before 75, it can be inherited tax-free. After 75, beneficiaries pay income tax as they withdraw.	Yes, counted as part of your estate. But any ISA can be inherited by your spouse (only your spouse) free of inheritance tax.
Lifetime allowance	Yes, you are likely to be taxed extra if the combined value of all your pensions goes above £1,073,100.	No

Source: GOV.UK.   ★Check evidenceinvestor.com/corrections for any updates

(All tax rates as of 2022/2023 tax year)

	Dealing/trading account	Other savings products
Income tax	Yes, on dividend income only.	Yes, interest is taxable. But there is a personal savings allowance of up to £1,000 (£500 if you pay the higher income tax rate).
National Insurance	No	No
Health and social care levy	Yes, on dividend income only, only above the dividend tax threshold (see below).	No
Capital Gains tax	Yes, if you make £12,300 of gains on the sales you make in any tax year.	.No
Tax on dividends	Yes, via income tax, if you receive more than £2,000 in a tax year.	No
Inheritance tax	Yes, counted as part of your estate. But whether tax is payable depends on the overall value of the estate.	
Lifetime allowance	No	No

The tax rules for the other products aren't affected by your age so they are relevant throughout your investing career, whether you are accumulating or decumulating.

If you only have a state pension and a DC pension pot, you won't have a very large range of choices to make:

- You will pay income tax on what you withdraw and you will get the income tax allowances and thresholds that working people enjoy.
- But you are entitled to take 25 per cent of your pension pot tax-free. This has a formal name: a Pension Commencement Lump Sum (PCLS).
- This sounds simple, but because it links to the lifetime allowance and the dread subject of 'crystallization', we must devote a separate section to it below so do read on to get a fuller (and more complex) picture.

Stocks and shares ISAs are, by contrast, genuinely simple. You pay no taxes on them until you die. When you die, you can pass your ISA on within the wider allowances for inheritance tax. Otherwise it gets taxed when it's passed on. ISAs therefore introduce a big element of choice. It is to your advantage throughout your working life to invest money in the following order:

- First of all, into a pension product (a final salary pension if it is available, but more likely a DC pension). You can now see three advantages that no other product gives you: extra payments from your employer, a tax subsidy and 25 per cent tax-free when you are allowed to withdraw (age 55 now, age 57 from 2028). But the maximum you and your employer can put in is £40,000 a year, so if you have more …
- … a stocks and shares ISA is the next best place for your money. You can invest up to £20,000 a year. Once that year has passed, its allowance has gone too, so it's important to keep up to date. Remember, once each £20,000 is invested, you can sell and withdraw the capital or the investment gains you make on it at any time with no taxes during your lifetime. This is both simple and attractive! If you are under

40, a special version of a stocks and shares ISA is available, called a lifetime ISA. We won't go into the details of this here other than to say that because the UK government adds money to what you put in, it's definitely the one to go for if you are eligible and want to use it for accumulating investments for retirement. It's not quite such a no-brainer (although worth looking into) if you want to save to buy a property.

Automating regular contributions to ISAs (then buying stocks each month) is the best way to use them. You will not forget to use up your allowance and you will not be buying all your shares at the same price, which will smooth things out a bit against the gyrations of the market.

Cash ISAs also exist, as do innovative finance ISAs. You may want to google these and find out more about them – but we don't think they can add much value to the simple rules of investment we are setting out in this book.

If you also have a trading or dealing account, you get taxed on it. Two types of taxes come into play:

- Dividends are taxed under income tax. Dividends occur when companies that you have shares in pay out a small slice of their profits and are paid out at fairly random intervals. You will be taxed on them whether you take the money out of your account or reinvest it. But you do get a special 'dividend allowance'. Your first £2,000 of dividends comes tax-free. After that, you add them to your income declaration and are taxed accordingly. The rates, confusingly, are not the same as income tax rates. If you are a basic or higher-rate taxpayer, they are 7.5 and 32.5 per cent respectively and this includes the 1.25 per cent social care levy.
- Capital Gains tax. You only pay this if you sell stocks, shares or bonds that give you a capital gain in any one year of more than £12,300. This introduces a further element of choice because you can choose to sell an amount that leaves you just below this capital gains tax threshold. Note

that other things you sell at a profit also count towards this tax threshold – for example, if you sell a piece of land. Or some collectables. (People living in Scotland have different income tax arrangements, but UK income tax thresholds dictate the capital gains tax they pay in Scotland. Other than this complication, the tax arrangements we cover here are currently uniform all across the UK.)

Savings accounts give you interest and you pay tax on that interest. But, similarly to dividends, you have to earn £1,000 of interest before you start paying tax – if you are a basic rate taxpayer. (For higher rate taxpayers, it's £500.) Although ISA savings accounts are tax-free, most people will not (or should not) park enough cash in an interest-bearing account to earn more than £1,000 of interest. For this reason, we don't advocate cash ISA accounts as their rates are poor and their tax-free status is not relevant to most savers.

Tax-free cash and crystallization
We now come to the part of pensions that is the most nightmarish to explain. Various metaphors have been put forward to make it simpler, including a Swiss roll, a cake and a jar of jam, and a glass of beer. Unfortunately, as the explanation proceeds, each metaphor breaks down and a new one has to get introduced and mixed in.

We're afraid that with us, the best we can do is give you a pint of beer … but one that you can not only cut up into slices, but which eventually hardens into cement! So we are going to walk you through a very ugly mixed metaphor.[3] But please bear with us and we'll do our best.

This explanation applies to defined contribution (DC) pensions only:

- If you hold investments in an ISA or trading account, they are not affected by any of this.
- If you have a final salary (DB) pension, you may get tax-free cash and the lifetime allowance *will* affect you, but the rules are very different, so you'll need to look into them with your pension provider or financial adviser.

If you have a mainstream, investment-based DC pension, you unfortunately have to engage with three overlapping concepts to make sense of it all:

- tax-free cash (or 'Pension Commencement Lump Sum' to give it its formal name);
- crystallization, which is in turn linked to ...
- the lifetime allowance (and this only comes into effect if you have a lot of money in your pensions).

In the graphic on the next page, we use a beer metaphor to get the message across.

Imagine a foaming pint of stout, well-known for its soothing qualities in Ireland and beyond. The foam settles so that it fills exactly 25 per cent of the glass. (So, you already know that it's a stout unlike any you've previously encountered.) The glass is your entire DC pension pot. Or if you have more than one DC pension, it is the total amount invested in all of them.

The foam, or head, represents 25 per cent of that total. Up to the value of the lifetime allowance (currently £1,073,100) you can take 25 per cent without paying any taxes. You can take it all at once, as soon as you access your DC pension, or you can take some of it. Either way, you pay no taxes.

Whatever is in the remaining 75 per cent, the dark but creamy stout itself, you *will* have to pay taxes on. Whenever you take a sip out of it, you will be assessed for tax. But it's assessed for income tax. So if your little sip is under the personal allowance for income tax, there will be no tax to pay.

And be careful. By contrast, if you take a very large gulp out of the dark stout (the taxable 75 per cent), it too will be taxed as income. So if you take £200,000 out in one year, you will pay an enormous amount of income tax, just like if you had earned that amount of money in a year of your working life. But had you been able to take the £200,000 you need from the tax-free part of your pot, you would have paid no tax. So it matters a great deal which part of your pension pot you withdraw the money from.

You might choose to take all the tax-free cash first, then dig into the taxable cash later. A lot of people choose a hybrid approach. See the vertical slice on the graphic. You can take a bit of income out of your pot each year and 25 per cent of it will have no tax payable, the remainder will be taxed under income tax.

Tax-free cash and crystallization ... in a glass of beer

25 per cent of your pension pot is tax-free (up to the value of the lifetime allowance).

75 per cent of your pension pot is taxable at income tax rates.

... *or* taking the tax-free cash first and leaving the taxable portion untouched

How you can withdraw money:

... in small slices that take a little of the tax-free cash in each slice ...

... and then taking small slices of the taxable portion later.

Warning:
If you take a large slice of the taxable portion in one year, your income tax will be correspondingly high.

Withdrawing money always crystallizes a part of your pension, but you can crystallize before you withdraw.

For defined contribution pensions. Defined benefit schemes have different rules.

Now we need to mix metaphors, to try to explain the dreaded crystallization concept. When a part of your pension pot has been crystallized, that means it's been assessed for the pensions lifetime allowance of £1,073,100 (which, contrary to its name, is in fact a distinctive and especially unpopular tax).

Now, if the combined value of all your pensions will never grow to be worth more than £1,073,100, this is nearly an irrelevance. You wouldn't need to grapple with the crystallization concept at all – except that your pension provider may still ask what you want to crystallize and when.

What is crystallization? Well, this is where we have to mix our metaphors. It's a bit like cement drying. Before the cement has dried, it can expand, or it can flow into unexpected nooks and crannies. Its future is somewhat uncertain. Once dried, it's hard and it's history. Similarly· when a part of your pension is crystallized, it is assessed for tax. As your pension gets crystallized, it is assessed against the lifetime allowance. If you ever exceed £1,073,100, you will pay a punitive tax on the excess above that amount. If you think this will ever be the case for you, we recommend you get a skilled financial adviser involved – while the cement is still wet! Because your options around crystallization and what you do with your money are quite complicated. And the events that trigger an assessment for the lifetime allowance also need careful explanation by your adviser. It is important to note that if you have a final salary (DB) pension, its value will get put in the mix for your lifetime allowance so a combination of a DB and DC pot might take you closer than you think to £1,073,100. If in any doubt, take advice on it.

An example of managing the tax mix
By an amazing coincidence, Adrian and Becky are both too young to draw their state pension, have exactly the same investments and both want to draw down an income of £35,000 a year from their portfolio.

- Adrian, although he has other products and a fair amount of money across his portfolio, draws the entire £35,000 down from his DC pension product.
- He gets 25 per cent tax-free: £8,750.

- He is then taxed on the rest. His personal allowance is £12,570. As he is drawing income that takes him well above that, he pays £2,736 in tax.
- His disposable income is therefore £32,264.

- Becky uses a handy *Which?* calculator that helps her to check what tax she will pay on a DC pension and draws down just £16,760 from her DC pension product.[4]
- She gets 25 per cent tax free: £4,190.
- The remaining £12,570 fits neatly inside her income tax personal allowance, so that's tax-free too.
- Becky now looks to the rest of her portfolio. She takes £4,120 from her cash savings account (her interest this year was under £1,000, so she paid no tax on that).
- She takes £4,120 from her tax-free stocks and shares ISA.
- She sells £10,000 from the stocks in her taxable trading account – leaving her well outside capital gains tax, which is not taxed on what you sell, but on the profit you make; she is nowhere near the threshold of £12,300 profit.
- She has paid little or no tax (like Adrian, she might have to pay a little bit of tax on income from dividends, or, if she's made a few mistakes with her other sums, it's only a few extra pounds here or there), so she has a higher disposable income than Adrian: £35,000.

Of course, it's possible that Becky's other funds will run out before her pension product does. If so, she will have to start digging more deeply into the taxable 75 per cent of her DC pension and she will be taxed like Adrian for a while. But by that point, Becky may not need to draw down as much as £35,000 a year. That would reduce the amount of tax she pays.

It's true that sometimes all you end up doing with tax is kicking the can down the road but then questions of inheritance do come into play. If you die having paid less tax, your heirs may inherit more and it might be tax-free.

As the example above shows, you can get a higher disposable income in ways that are perfectly above-board and legal. It just takes a bit of planning, probably with the help of an adviser.

Switching providers and keeping fees low

We feel you may have heard more than enough from us by now about keeping fees low so we don't think there's too much more that needs to be said about this element of your dashboard. Keep reviewing your fees! But we do want to say a very small amount about shifting providers when you find one that offers lower fees – above all, the provider that holds your precious DC pension investments.

It used to be said that we in the UK were more likely to get divorced than switch to a new bank.[5] This has changed in recent years as rules were introduced to make switching banks automated and less hassle. But this inertia will probably carry through to our pension providers. There are two barriers to that, which we want to demolish in this short section.

The first is the fear that you might have to pay a prohibitive exit fee. Exit fees for pensions providers were banned in the UK in 2017. This applied to people entering into new contracts from the time of the ban. Those in existing contracts had their fees capped at 1 per cent, but some big providers got rid of fees even for existing contracts so it's mostly free to leave. And if it isn't, you will be able to calculate how quickly you can recoup the low cost.

The second is a psychological barrier – the fear associated with the transfer of the biggest amount of money you've ever had. What if it goes wrong? The important point to make here is that you don't have to take legal responsibility for it: you instruct your provider to transfer your DC pension to another provider. You must check that your destination provider is FCA-regulated but beyond that, leave it to your existing provider to verify the transfer destination details. The money never goes through your bank account, so it's very hard to see how a mistake on your part could ever affect the result. There is an outside chance that a fraudster could somehow insert themselves in the chain of transfer, but it is your provider's responsibility to ensure that the destination details match to you.

We hope that transferring pension providers two or three times in the course of a retirement will become a normal part of people's financial lives. If it does, it will continue to drive down costs.

Keep your provider's costs under review and shop around each year. And we recommend you look into consolidating

> **Rule 6: Keep investments simple, cheap and automated**

all your different defined contribution (DC) pensions with one provider, following Rule 6. It will be easier to manage your mix, easier to know what fees you are paying and easier to switch again if you need to. But only do this if the fees are equal or lower, and never do so if it means your employer will stop paying contributions.

Using your money to influence society and the future

In Chapter 1 (*Your Money or Your Life?*, see pages 13–26), we pointed out that the amount you pay in taxes during your retirement will add up to a small fortune. We noted that you can simply pay and forget, or you could use your vote and other influencing techniques to try to ensure that this huge sum is spent in line with your beliefs and values.

As you approach death, thoughts about the world after you are gone will loom larger in your imagination – and so the legacy you leave behind for future generations. If you treat every pound of tax you pay and investment you make separately, they won't add up to much. If you add them all up and consider the clout that they give you, it will be considerable.

You will have seen from Chapter 6 (*Take the Right Risks*, see pages 114–51) that your financial future depends primarily on equity investments delivering more than 4–5 per cent average growth over the long term. The reality of climate change, and the mass extinction of wildlife are, to put it mildly, the dark side of this economic growth. If this is not reshaped, it seems there will be terrible consequences for everyone's future so there is a fierce debate about the sustainability of economic growth. But we're not going to start addressing that very wide-ranging debate here – it's beyond our expertise and it's not what you bought this book for. We simply note that under the system we are guiding you through in this book, our personal futures truly do depend on economic growth and sustainability 'getting married'. The stakes are far too high if they go their separate ways.

The latest business acronym for companies that want to maximize their reputation for long-term sustainability is ESG. This rather unwieldy abbreviation stands for 'Environmental, Social and corporate Governance'. There is a reasonably well-established body of thinking behind it, going back more than 30 years (and several name changes). It gives investors pointers and measures that they can use to assess companies' ESG performance. In this section we want to take a look at the pros and cons of investing from an ESG perspective. Should you do this because it is more financially viable, or would you do so only to improve the legacy you leave for the future and take the financial consequences as they come?

Let's look at the evidence. We will start with the financial question. It is this: is there any reason why high-sustainability

> **Rule 3: To dilute your risks, add lots of time**

companies should produce higher returns than low-sustainability ones? Many believe this: companies with bad business practices and poor environmental records (so-called 'sin stocks') will be called out by employees, shunned by customers, rejected by local communities, punished by regulators and – sooner or later – abandoned by the market. If so, over the long run, investing only in companies that have the *opposite* characteristics and values *should* bring a higher return. This would be a classic case of where you need to apply Rule 3 and see the effects of lots of time added to the risks.

What does the evidence show so far?

The financial case, so far, is more or less neutral
There is not a long track record of data to provide evidence, so any conclusions we offer here have to be quite tentative. We have looked at academic studies from Harvard (measuring 190 companies) and Hamburg (a meta-analysis of 2,000 studies) that concluded high-sustainability companies 'significantly outperform their counterparts over the long-term' and that 'the business case for ESG investing is empirically very well founded'.[6] We have also looked at studies from Princeton and the highly respected investment author Larry Swedroe that suggest 'sin stocks' in fact do better, as do tracker indexes that include them.[7] But we also noted that the S&P 500 ESG index, which deliberately excludes 'sin stocks', had a slightly higher return

and slightly lower volatility when measured over a nine-year period, compared to the standard index that includes all companies.[8] This relatively short-term evidence so far does seem to suggest that, even if there is a performance penalty for ESG investing (and there may not be), then it's probably very small. We don't think there is compelling evidence that you can expect a big loss. You might, over the long term, get the same as the market return. Or you might receive a modest performance premium. That leaves the choice pretty neutral from a financial point of view, if you invest in ESG-screened passive funds. As a 2021 paper from Arizona State University concluded, 'implementing ESG strategies can cost nothing'.[9] A longer view of risk will unfold over your investing lifetime, so please keep watching the evidence.

So, what about the non-financial case for ESG?

The non-financial case

Although this is a book about money, we started by pointing out that there's much more to life than money. We certainly don't want to leave that thought behind here. If you want to take an ESG route, you can still invest passively. There are plenty of sustainable funds that are broadly passively managed. Most of them simply screen out companies that engage in particular activities. But of course, you can take a more active approach: it's all about what you choose to do with your money.

We think we've provided plenty of evidence in this book to point out the financial risks of lower returns if you put your faith in active investment managers. But now you know that price. You can make an informed choice about whether you are happy to pay it in order to get something else that you value. Although the majority of active investment managers don't outperform the market, this does not mean none of them delivers any growth at all. If that were the case, they would have gone out of business decades ago.

As we pointed out at the end of Chapter 5 (*Avoid Charlatans and Sharks*, see pages 87–113), there is a big difference in the message you send to companies by buying into a passive fund, compared to making an active investment. If you buy ESG-screened passive funds, you do send a price signal to all 'sin stock' companies that you value them less. That is not a trivial signal but it is relatively subtle and it is certainly indirect.

By contrast, and in theory, a highly ESG-focused active investment manager could go much further. They could attend the AGM of a particular company and point out its failings. They could play their part in the mobilization of unfavourable media sentiment against the company. They could engage in dialogue with regulators. And they could sell stocks outright and point out why they were doing so. We say 'in theory' because there are many different factors and motivations driving active managers. There is no guarantee that any or all of these actions would be taken just because of your investment. It would likely require careful shopping and a lot of pressure on your part.

Another approach you could take is to forget active managers and buy a small portion of stocks in a company directly. This would give you the right to vote and attend the company's AGM directly yourself. However, it's important to be self-aware. By this point, you're not buying stocks as an investment – you are buying them as a point of access, to make your voice heard. And that's a perfectly valid use of your money.

The delightfully contrary Merryn Somerset Webb made this point very well in her opinion piece for *The Financial Times*, 'Want a greener world? Don't dump oil stocks'.[10] This is a thought-provoking read. She points out that when you sell shares in an oil company, someone else buys them and the business carries on: 'What we want, then, is not no oil, no tin and no copper, but more carefully produced oil, tin and copper. How do you get that? Probably not by making a show of flouncing off in a huff. Enter impact investing, the idea that instead of divesting, big investors should stay invested and encourage better behaviour.' Of course, you will need to feel very strongly about climate change, workers' rights, social justice, etc. – and have a lot of time on your hands! – to be a proper shareholder activist.

If you decide to stick to passive management for all the reasons we've covered so far, it's worth knowing that some passive (or systematic) fund managers have been making inroads into corporate governance and holding boards to account. LGIM have the best record in this regard, followed by Dimensional. Vanguard's ESG credentials have long been questioned, but their record has improved and it is certainly no worse than that of the average active fund house.

If you do decide to put ESG on the 'dashboard' of things you will come back to regularly over your investing lifetime, we put forward some final points to consider. The first is this: the very purpose of ESG is to go further and faster than governments and regulators want to go. If the law requires a company to emit less carbon and shun modern slavery, why should investors also need to exert pressure on it to do these things? So if you do dip into the world of ESG, be aware that plenty of companies will be marketing their compliance with regulations that already exist, or soon will. You will encounter no end of 'greenwash'. Regulations come about because of years of societal debate and pressure. This means that at any one time, there may be a public perception that something already illegal is still a voluntary choice on a company's part.

Climate change is a great example. For many years, it was the subject of pressure and debate. Now governments are changing regulations in dramatic and surprising ways, to drive change at pace. It may be too little, too late; the ESG 'bow wave' of pressure can still up that pace, and that may be very much needed. But there's not much point in celebrating companies who are simply up to date with their carbon emission obligations.

As a result of many factors, but especially climate change, ESG is becoming more and more mainstream. This has its pros and cons. By 2020, 72 per cent of institutional investors and 77 per cent of fund selectors said they were using ESG principles in fund selection.[11] This means that even if you don't feel very strongly about ESG, you'll probably find something is being done on your behalf anyway. But how much that is applying real 'bow wave' pressure and how much is 'following the boat's wake' will get harder and harder to tell.

A new and very interesting campaign, which aims to up the pressure on pension funds to reduce carbon-intensive investments, is 'Make My Money Matter'. Its figurehead is the filmmaker Richard Curtis and there are various other well-known figures involved. They commissioned research that suggested focusing your pension savings on sustainable funds was, on average, 21 times more effective than 'the combined annual carbon savings of switching to a renewable electricity provider, substituting all air travel with rail travel, and switching to a vegetarian diet'.[12] Their website provides an easy way of sending a message to your pension provider to pressure them to make this switch.

Laws change things *much* faster than ESG pressures will. This line of thought takes you back to consideration of your vote and the vast sums you will pay in taxes. What role do you want them to play in pressure towards a sustainable future?

Sharia-compliant pension funds have similarities to ESG
The principles of Sharia shape pension funds that are intended for Muslims but anyone can invest in them. In many ways, Sharia pension funds resemble ESG funds, so it's worth explaining them here. For the general investor, they may be useful. For many Muslim readers, they will be essential.

Sharia-compliant pensions cannot invest in 'sin stocks', but in some areas they go further than most ESG funds. For example, they cannot invest in companies that make money out of pork products. Nor will they invest in financial services companies. On the other hand, they are not prohibited from investing in oil and gas. Many ESG funds would not make such investments.

There is one further, very important difference. Because of the principle of not profiting from interest on debts, Sharia-compliant pensions will invest mainly in equities and won't buy conventional bonds. It also means they invest only in companies that have low levels of debt. This gives Sharia-compliant pension funds some very interesting properties. They are high-risk, high-return, because of their focus on equities but they are also focused on companies that are potentially more sustainable, not least because of their low levels of indebtedness.

There can be performance opportunities from such funds, although volatility will be higher. For example, Nest's Sharia fund[13] (which is 100 per cent equities) has grown more rapidly than any other fund Nest runs. It enjoyed a 16.3 per cent (pre-inflation) return over 10 years.[14] A 2020 study asserted that funds merging ESG and Sharia principles offer a more competitive return in both rising and falling markets, but sadly, its geographical scope was quite narrow.[15] Although there is not a great diversity of Sharia-compliant funds available through UK platforms, their number is growing.

Why your portfolio may need rebalancing

Even after you decide on your asset allocation, you can't just put your portfolio in a drawer and forget about it. That's for two reasons. First, investments change over time. Some grow faster than others. The second reason is that you are changing, getting older and closer (or perhaps further away) from your desired goal. This is where rebalancing comes in. That means bringing your asset allocation back to your original plan, or changing your asset allocation because your plan is not delivering your goals.

If you started with our ambitious portfolio, but for two or three years, small- or micro-cap companies enjoyed a periodic spurt of growth, you might find that instead of making up 20 per cent of your portfolio, they were now 35 per cent. And your bonds might be down to 14 per cent, from your desired 20 per cent. You would have moved away from your original risk mix and would expect to experience more volatility as time goes on. So if you still wanted to keep to your original plan, you would want to sell some of your small company equities and reinvest them in bonds.

The point about this process is that it should be disciplined and scheduled, not a knee-jerk response to external events. Doing it once a year is a sensible rhythm. And you don't *have* to do it yourself. As we pointed out in the last section of the previous chapter, there are plenty of pension providers who provide this as an automated service.

This works if you put all your money into a single product that offers readjustment. If, within your portfolio, you mix and match different investments that themselves are automatically adjusted, then you will have to take care of their overall mix. Fortunately, many providers – Aviva is a good example – will provide an 'X-ray' of your entire portfolio, which gives you a pie chart: how much is in bonds, equities and so on. So you can analyse and adjust accordingly, getting yourself back to your original desired mix.

Geographies and sectors

More complicated is the issue of developing too much exposure to different geographies or sectors. The problem is easy to grasp.

If you are investing in a fund that buys equities worldwide, a spurt of growth in one region, or a decline in another, might mean that over time you get a disproportionate representation of (for example) European equities, or equities from Latin America. Or, take a relatively recent example. The mammoth tech companies such as Google, Amazon and Facebook grew enormously during the 2020 pandemic. As a result, passive investors automatically held substantial investments just in these four or five companies, reducing their overall diversification.

These higher exposures might run well for a while but markets will change again and you may find you are less diversified than you would like to be. So it's easy to see how overexposure could come about. Less easy is diagnosing what matters – and fixing it – if you are following a passive, indexing approach.

Pension providers and investment platforms do sell products that are focused on particular regions. So, for example, you can buy funds that invest in Europe excluding the UK. Or investing only in Japan. So it is relatively easy to positively demarcate some regions and to avoid buying funds that accidentally double your exposure in your home market.

You can also buy investment funds that hold equities in a wide range of technology companies, or focus on the health sector. So again, focus and demarcation by sector is possible. But beware the more fashion-driven 'themes', as we pointed out in Chapter 5 (*Avoid Charlatans and Sharks*, see pages 87–113).

At the moment there are no mass-market passive funds that allow you to say: 'I like your index approach, but please remove everything from my personal index that's based in Germany, or from the hotel sector.' But we are sure these will come within this decade. OSAM, a relatively boutique US-based asset management business, have developed exactly this approach for their clients. They predict it will be a common approach by 2025.[16] But take care. Consider that as soon as you start picking, you are beginning to try to pick winners and applying 'active investing' principles – 'I think tech companies are in a bubble ... I think Japan will see a resurgence of growth.' This is a lot harder to do well than to mix and rebalance asset classes. In our view, more and more of this won't end well (or rather, if it does, it will be largely because of luck), for reasons we've rehearsed many times so far here. Probably the best use of this kind of 'direct indexing' approach, when it becomes mass-market, will be to give a pick-and-mix approach to removing 'sin stocks' (for example, companies that make money from tobacco, alcohol, gambling or highly polluting activities) from your portfolio. This will make it easier to apply pressure on the environmental and social governance of companies.

To the extent that it's practical to combine with a largely passive approach, we think it makes sense to look at your portfolio and apply these two principles where you can:

- Try not to be overexposed to sectors or markets that replicate your job, or replicate your investments outside your portfolio;
- Try not to be overexposed to your home market (more on this in the next section).

But we don't think you should do this by trading off a passive, index-based approach for the pick-and-mix of active investing.

Rule 5: Only focus on what you can control

And if you agree, Rule 5 comes into play. Keep an eye on the controls that are becoming available to you as the marketplace changes. But if you can't control it, don't worry about it!

How much should I invest in my home market?

Our second point above takes us into the pros and cons of investing (or over-investing) in your home market. By this we mean the country where you live and in the currency of that country. An extreme example: a 2016 study found that although Singapore's stock market was only 0.4 per cent of the world total, Singaporeans were investing about 39 per cent of their portfolios in Singaporean equities.[17] They were therefore significantly over-exposed to the risks of that market under-performing. (You will see that Singapore does not even make an individual category on the summary graphic that follows and Switzerland, surprisingly, has more of a footprint than Australia.)

FTSE All-World market weightings

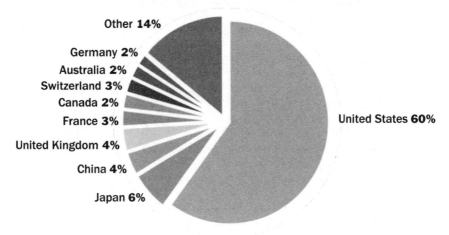

A 2021 weighting of global stock markets. Source: Vanguard

There are plenty of positive behavioural biases that take people in the direction of home market investing. They tend to invest in what they know; they also tend to be over-optimistic about the economy in which they live. (Remember, UK stock markets have a lower long-term performance than the US stock market.) And there are negative barriers and complications that put people off investing in foreign markets:

- Investing in foreign markets usually attracts higher fees – although costs are coming down and it is cheaper and easier than ever to do so.
- Following the trail of business activity is complicated. Just because a company has its head office in a particular country, that doesn't mean its exposure is in that country too. It may do most of its day-to-day business in other markets. The UK stock exchange, for example, is well known for headquartering companies that do business all over the world.
- A further complication is exchange rates. When you invest in companies that operate mostly in the UK, you are taking on the risks associated with equity investing but you are not adding much extra risk linked to major fluctuations in the value of the pound. If you invest in companies abroad, you

are adding that complication. However, the complication has a complication! There can be upsides to exchange rate movements as well as downsides.

Based on the peer-reviewed academic evidence, these are some of the issues to bear in mind:

- The UK represents just 4 per cent of the value of global stock markets. So if you were going to take a strict approach to allocation based on how much wealth creation happens in different parts of the globe, just one in 20 of your stocks would be UK-based and 60 per cent would be in the US market. You would match up to the pie chart above. However, very few UK investors are this stringent.
- It's worth being aware that global markets move more in step than ever before. This was particularly obvious in the 2020 pandemic. Diversification did not help much at that point. Covid-19 struck all regions more or less simultaneously.
- But diversification does still matter for all sorts of reasons – not least because countries specialize in different types of economic activity. If you invest almost entirely in the UK, you will miss out on great technology companies and manufacturing. You do have to dip into global markets to ensure you are getting a slice of everyone's business and future innovation.
- It is possible to 'hedge' against currency risks. However, research by Vanguard suggests that over the long term, the benefits of investing in foreign markets outweigh any temporary problems caused by the ups and downs of exchange rates.[18]
- Funds that invest in foreign markets sort out tax and regulation on your behalf so there is no danger of becoming entangled with other tax regimes if you buy into (for example) an Exchange-Traded Fund (ETF) that invests in foreign markets.
- However, it is important to note that some foreign markets are regulated very differently from the UK markets. At an extreme, you could lose money to investment frauds that would be detected and prevented in the UK.

Our suggested rule of thumb, digesting all of the above, would be to allocate at an absolute minimum 80 per cent of your portfolio to companies outside the UK. If you turn the dial up any further towards 95 per cent, expect more volatility, watch out for more unusual risks and for higher fees. For all the reasons we've previously set out, if the fees rise too high they will begin to cancel out your benefits from diversification.

So that you can know whether you are matching up to your rule of thumb, part of your portfolio thinking should be to avoid double-investments in your home country. You can avoid being accidentally overexposed; you can do this by buying funds explicitly *focused* on your home country, at the same time as buying worldwide or regional funds that explicitly *exclude* it. Or Vanguard sell a low-fee fund – Global All-Cap Index – that gives you exposure to worldwide stock markets in the proportion to the wealth they contribute. If you want to keep life simple, you could invest in this. It will be automatically balanced to the current proportions of wealth creation around the world.

Robin writes: Tempted to swap the home market for the homes market?

Brits are obsessed with houses and homes. Think of all those tedious dinner party conversations about rising prices, or the endless column inches devoted to the housing market in the media. And don't get me started on those property makeover and escape-to-wherever shows on television. Houses aren't just seen as places to live in, they're seemingly a way to make us rich. To many people they appear simpler and more lucrative than investing in equities. But there is a bigger picture to consider before you bet your savings on housing.

It's true that residential property has generally provided higher financial returns than equities over the last 30 years but that hasn't always been the case. Over the very long term, shares have been the better investment. And on their own, property *prices* don't tell the whole story. Even after you've taken account of all the interest you have to pay to the lender, houses aren't cheap to maintain; nor are they cheap to buy and sell. Then there's the hassle factor. Equity investing is as simple as setting up automatic monthly payments into an index fund. With property, there are always bills to pay, jobs that need doing, contractors to find and, for landlords, the prospect, or reality, of awkward tenants.

The consensus is that house prices have risen for three main reasons – a lack of supply, the willingness of successive governments to support the housing market and, since the global financial crisis, rock-bottom interest rates. None of those things will continue indefinitely. In recent years, the tax advantages that made it attractive to buy and let second homes have been considerably tightened or eliminated. This means that the truly attractive tax advantages have narrowed down to owning the home you live in.

Although it sometimes seems that UK house prices are immune to gravity, at some point that will change. If you're too young to remember a housing crash, take it from those of us who can that prices can fall very quickly. Spending several years in negative equity – in other words, owing more than your house is worth – is no fun.

Finally, if your main home is your pension, where are you going to live when you retire? To realize the capital you're likely to need, you will almost certainly have to sell. And if that's in the middle of a housing slump, or if your home is blighted by plans for a business park or sewage works on neighbouring land, you may strike a very disappointing deal.

Financially speaking, there is much to be said for buying your main home, especially if you plan to live there for a long time. We also think that parking the funds you may need for social care in your own home is a reasonable response to that complex end-of-life dilemma (more on that later in this chapter). But sinking all your pension savings into an enormous main home, or further properties, simply over-exposes you to all the disadvantages we've set out above. Remember, if you already own, or have a mortgage on, your own home, you're already significantly exposed to the housing market. And if you're invested in a total-market index fund, you should already have exposure to property firms and housebuilders.

If you do want more exposure to housing, a property fund or real estate investment trust (REIT) is a sensible option. You could also consider this route for exposure to commercial property, which would give you the added benefit of greater diversification. But a word of warning: funds that invest in actual buildings, either residential or commercial, have not been a good investment in the past. Some funds in particular have had liquidity issues; in other words, when large numbers of investors headed for the exit, there wasn't enough cash to meet redemptions and the funds were suspended for long periods. Be aware of this limitation.

In conclusion, don't be unduly influenced by friends or relatives who appear to have made a mint out of property investing. It's not the route to riches it's often made out to be.

Homes are primarily for nesting, not investing.

State pension and pension credits

This section is brief, easy – and important. If you don't pay the required number of years of National Insurance, you won't get the full state pension in the UK. Because this is a guaranteed income, topping up any unpaid years is typically a no-brainer. It costs about £700 to pay up for any year you've missed, but you get a guaranteed pay rise to your state pension as a result. Checking has never been easier – you create an account on the GOV.UK website and you can rapidly check your state pension forecast.[19] If you've missed a year, you get a four-year window to make the extra payment. So, part of managing your mix should be checking this at least every few years.

As mentioned earlier in this book, after state retirement age, if you end up with a very low income, the UK government will pay you pension credits. If you're investing in any other kind of pension mentioned here, it's unlikely you'll be eligible for these, but we do mention them for completeness.

Pensioners miss out on £1.8 billion a year in pension credits that are left unclaimed.[20] Even if you are not eligible, you may know people who could do with a nudge because they are missing out.

If you're single and all your retirement income adds up to less than £177.10 a week, you get a top-up to reach that amount. If you're a couple, it's £270.30 a week. There are additional top-ups for special circumstances.[21]

Keep social care costs in your line of sight

In Chapter 3 (*Manage Your Money*, see pages 42–66), neither the table of living expenses nor our 'mountain' graphic included the cost of paying for social care, if it is needed at the end of your life. We said we would return to this difficult topic in this chapter.

Although in September 2021 the UK government announced very significant changes to the way social care is funded in England, its financial burden can still be very heavy, wherever you live in the UK. New rules don't change as much as people will probably hope or believe. And they may keep on changing. At the time of going to press, the social care tax rise was the subject of bitter debate in the 2022 Conservative Party leadership election. We will post any updates to evidenceinvestor.com/corrections. Meanwhile, we try our best to set out this complex issue by considering your odds and the fundamental costs. We then look at how means-testing and caps *might* reduce the proportion of those costs you will eventually pay.

Social care: your overall odds and the high-level costs

1 in 6	**But 5 out of 6**	
people aged 80 or older live in a residential care home.[22]	people aged 80 or older remain in their own, or a family, home.	

Some will need nursing care in the home	**Others will need only residential care**	**About 2 in every 6 adults over the age of 80 take up paid-for residential or nursing care provided at home**	**Happily, nearly 3 in every 6 adults over the age of 80 do not feel the need to take up paid-for social care.[23]** **But to note … some of these people will receive care from family and friends that is equivalent to social care, yet is unpaid.**
As a guideline, higher-quality private nursing care in a home can cost up to £60,000 a year.[24] Residential care without nursing costs about 20 per cent less – so in round numbers, assume £50,000 per year. These are figures for the top tier of homes – homes with more modest facilities charge less. And prices vary from region to region of the UK.[25] The average length of stay has been measured at 12 months for someone who needs nursing care and 24 months for someone who doesn't need nursing care.[26] So looking at a reasonable worst-case scenario, that would mean a cost of up to £100,000 in some of the more expensive parts of the UK.		Lighter-touch care received in your home (for example, one or two daily visits) will usually cost a great deal less than the residential costs. Two hours a day would be around £16,000 a year. So it can still easily cost £20,000+ per year. But be aware that once it goes up to the level of 24-hour support, it's much *more* expensive than residential care: at least £2,000 a week. [27]	

Sources: multiple

So the table gives the possible scenarios. What are the mitigations? The means-testing and caps that are coming into place across the four countries of the UK are intended to stop people being financially overwhelmed by unlimited social care costs but they can still leave them with huge sums to pay.

For a start, to benefit from any of these rules you have to have a level of need that is high enough for your local authority to agree that you *need* social care. If you think you need it, and they don't agree, you'll have to self-fund or do without. And very importantly, means-tested support only addresses the 'care' costs of social care – the specialist support you need. If you keep on living in your home (so your care comes to you) that will probably be the main extra you need to worry about from a financial point of view. But if you stay in a care home, you yourself must pay for the costs of your food and shelter – 'hotel' costs. The state support will only assist you with your 'care' costs.

We have not been able to find reliable data about the proportion of residential care home fees that are 'hotel' costs but there seems to be industry consensus that these are the majority of the cost – perhaps as much as two-thirds. By contrast, the UK Government's official publication about the change in the rules optimistically has the proportion the other way round – less than one-third – and claims the state pension is nearly enough to cover most people's 'hotel' costs.[28]

Provided your local authority agrees that you do need social care, the rules are designed to protect people with the smallest assets from paying anything at all and they put an absolute limit on what anyone will pay. For example, the new rules in England (taking effect from 2023) will mean that:

- Anyone with assets of less than £20,000 will pay nothing for agreed care costs – although they will still need to meet 'hotel' costs if they go into residential care.
- People with assets of between £20,000 and £100,000 will pay partly subsidized costs for their social care, but up to a cap of £86,000 across their entire lifetime.
- People with assets of over £100,000 will pay full care costs, but only up to the £86,000 cap. Beyond that, the state will pay.

It all sounds fairly positive but to give worked examples for people with assets of more than £100,000:

- If you end up staying in a care home and if 'hotel' costs are indeed two-thirds of the costs of your care, to start benefiting from the £86,000 cap you would need to first spend £258,000 of your own money.
- If you were staying in a care home needing residential care only, and this cost £50,000 a year, you'd need to be there more than five years before the state support would kick in.
- If you were receiving £20,000 per year of care in your home, it would be just under five years before your state support kicked in.

And the meter starts ticking up towards £86,000 not at the rate that you choose to pay, but at the rate that your local authority agrees is appropriate to pay for your needs. These rates may not coincide.

Despite all the political fuss and emotion about people 'having to sell their homes' for social care, we think that the most rational way to fund these costs, if you can, is *still* to hold funds in the equity of your main home. By definition, if by the time you move into a care home you are living alone, you won't need your home to live in any more. And if you have a partner, they will be protected because, as Age UK puts it, 'jointly owned property is disregarded from the financial assessment for as long as your partner remains living in it after you have moved into residential care.'[29]

Should you need the money from your home while you or your partner is still living there, that can be arranged through something called 'equity release'. Effectively, a new mortgage is generated against the value of the home and paid off when the home is finally no longer needed by either of you. If your council agrees you need residential care and you end up paying for it through your home, the council must offer you a form of equity release called a 'Deferred Payment Agreement' or DPA.[30]

If you don't own a home and don't think you ever will, or the value of it will be below what you would need, you will need to hold £100,000 or more in savings over and above your pension needs. Or, depend on the rules supporting you and mitigating the costs.

We think the rules of this gloomy and complex area will continue to change. That's why they are on our checklist to keep under regular review as they may have a substantial impact on your financial plan. It is possible that an insurance market will arise whereby you can insure yourself against your risk of paying what the state will not pay for. If it does, its products will be well worth looking into.

The case for a late-life annuity

Finally, in this chapter, back to annuities. We have been fairly disparaging about annuities bought at the point of retirement. This is not because we dislike them in principle, it is because since the pension freedoms were introduced, the gap between what an annuity will pay you and what you can reasonably hope to draw down from an invested pension pot has widened so much, we're hard-pressed to recommend them. If you've read so far and feel that, as you look at the whole of your retirement:

- you just can't face the burden of managing your investments yourself;
- nor do you want to pay the cost of getting a money manager to manage them ...

... then buying an annuity at the point of retirement is a reasonable response to your dilemma. But there's a big cost. You will see from the figures we give below that you will be trading off getting on for 20 per cent of your income. In return, you will receive something as close to financial certainty as you can get. For some people that will be a reasonable trade-off.

For most of us, it will create too great an income gap. However, we do think it's wise to at least look into buying an annuity when you reach much later life. Because at that point the trade-off becomes less stark.

Annuities that take effect from age 85 (as an example) are vastly better value than those you might take out at a much earlier age. For example, using the MoneyHelper 'Compare guaranteed income products tool', we find:[31]

- A healthy, single 65-year-old spending £250,000 to buy an inflation-linked annuity, with no inheritance, could expect to get roughly £6,500 a year guaranteed income for the rest of their life.
- By contrast, if they invest the £250,000 and spend 3.3 per cent of it each year, they will get 25 per cent more income – £8,250 a year.
- But a healthy, single 85-year-old spending £250,000 on the same type of annuity could get roughly **£21,200** a year for the rest of their life.

So, taking a look at annuities at age 75 and again at age 85 is a good idea. Your spending will likely go down naturally around these times anyway so it's likely to be more predictable and an annuity could make a good contribution to it. But sadly, and unavoidably, there is another reason to consider: your cognitive abilities are in a continuous state of decline from your mid-twenties.[32] This decline will pick up speed after you are in your early seventies. This means that, even with good mental health, you may be less able to manage your investments in your later years. Having a guaranteed, inflation-adjusted income will remove one of the things that might at some point overwhelm you. And of course, if you begin to experience a condition that affects your mind, such as dementia, an annuity will solve a major practical challenge.

We don't think this is an argument for buying any old poor-value annuity and there may be a difficult trade-off between the large sum of money you might put into an annuity and the large sum you might still need for care costs. Other options are available. You can appoint someone else to manage your money, for example, but in managing your mix, reviewing your annuity options in later life is a sensible approach.

Now take action

Our workbook will help you to:

- Review the points we have set out for your financial 'dashboard'.
- Set up a cycle and reminders for returning to them – regularly, but not too often.

8

Face Your Feelings

At the end of all the other chapters in this book, we've asked you to take action. This chapter is different: it's about helping you to do ... nothing. Taking no action when your feelings are screaming at you because of a massive plunge in the stock market will be very difficult but if you can face those feelings, you *will* do better than those who let their feelings do the investing.

If you're pursuing the right investment strategy, based on what we've written in the earlier chapters, our job is to help you become a great investor. How can you do that? In our view, by learning to apply the right behaviours so that you worry less and then do even less than that. So this chapter is about helping you to face your feelings. Frankly, to trick your emotions. Here, we will show why behaviour matters so much. We'll give you a guide to the main behavioural biases that all humans suffer from and then prepare you for the feelings you will face. We'll face up to the roller-coaster ride markets may give you over an investing lifetime then give you some simple, practical tricks you can use to face your feelings throughout that ride.

Why behaviour matters

We greatly admire the work of a personal finance cartoonist (yes, there is such a thing!) called Carl Richards. He wrote a fascinating book called *The Behavior Gap: Simple Ways to Stop Doing Dumb Things with Money.* Carl used to work as an active manager, trying to spot opportunities in the market. One day he spotted a statistic that stopped him in his tracks. He couldn't understand why everyone around him wasn't obsessing about it. But he did. He spotted the difference between investment returns – what would have happened if people had bought and held investments – and investor returns. This is what people actually get, based on their real buying and selling *behaviour*.

> For the 20-year period ending 2007, the average investment return was 11.81 per cent. The average investor return was 4.48 per cent. When I realized the implications [of this gap], my entire job changed. I realized that investment success is not about skill – it is about behavior.
>
> It turns out my job was not to find great investments, but to help create great investors. If all you had to do was buy good (versus great) investments and then behave correctly, that changes everything. ... I decided to leave the complex task of finding the best investment to the smart guys with the big computers; I was going to focus on the simple problem of helping people behave correctly.[1]

Carl wrote his whole book about this insight and we highly recommend it.

Another great way of summarizing the problem is a famous saying attributed to Warren Buffett: 'Be fearful when others are greedy, and greedy when others are fearful.' What he means is: when markets slump, shares are effectively 'on sale', so that's a good time to buy. You certainly shouldn't stop investing, or reduce the amount you invest each month, just because markets have fallen sharply. Similarly, when markets are at all-time highs, beware the temptation to go all-in. Although a little too much on the active side for our tastes, it is still a powerful saying, well worth quoting, because it encapsulates a truth. It also shows how difficult the behavioural challenge is. You have to separate yourself from the feelings of the rest of the crowd – that's a very lonely place to be.

You've already gained a lot of actionable knowledge from this book about how to invest, but knowledge and behaviours are different things. This seems so obvious, but it is worth emphasizing.

Morgan Housel, the author of another great book, *The Psychology of Money*, likes to give the example of a highly educated doctor, who knows more than virtually anyone else about how the human body works and what is good for it. Yet if that doctor smokes and eats a bad diet, his knowledge is doing him no good whatsoever.[2]

Knowledgeable investors can suffer the same behavioural gaps. The table below illustrates this. It shows that in a group of people studied, the most active traders turned over 21 per cent of their portfolio every month and the least active turned over just 1/100 of that amount. The figures for the investment outcomes are remarkably stark – the least active traders were getting on for doing twice as well! But you can be sure that the most active traders were gathering a lot more knowledge about companies and markets.

People who trade more frequently get a worse return on investments than those who trade less frequently		
	Monthly transactions as a percentage of their portfolios	Annual return on their investment portfolios
Least active 20 per cent of traders	0.19%	18.5%
Most active 20 per cent of traders	21.49%	11.4%

Source: Barber and Odean[3]

The most common behavioural biases

Behavioural science over the last three decades has identified six weaknesses. These affect most of us, most of the time. They are all likely to impair our ability to make good financial decisions. Having read so far, you won't be too surprised to see what's on the list but it's useful to bring it all together.

1 **Herd influence**. This is the tendency to follow what the crowd does, rather than take independent decisions based on your own research or talking to experts you select.
2 **Confidence bias**. Just as many people think they are better drivers than they really are, many investors think they are

smarter than average. This is related to self-serving bias, where people tend to attribute their successes to their own skill and their failures to the system. We have bumped into this bias with Neil Woodford earlier in the book (see pages 103–4). It's one likely to be present in most professional active investors. Otherwise, how would they get up in the morning and go to work on their jobs?

3 **Narrative fallacy**. Humans like stories. We are tempted to force random events into tidy narratives and mistake correlation for causation: 'The market fell today because...' Who knows why it fell? We came across this bias when we reflected, in Chapter 5 (*Avoid Charlatans and Sharks*, see pages 87–113), on the ways we can fall for stories in the financial press about investment themes or star managers.

4 **Anchoring**. When we anchor, we take one piece of information, which may be only partially relevant, and use it to frame other decisions. Recency bias (see below) is a close cousin of this trait.

5 **Loss aversion**. This is where we put a greater weight on the possibility of a loss than we do on a gain. An example is someone who worries so much about the risk of losing money in the market that they invest in 'safe' assets which, in the long term, leave them poorer.

6 **Recency bias/projection**. This is where we are overly influenced by recent events and extrapolate them into the future. You see this when investors act on whatever has been dominating the media. By the time they sell, the markets are worrying about something else.

These last two points are such serious threats to your best financial behaviour that we'll give a bit more background to each of them now.

Avoiding loss, avoiding regret

Regret has been cited by Nobel laureate Daniel Kahneman as probably the greatest enemy of good decision-making in personal finance. Investment regrets are often the driving force behind panicky attempts to time the market, buying at the top or selling at the bottom. Regret can prompt us to place a far greater weight on the possibility of suffering a loss than the prospect of a win.

Landmark research by Kahneman and his partner Amos Tversky in the 1970s found that when confronted with several alternatives, people tended to avoid losses and choose the sure wins. This is because the pain of losing is greater than the joy of gaining.[4] In one famous experiment, students were given the choice of being certain to win $1,000, or having a 50 per cent chance of getting $2,500. When the focus was on gain, people chose the safe option of money in hand.

But if the stakes were reversed and reframed around loss, people behaved very differently. They were given the choice between certainly losing $1,000, or trying a 50/50 gamble. On one side of this gamble, they would lose nothing. On the other side, they would lose $2,500. Confronted with this choice, they tended to choose the gamble.

In other words, we tend to switch from being cautious when we can see possible gains to risk-seeking behaviour when we fear losses. This has obvious implications for how we deal with rising and falling markets. What's more, regret, at least in the short term, tends to be stronger when it relates to what we did, rather than what we didn't do:

- Imagine Jane has held a particular stock for some time. She thinks about selling it – but does not follow through. The stock subsequently slumps in price.
- By contrast, John sells the same amount of stock, only to see it rise in value.
- Both lose exactly the same amount of money.

Which of these two people will have stronger feelings of regret? Behavioural psychologists have shown it will typically be John. And the reason is because he himself took an action that caused his loss whereas Jane can tell herself she is the 'blameless victim' of a loss – she didn't do anything to cause it, after all ...

The root of all this is *taking the current situation as a reference point* (and being invested in it emotionally), rather than being able to step outside it and view its pros and cons impartially. This can greatly distort our investing behaviour. As the US Supreme Court Justice Oliver Wendell Holmes expressed it as far back as 1897, 'It is in the nature of a man's mind. A thing which you enjoyed and used as your own for a long time, whether property or opinion, takes root in your being and cannot be torn away without your resenting the act and trying to defend yourself, however you came by it.'[5]

Last year's thing

You're sitting in your favourite restaurant, feeling famished. The waiter arrives and reads out a long list of mouth-watering specials. Yet the moment he walks away, you find you can recall only the last item or two on the list. Congratulations, you've been struck by the 'recency effect'.

In psychology, this refers to a human tendency, when asked to remember a long list of items, to have a sharper recall of the last items on the list. No doubt you've experienced this at a party. When introduced to 10 people, you only recall the name of the last one or two.

The recency effect occurs in finance, too. If you are making investment decisions based on what happened in markets in the last week or the last day, you risk chasing past winners or perceiving as the greatest risk something that has already occurred and been priced in – you project from the recent past to the far future.

There is an evolutionary reason for the recency effect. Just as when we were hunter-gatherers more than 10,000 years ago, our brains are programmed to respond to what we perceive as the most immediate threats. Equally, we are likely to see as the best opportunities those that proved themselves in the immediate prior period.

During particularly traumatic markets, or rapidly rising markets, this effect can be magnified. Our short-term memories dominate our decision-making process, extrapolating recent returns into the future. The consequence is that all too often people buy stocks near the top of the cycle or sell them near the bottom. In rising markets, this equates to fear of missing out, while in falling markets, the overwhelming imperative is loss aversion.

Jonathan writes: Money hacks

Often, we know what we need to do about money, but find it hard to do it. Working for the Money Advice Service, I came across some pleasing money 'hacks' that people have used to help nudge themselves into doing the right thing. Not content with playing tricks on their mind, they had some physical tricks to back them up.

Monzo Bank was a simple tool that helped many of our target customers – so good that I had to pass it on in Chapter 3 (*Manage Your Money*, see page 44). It was one of the first banks to introduce gambling blocks – enabling you to cut your account off from any gambling business. Other banks have followed its lead. This is helpful with a very specific form of addiction.

I also came across less dramatic situations, but more intriguing hacks. Some people put a credit card in a ziplock bag, then a Tupperware full of water, which they then froze. That way, they had access to it, but only after a substantial and inconvenient delay. Given this delay, the spending impulse that they were battling often cooled off while the credit card warmed up! There are lots of useful variants on this. Put it in a friend's freezer if you want an even greater barrier between you and the card … If you want to preserve the integrity of your 'bills' account, so that it can only be used to pay direct debits, simply destroy the card that comes with it.

Some of the wilder examples I came across were from behavioural science experiments in other countries. An experiment in India took place to see whether employees could be encouraged to save more of their wages. They were given wages in cash and in two envelopes. The 'savings' envelope had a personalized photo of each employee's family on it. The employee had to tear apart their family to access the savings money. Unsurprisingly, this did lead to an increase in saving!

We hope that people reading this book will have a reasonably comfortable line of sight between what they *want* to do about money and what they actually do. If, by contrast, you feel there is a serious disconnect, you might want to consider contacting Mental Health and Money Advice. They can put you in touch with different forms of support to help you address it.

What to expect

Depending on your age, you may be investing for 30 to 60 years. This means you *should* expect to experience many recessions and a major market fall, such as was seen in 2022. Each time, you will see your savings fall in value. At the extreme that history has given us, which we can hope might not be repeated, they may fall by as much as 90 per cent. This was the 'trough' of the Wall Street crash in 1929. A lot of myth surrounds this, so it's good to have the actual figures. In fact, it took about 2.5 years for the index to fall that far from its peak. The biggest one-day fall of the Wall Street crash was nearly 12 per cent.

Let's look at more recent history. Patrick Cairns from the Evidence-Based Investor summed up the US stock market story since 1955 as follows:

> Since the S&P 500 officially became constituted of 500 stocks in 1957, its annual average return has been a little over 8 per cent. Over all that time, however, it has never actually produced an 8 per cent return in a calendar year. In fact, in all of those 63 years, the index has only returned between 7 per cent and 9 per cent on four occasions. It has more commonly produced an annual return of between 19 per cent and 21 per cent. That has happened five times.[6]

If we take a look at this visually, a long slice of history for the main US index, the S&P 500, looks like this:

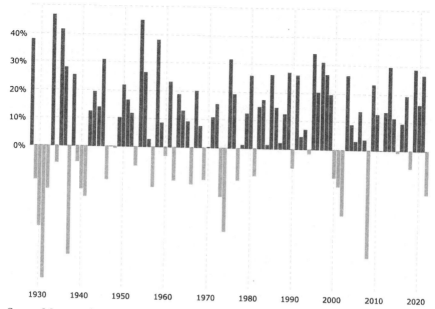

Source: Macrotrends S&P 500 Historical Returns[7]

Look carefully at the heights and depths of the up and down lines. The emotional effects of these ups and downs are going to be fairly obvious to anyone who thinks themselves into what each swing would feel like.

Now, here's something to think about that will help you to understand why it may *feel* even worse. For most people the amount of money they have invested in their DC pension will be the largest single sum of liquid money they have ever touched. True, their house may be worth more, but most houses are not paid for with cash outright.

If you integrate all your pensions into one account, this will mean that when the market does swing down, you will see all your 'losses' in one place so they will be 'losses' that are bigger than the largest sums you have ever lost in real life before. Towards the end of your working life you might even see 'losses' that are larger than the annual salary you are earning.

We use the word 'losses' in scare quotes, though because it can't be said often enough: if you are investing for the long-term, *it's only a loss when you finally sell*. For all the years up to when you sell, you could call it a 'paper loss', but it's probably better thought of as just 'volatility'.

If you are drawing down income each month at the time that a major market fall happens, you will indeed realize a loss but that real loss will only be a tiny sliver of your whole portfolio. It is best if you can hold your focus on the smaller losses when you sell – the real losses – rather than fluctuations in the overall value of your portfolio. And that's why it's worth thinking carefully about the different meanings of the word 'risk'. When bad things happen, ask yourself what kind of risk has actually materialized and what it means.

The three flavours of risk

Risk is an aspect of investing that most people are confused about. That includes pension fund trustees and indeed many financial professionals. If you've read so far, you will certainly know that you can't avoid risk – you have to learn to live with it. In fact, you have to learn to live with three flavours of risk.

The first and most dangerous flavour of risk is permanent loss of capital. This clearly needs to be avoided. Now, every investment advert warns you that your capital is at risk. That's right, and it's true. And it's pretty misleading, in our view. Here's the more important truth to be aware of. Probably your biggest danger for loss of capital isn't in the mainstream markets – it's losing large chunks of it to fraudsters. That's why we devoted most of Chapter 5 (*Avoid Charlatans and Sharks*, see pages 87–113) to warning you about it.

Over any one year, with any one equity, you do have a chance of losing your capital. But with almost any mainstream investment strategy that is truly diversified – over the long term – you would have to be spectacularly unlucky to lose all, or even most, of your capital so the warning is only accurate if you think about buying one stock and selling soon. If you think about buying slices of tens of thousands of companies and selling after a long time, it's a lot less relevant.

The second flavour of risk is returns that don't outpace inflation, costs and eventually, the income you want to draw down. We've mentioned before that inflation is like a silent killer, gradually eroding your capital over time. It's quite useful to think of it as a 'wealth tax'.

More generally, you want to be sure that your returns, over time, are keeping pace with your plan and your needs. Even a small braking on returns will build up, for a big effect over the long term, so this is a very important risk for you to focus on.

The third and final flavour of risk is volatility. It's the least dangerous flavour but the one that will most shape people's experience, consume their focus and drive their behaviour. We have seen in the graph above that there will always be volatility in the financial markets, especially equities, but bailing out once markets have fallen can do enormous damage. Given that equities have a long history of providing rising capital value over the long run, the logical course is to take that long view and ride out any volatility.

Volatility will affect your feelings but until you sell, it's a wholly theoretical problem. In the next section we will look at ways of avoiding the traps that your feelings will set for you.

How to overcome your behavioural biases

We have found there's a lot more evidence about the problems created by all these biases than there is on clever research into how to overcome them. But we have looked over a great deal of material and tried to synthesize some simple, practical methods you can use to help yourself to not succumb completely to their effects.[8]

You won't be surprised to learn that our six rules already embed some of this thinking. We'll remind you of the three most important rules relevant here and then give some more detailed practical suggestions about how to apply them in particular circumstances.

Remember the rules

Our first rule is number one for a reason! If you know what your plan is, and you have a method for achieving it, you are less likely to

Rule 1: Have a purpose, a plan and a method

be buffeted about by your emotions at difficult times. If you know *why* you have chosen a particular mix of asset classes, and you know the long-term history of their performance, you can match them up to what the market throws at you. If it fits the long-term plan, stick with it.

If the market messes up your long-term plan, make the necessary changes. In each case, the plan, not your emotions,

> **Rule 3: To dilute your risks, add lots of time**

should be the principal driver of your actions. Of course, this links very closely to Rule 3. Most of the literature about the penalty people pay for succumbing to behavioural biases shows that, heated up by emotional pressure, they take short-term decisions. Had they taken a long-term view and done nothing, they would be much better off.

Other people's views, or even giving other people control, are a further way of ensuring that you take the heat out of such

> **Rule 4: Phone a friend, especially when times are taxing**

moments. In the next chapter we will look at the advantages of using a financial adviser to take away the direct levers of control over your finances. Ideally, they can take a dispassionate view.

Handing over control ought to be necessary only if you are sure you can't keep on top of short-term feelings yourself. Friends and family could fill in for some of the help you might get from a financial adviser. If, for example, you 'only' need to vent your worries and emotions (and don't at that particular time need technical support or recommendations), you don't necessarily need to pay an adviser to listen to you.

Play some tricks with your mind

Again, you won't be surprised to learn that some of the tricks we're about to note here have cropped up before. We start with some tricks that will help you to do nothing. The most important one is 'cash for a crash'. We covered this in Chapter 6 (*Take the Right Risks*, see page 134). If there is a financial crash and you are able to switch to a fund of cash to cover your spending for a year, two or even three years, then you won't need to cash in any paper losses on your investments until you have drained your cash. This means that the paper losses may never materialize as real losses, or they may have significantly diminished by the time you have to start to make them real.

Another trick came up in our review of the products from Nest Pensions. You will remember that their pension product has three named parts: the wallet, the safe, and the vault. You don't need to have a Nest product to use the same thinking about using mental accounting labels to divide up your savings. We are not so sure the Nest language is self-explanatory, but here's an example based on the 'ambitious' portfolio we covered earlier (see page 132). Play around with the language and find what works for you.

	Mental accounting for an ambitious portfolio		
Proportion of your portfolio	Asset categories	Labelling you might use	Thinking behind the labelling
30%	Micro- and small-cap equities Emerging market equities	'Rocket fuel' 'Rollercoaster' 'Dreaming'	'I have this in my portfolio to drive high growth over the long term and I won't mind if I see big swings and ups and downs.'
50%	Developed market equities Large-cap equities	'Defensive play' 'Bread-and-butter' 'Vanilla'	'I have these in my portfolio to keep growth going through good times and bad. I should allow myself to worry a bit more if these suffer big falls at the same time as what's above.'
20%	Government bonds	'Safety' 'Foundations'	'I have these in my portfolio to provide solid, safe ballast to what's above. If the other assets are going down, I need to focus my mind on the security these provide.'

Another approach is the 'envelope trick'. If you are tempted to sell because you are worried about a sliding market, write down your decision (and why you think it's a good one) and put this in an envelope. Date the envelope six months from now, or three months, even one month away. Any reasonable distance of time is going to stop you from acting on the spur of the moment. If on the day you open the envelope it still looks like a good decision, go ahead and do it.

Some cautious investors take a more disciplined approach. If they are thinking of selling an asset, they look at whether its price has dropped below a 10-month average. When it has, they sell. This is a deliberate attempt to make their investment decisions in 'slow motion' – something the envelope trick echoes in a less mathematically driven way.

Sometimes, however, you will need to do something rather than nothing. What if you decide parts of your portfolio were based on the wrong decisions and you need to sell? The challenge here will be your emotional investment in what you have already managed for years or possibly decades, nursing it through good times and bad. One trick people recommend is to self-identify as someone who is renting your investments, not an owner of them. Imagine you were renting them like a car or a holiday property. Tomorrow morning, you could wake up and easily make a switch to something better. Would you indeed switch to other 'rented' investments, or would you take up the same ones all over again?

What happens if you come into an inheritance and need to invest it? An issue many people face here is the emotional baggage that comes with inheriting a property, or valuable items, or even somebody else's share portfolio. The sense of what that other person intended, or what they meant to you, can outweigh rational thought. Behavioural economists call this 'the endowment effect' and it's a powerful driver of inertia. If what you have inherited stands to make a crucial difference to your financial future, pretending that you have inherited cash, rather than any other type of asset, can help you to think about what is the most reasonable course of action.

Finally, it can't be said often enough that talking to others about decisions is one of the most sensible ways of managing your emotions and making better decisions. Especially if you are brave enough to seek out the views of people who are likely to give contrary

Rule 4: Phone a friend, especially when times are taxing

opinions to your own. And it is in our final chapter that we will turn to this subject and how to implement Rule 4. Who can you turn to? Who can you trust? Who is it worth paying for advice and on what subjects? How can you find a first-rate adviser?

Now take (no!) action

Our workbook will help you to:

- Do a behavioural bias test.
- Rank yourself against the six behavioural biases.
- Mark which of our behavioural tricks are more appealing to you to use when markets are falling – or rising.

9

Find a First-Rate Adviser

Congratulations, you are on the final chapter of the book! And having read this far, you're in a very good position to make best use of this important final chapter. We think there are very few investors, if any at all, who can afford to go for a lifetime without taking some regulated financial advice. It's not a matter of *if* you need an adviser, what needs careful consideration is *when* you need them and *how* to engage them. We deliberately left discussion of advisers to the last chapter – we felt that if you have an overview of the whole territory your adviser might need to cover, you'll have two advantages over most people:

- The first is that you'll know exactly what you need to ask them about.
- The second is that you'll have a good instinct for which areas you will find easiest to handle yourself – and so which you'd most want an adviser to take on. This does open up some options to save money – by getting an adviser to work on some things, but not others.

Here, we'll set out some of the problems with the adviser market – because, sadly, it doesn't work for everyone. We'll then look at all the ways you can get meaningful help – for at least some of the areas that might defeat you – instead of paying an adviser. And we'll look at online alternatives, and hybrid alternatives, to traditional ways of giving you advice. Finally, we'll look at the practical steps to choosing an adviser. We'll give you the questions we suggest you ask them at your first meeting and at regular intervals after that.

General principles for using a financial adviser

We think the flow chart on the next page will be helpful to you as you think through your advice needs. They will be expanded on through the rest of this chapter.

In the ideal world, everyone would be able to afford to use a financial adviser but for the reasons we'll set out in the next section, we don't live in that ideal world. In the non-ideal world, we think the two key points you need to consider are whether (having read the book so far):

- you think you can manage your investments;
- you can afford the 0.8 per cent, or 80 basis points – or more – that an adviser will charge for *ongoing* investment management.

In thinking about managing your investments, there are two big considerations. The first is the level of your knowledge and skills. The second, probably more challenging to evaluate, is behavioural. We don't think that the knowledge and skills required to manage a simple passive portfolio of investments will be beyond anyone who has read this whole book so far but whether you need a 'financial bodyguard' to protect you from the ups and downs of your emotions, only you can judge. That's why we dedicated the whole of the previous chapter to considering all the ins and outs of the behavioural challenges you will face.

Even if you can – and do – manage your money yourself on an ongoing basis, we believe almost everyone who is investing will need to use an adviser at some point in their life. Whether it's taxes, inheritance or a financial plan at a particularly critical stage, there are some areas of expertise that you will need from an adviser to make a good decision so you should expect to need to engage one at least at a moment in time. The alternative – ongoing money management by an adviser for every single year you are investing – is not cheap. We'll show that below. But cost and value are two different things. If it prevents you from selling when shares are low and buying when they are high, it will save you much more than the fees you pay. After the flow chart, let's look into the financial advice market and all your options for getting help thinking about and managing your money.

Thinking through your adviser needs

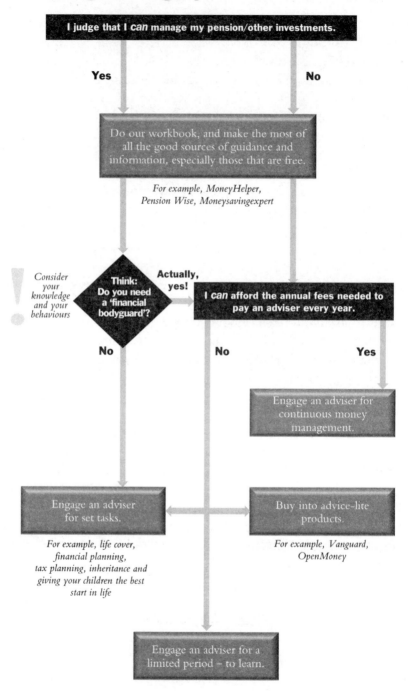

I judge that I *can* manage my pension/other investments.

Yes   No

Do our workbook, and make the most of all the good sources of guidance and information, especially those that are free.

For example, MoneyHelper,
Pension Wise, Moneysavingexpert

Consider
your
knowledge
and your
behaviours

Think:
Do you need a 'financial bodyguard'?

Actually, yes!

I *can* afford the annual fees needed to pay an adviser every year.

No   No   Yes

Engage an adviser for continuous money management.

Engage an adviser for set tasks.

Buy into advice-lite products.

For example, life cover,
financial planning,
tax planning, inheritance and
giving your children the best
start in life

For example, Vanguard,
OpenMoney

Engage an adviser for a limited period – to learn.

A broken marketplace for advice

When we wrote about the costs and risks of social care, we concluded that the best recommendations we could give you were practical, but imperfect. We described a messy, inconsistent marketplace that numerous governments have shied away from sorting out. Regulated financial advice is not quite so much of a basketcase as social care but we have to be straight with you: it's challenging to find affordable, high-quality financial advice at a price that will feel proportionate to the money you have invested.

It's not just we who say this. The Financial Conduct Authority is the regulator responsible for the marketplace. Its 2020 report on the marketplace it regulates said: 'Advice firms appear to face little competitive pressure to innovate and offer new, more affordable services, or to try to attract less wealthy consumers. Competition does not appear to be operating effectively in the interests of consumers.'[1]

What drives advice costs?
If you get regulated financial advice, you are paying for two things you will like and both are expensive. And you will inevitably pay for other things that interest you much less, such as offices, overheads and marketing. These too can be expensive drivers of cost.

The first good thing you will want, above all, is the skill and qualifications of the adviser. This book is the tip of a very large iceberg. A wealth (no pun intended) of rules and opportunities lies behind what we have set out in each chapter. Acquiring that knowledge, and keeping it up to date, so that it can be applied to your circumstances is never going to be cheap. The second is a guarantee (of sorts) if things go wrong. We mentioned this right at the beginning of the book.

- If a regulated adviser gives you advice that is wrong for your circumstances, you have a right of comeback.
- Ultimately, you can raise a complaint to the Financial Ombudsman Service and if it is upheld, the adviser must compensate you.

- And if they have gone out of business, the Financial Services Compensation Scheme must compensate you instead.

This guarantee is pretty helpful, but it's vital to understand what it's not: it's not something you can call on if you get sensible advice, yet your investments perform badly in the natural course of things. Of course, if people are dissatisfied with their adviser-led investments, 99 per cent or more of the time it will be because their investments haven't performed quite as well as they hoped. Only a tiny minority will experience objective incompetence. But every time you are paying a regulated adviser, remember that part of what you pay goes into insuring them – so that you can have this right of redress.

Who pays for the advice?
This may seem like a strange question because *you* do – of course you do! But there is confusion among consumers because the business model of advisers was radically different very recently – less than a decade ago. Up to 2013, it was entirely legal for advisers to depend on 'trail commission' to pay advice costs. Most did. Translated into everyday language, this meant that when you bought a financial product because of an adviser's input, they got a small payback from the amount you invested in that product, for as long as you invested in it. Typical 'trail' commission was about 0.5 per cent, or 50 basis points. And of course, financial services providers ultimately got the money to pay this commission from the prices they charged consumers for products.

The regulations changed radically in 2013. Trail commission was banned. There was a very good reason for this: advisers were, or at least could be, driven by the wrong incentive. This was to get you to buy products that gave them more commission, rather than the products that were right for you and gave you the best results. And too many only considered products from one financial services provider, rather than the whole market. However, although the old system was very bad for those reasons, it did have one enormous advantage. The removal of this advantage has been the cause of fierce debate ever since. For most consumers, the advantage was that financial advice appeared to be 'free' – it had either no upfront cost, or much lower ones than you face today – so more people took it.

A further advantage was that banks offered an in-house advice service under the old model. Because of their frequent interactions with banks, this gave consumers regular prompts to seek financial advice. As a result of complete upheaval, four things have now been lost:

- There were many more advisers under the old system. When the changes came in, about 25 per cent of advisers left the marketplace. (Numbers have crept back up a bit since then, but not much.)
- More people took advice in the past, because it appeared to be 'free'.[2] By 2017, fully 94 per cent of adults *weren't* taking financial advice. By 2020, the position had improved slightly, down to about 92 per cent. But regulated financial advice remains very much a minority pursuit.
- Advisers were happier then than they are now to serve people with much smaller investments (£50,000 or less), because their business model made it more attractive.
- By and large, the main banks exited the advice market.

We are not saying that the old model was better, it was a different kind of broken market. It has been replaced by something that is a much closer fit to most people's idea of a free market: people pay for what they use. The result, however, is that too many people are priced out of it.

How you pay for advice today
All that is history and there's no prospect of anyone turning the clock back. Today, you pay for advice directly and there are three main ways:
- An upfront, one-off charge to analyse your financial circumstances in the round, based on the total value of the money you want to consider investing. The average fee for this is 2.4 per cent – known as 'onboarding'. It typically includes the cost of the adviser implementing their recommendations, by buying investments for you.

And then either:

- An ongoing management fee, for managing your money. This is a fee you will pay every year. The average charge is 0.8 per cent of what is invested. As it is an average, you can expect to encounter higher rates. This is on top of all the other types of fees we covered in Chapter 4 (*Capture Market Returns*, see pages 67–86). Remember, it's like paying for a personal shopper. On top of what you pay them, you still have to pay for the goods they buy.

Or:

- You may be able to pay an hourly rate, or agree a set sum, for specific work on specific issues. The average is £150/hour, or £1,100 a day.[3]

If most advisers charged by the hour, the scales would not be tipped against small investors – but most don't and so they are. Nine out of 10 clients of regulated financial advice pay the ongoing percentage charge. As the FCA itself points out, this means that if an adviser has to choose between one person who is going to invest £250,000 and 10 people who each have £25,000 to invest, they are naturally going to have an inclination to serve the wealthier client because they will get the same amount of money for considerably less work.

So let's think about a couple who have saved a pension pot. It is not all the way up our pensions mountain at the £860,000, 'luxurious' level. Let's say they have a pot of £680,000 – somewhere between moderate and luxurious. When they approach drawdown at the age of 57, they want to decide what to do. Here's what they will pay:

- If they approach the average adviser, they will pay £16,320 for their onboarding and initial advice, then £5,440 for the first year's money management fees. All this before they have paid platform, product and transaction charges, which will add up to several thousand pounds more.
- If they are taking 3.3 per cent out of the pension pot they have saved up, they can safely take an income of £22,240 each year – and their adviser will be getting a quarter of it.
- Suppose their pension pot maintains its value for 40 years. They will have paid the adviser nearly £218,000.

- Suppose they inherit £400,000. An adviser managing all their investments will be getting nearly £9,000 a year – close to the level of having a full-time permanent employee (albeit a very badly paid one) working for their family.

As we said earlier, cost and value are not the same thing. For this money, they would expect to receive a very comprehensive service, covering anything from investment to inheritance and lots of other matters in between. It's entirely possible that the adviser will save them all of the fees they pay by giving them great advice about inheritance planning, or other aspects of taxes, during that 40-year period. Many advisers bring significant expertise and value and so prove their worth.

On the other hand, the central part of an adviser's mission is to manage your investments. Remember all the evidence about active investing from Chapters 5 and 6. We don't think that any adviser can reasonably claim that, in order to balance out the fees you pay them, they will simply outperform the market. If you come across one who hints at this claim, steer well clear!

We're not blaming advisers for the costs they charge. They operate within a market, and as we have said, it is now closer to a free market than it was before. And we're certainly not saying there's anything wrong with people wanting an adviser to manage all their money, so that they can focus on other things they enjoy more. We think the awkwardness comes from the fact that for many people, the sums they would need to pay an adviser to manage their retirement money represent an unaffordably high proportion of a not-very-high retirement income yet the overall system (not just investing, but investments within a tax and legal system) remains sufficiently challenging that you need a book of this length to decipher it.

Less wealthy people are therefore caught between a rock and a hard place. As we said in our introduction, this is why we have written this book. We aim to put self-management of your portfolio, or at least parts of it for long periods, within the grasp of as many readers as possible. One silver lining we should note is that if you need to seek regulated advice about your pension, there is a tax benefit available to you. You can withdraw £500 from your DC pension pot, up to three times (so long as each time is in a different tax year), to pay for advice regardless of whether you've started drawing down a pension from it. This amount of advice therefore has a tiny tax subsidy because you don't need to pay for it from your post-tax income. Given the costs we've set out above, it won't go very far, but it is there to be taken. It's called the 'Pensions Advice Allowance' and your DC pensions provider can help you access it.

Alternatives to regulated financial advice

We will immediately attract controversy by talking about alternatives to expensive regulated financial advice. Many who practise it say there is no alternative and it is a unique 'gold standard' offer in the marketplace. But people who hand over all their money management to a regulated financial adviser receive a wide range of services from them. Some of these services are things only a regulated adviser can do and indeed 'gold-standard', but some will be:

- a listening ear, on a topic many people find embarrassing;
- explanation and education;
- factual information equally available a few clicks away on the internet;
- what industry jargon calls 'guidance' – helpful information that falls short of a regulated, personally applicable recommendation.

Regardless of what anyone says, you can find these elsewhere and you don't have to pay £150 an hour to receive them. Here, we go into some of the sources and options you can use but of course there are pitfalls you need to look out for, as well as the advantages – we'll point these out in each case.

Friends and family: talk is free!
A constant theme of this book is encouraging people to talk more about money to friends and family. The less money becomes an embarrassing, private topic, the more chance people have to learn from each other's experiences. That said, we really do want to warn you against a major pitfall: we don't think that relying on friends and

family for investment recommendations is a good idea at all. Perhaps, if the person you're talking to is fully bought into the principles in this book, and much more experienced than you at putting them into practice, there might be an exception, but that is going to be very rare.

A dangerous source of bad investment decisions, and in the worst cases scams, is talking to someone you know who has

> **Rule 4: Phone a friend, especially when times are taxing**

made 'this one great investment'. It will be very attractive because it's based on someone you trust. Trust is that vital lubricant which moves people to invest. But as we've seen from Chapters 5 and 6, the recent past performance of a single investment is a poor guide to its future performance. So what do we think are good opportunities to lean on friends and family? Well, from the arguments we've made so far in the book, you would expect us to emphasize the following:

- comparing notes on platforms, fees and highly diversified passive funds;
- a listening ear when you are worried about a fall in the stock market and trying to hold your nerve;
- comparing notes about your future income needs and retirement timeline;
- double-checking the bank details so that a life-changing sum of money doesn't get transferred to the wrong destination;
- talking over something that sounds too good to be true to see if it's a scam.

Of course, a good adviser will be an excellent expert who can cover all these topics but they may also be an expensive way of fulfilling them – above all, if you pay them by the hour. And there are very good reasons to keep on seeking a wide range of opinions. Human beings, even the very smartest ones, are naturally inclined to view the world through the prism of their circumstances, beliefs and experiences. All of us, no matter how high our IQs, have our blind spots. This is why it is so important to seek an outside view – preferably more than one. An objective view can help you uncover your assumptions or blind spots. It can also anchor your beliefs and help you to be better prepared in case things don't turn out the way that you expect.

Sources of self-help information and guidance
So how can you widen your range of informed insight?[4] This book, obviously, is intended to be a great source of self-help guidance and factual information. Earlier, we talked about the pros (and cons) of media coverage of money matters. But there's more. Some of the most notable free-to-access sources outside the news and current affairs space are:

- Robin's website, *The Evidence-Based Investor.*
- Martin Lewis's remarkable moneysavingexpert.com. The detailed topic guides it gives to bank accounts, saving accounts and pensions products are world-class, practical and free.
- The *MoneyHelper* website. Not just a source of explanation, it has some excellent tools, linked throughout this book.
- The which.co.uk money pages (from the Consumers' Association).
- The US-based *Investopedia.* It has 36,000 articles on investment topics and some robust editorial processes to keep them from bias. Because of its US provenance, it will not be useful for looking into the kinds of UK-centred practicalities we cover in this chapter or Chapter 7 (*Manage Your Mix*, see pages 152–86), but for general investment explanations it's a good source.

There are hardly any pitfalls to using the UK-based sources of information. None of them tells you exactly what you need to do, but the more time you invest in them, the better educated you can become. You now have a framework of knowledge and understanding from this book, which will help you to focus and filter your learning.

More generally, digital publishing and Google meant it's never been easier to find the facts and explanations you need. There are tens of thousands of reputable organizations in the English-speaking world publishing free explanations, free market data and highly useful tools. It truly is a golden age for people who want to help themselves. But ... we also said it's a golden age for scammers trying to reach their next victim. Google ads are one of the tools they use so do look for objective sources of information and/or large, well-known organizations. If you are doing a financial search on Google that doesn't take you straight to an established source, it's best to avoid the links marked as an 'ad' and plough through to the naturally-appearing search results.

Pension Wise and MoneyHelper
When the UK government introduced the pensions freedoms we talked about in Chapter 2 (*Invest in ... Yourself*, see pages 27–41), it also introduced a guidance service called Pension Wise – a free service for people over 50. Pension Wise offer a website with a self-help tutorial, a telephone line or you can book face-to-face appointments. All three ways of accessing Pension Wise are designed to help you understand your pension options within the legal framework of the 2015 pension freedoms.

Nobody from Pension Wise will give you any recommendations about what you should do. That would cross a line into regulated financial advice. A Pension Wise appointment will likely help you understand the finer details of accessing your DC pension. If you want to take the discussion deeper, towards what is best for you, you may get frustrated with the limitations placed on a Pension Wise adviser but the appointments are free, the pension freedoms are not easy to understand and it won't hurt to have someone new explain it to you who has done so many times before. We recommend booking an appointment.

However, there is another government service that is not very well known, available to people of any age and very helpful. Also a MoneyHelper service, it used to be known under the name of 'The Pensions Advisory Service'. They have a website and a remarkably good telephone line – 0800 011 3797. The line is staffed mostly by people who used to work as professionals in the pensions industry. Mostly volunteers, they are there to explain, not recommend, and can answer highly specific questions about truly niche pensions topics so they won't tell you what you should do, but they are very good at demystifying things. And if your topic is long and complex, they won't watch the clock. Nor do they take reams of irrelevant personal information from you before they start answering your question!

All of the above services are free. Now we move on to services you can pay for. Because these mix or replace expensive, comprehensive, regulated face-to-face advice with digital methods, they are cheaper.

Money helplines

Which? run a financial guidance helpline for its members. *Which?* membership costs about £10 a month. Of course it gives you a great deal more than access to the helpline. The helpline covers virtually all key money topics. But it doesn't offer regulated financial advice, so it won't offer recommendations specific to your circumstances. You should probably think of it as a service that can help explain things to you and narrow down your options somewhat, but not something that will take you to the exact course of action you need.

(MoneyHelper offer a free financial guidance helpline on 0800 138 7777, different from their pensions line noted above. You might try this before you pay for a *Which?* subscription.)

Robo-advice

'Robo-advice' is an expression we both dislike intensely because it's so unhelpful and misleading – doubly irritating when the services it disguises are useful innovations. It's shorthand used to identify a category of new digital services that began after regulated financial advice was reformed. In essence, these online services will take you through a series of questions to build up a picture of your finances and identify your risk appetite. They then programme a 'set menu' of typically passive investments that you can buy and manage through the same account. Because it largely removes human interactions from the equation, it's less expensive – hence the 'robo' bit of the nickname.

But is it a good idea to call it *advice*? Sure, it produces personalized recommendations. But at the time of writing, the questionnaires are far from taking a comprehensive view of your whole financial world. That view, if you think back to the start of this book, should include a fuzzy, wide-ranging conversation about your purpose, your goals, your expected longevity, your retirement timeline, your relationships and need for life assurance or income protection, your inheritance wishes – and any peculiarities that would shape your tax situation. A good regulated financial adviser, by quizzing you on all of these matters, will not only be able to give you truly comprehensive advice. They will also know from the answers you have given what further questions they should ask, which may not be on their usual list – try getting a machine to do that!

Robo-advice has its place. It's a cheap way of selecting a basket of broadly suitable passive investments but it's essentially a self-selection service. Think of it as *robo-selection* and remember that it is taking an extremely limited 'view' of you and your life. There are many robo-advice services. Some of the UK's best-known are Nutmeg, who we covered a little in Chapter 6 (*Take the Right Risks*, see pages 148–9), Moneyfarm and Wealthify. They are all worth looking into but as ever, make sure the 'robots' do their job and keep your fees low.

'Advice lite': a hybrid of robo-advisers backed by financial advisers on the telephone
We devote a whole section to two providers here because they are the best examples of genuine innovation in the marketplace. They offer a combination of robo-advice with access to qualified human advisers and extremely low fees. We think these could be good solutions for a lot of people and encourage you to look into them. Please remember, as with the earlier buyer's guide, we include them to help you understand what to look for in the marketplace, not because we think they're automatically the best of the best. And because we have to base our 'buyer's guide' notes on their sales information, we might have misunderstood something important.

OpenMoney is a Manchester-based firm that offers self-invested pensions, alongside stocks and shares ISAs. Their service combines a financial healthcheck questionnaire, an app and access to advisers online and over the telephone. The app can even link to your bank accounts (and recommend utility switching offers). Based on your circumstances, you can then invest in portfolios structured as *cautious*, *balanced* or *aggressive*, which dip into funds supplied by iShares, Vanguard and some other providers.

OpenMoney get rave reviews for the service they provide. Their all-in fees for each of their three portfolios are among the lowest in the marketplace. Fees range from 0.49 to 0.46 per cent. Each fee includes the financial advice, the platform charges and transaction charges. We hope this will spark a revolution in lower fees, but at the moment OpenMoney stand almost alone – apart from Vanguard.

Vanguard very recently launched a dedicated financial planning service in the UK. As we pointed out when we referenced Vanguard earlier, they are a mutual organization that doesn't seek to make a profit from its activities. The offer has significant limitations, which we'll go into below, but it offers an all-inclusive fee of 0.79 per cent, which covers the advice, the platform, the management charges – everything. What you get for that depends on how much you invest. If you are investing under £100,000 (with a minimum of £50,000), you essentially get a robo-advice service, but with claims that Vanguard will do genuine, tax-efficient financial planning and not just give you some tailored investments. Above £100,000, you get all of that and access to real qualified people by telephone or video and above £750,000, you get a dedicated financial planner. Their service will only invest in Vanguard products – a big limitation. But as these are among the lowest-fee products in the marketplace, it's not one that draws a sharp intake of breath from either of us. Unfortunately, neither service extends to managing the process of drawing down your pension. They only currently exist to help you in the accumulation phase. But, for millions of people, that's a relevant offer.

Choosing a regulated financial adviser

So now we have given you a 'buyer's guide' to some of the ways you can address financial problems. They all fall short of buying the most costly forms of 'face-to-face' regulated financial advice. Use as many of these as you can. Here, we'll set out a process to help you find a first-rate financial adviser for your needs. Just so you understand the shape of the market, here is the FCA's overview from 2020:

> There are over 5,000 advice firms and 27,000 regulated professionals advising on retail investments and pensions. The advice market remains dominated by holistic advice (where an adviser considers a consumer's overall financial circumstances and objectives, and makes recommendations to meet them), accounting for upwards of 90 per cent of revenue, and target customers remain largely wealthier consumers. The average advised customer has over £150,000 of assets under advice.[5]

We think the main steps you should go through in venturing into this marketplace are to:

- Write down your needs and decide how long you need advice for;
- Document your 'money world' clearly;
- Go for the best by shopping around;
- Ask tough questions;
- Get a good price;
- Finally, be 'promiscuous', leaving or switching services when it suits you, not your adviser.

What do you need, and how long for?

Now is a good time to look back to the flow chart on page 204. Where do you now stand with your need for regulated financial advice?

We suggest that it will be very helpful for you, and even more helpful as you choose between advisers, if you write down your needs – in a way that you can easily paste into an email. (You might want to keep to yourself thoughts about timescales. The optimum client for many advisers is the one who stays with that adviser forever.)

Our downloadable workbook will take you through these.

Now is a good time to set out the distinction between financial advice and financial planning and complications around tax advice. In many countries, to be a financial planner is defined in regulation and it is different from being a financial adviser, but in the UK, any financial adviser (which is a regulated profession) can call themselves a financial planner (which is not).[6]

We would expect a financial planner to take the kind of approach that follows the logic of this book. They would provide a comprehensive service: asking you about your goals, then helping you to develop a life plan; your entire assets; your relationships and your legacy. The best of them can produce a year-by-year financial plan to cover the rest of your life. It will take account of milestones such as state pension age and tax events triggered by your age or your death. Many will have access to software that will model all this and carry out risk analyses on it. It will even calculate the most tax-efficient path through it all. We know plenty of people who use advisers that say the financial plan, with its detailed tax and cashflow modelling, is the most helpful thing they have taken away from the advice process (Robin says a bit more about the qualities of a good financial plan later in this chapter.)

If you want a more limited service, the type that would be labelled financial advice, this will usually mean helping you to solve a pinpoint problem, such as how to invest a particular sum of money. But you can probably sense the difficulty: because the language is loose and unregulated, some advisers will say they are offering planning and some planners will describe what they do as advice. This underlines our point that you need to be very clear about what your needs are so that you can check them against your adviser's experience.

Then there is a further complication with tax advice. We have said earlier that we think help with tax is one of the most valuable services you can get from professional advisers. It is so much harder to understand and get right than the basic rules of investment. Hence our pun in Rule 4 about 'taxing' times. When you're dealing with the tax, an adviser is probably the 'friend' you should be phoning!

Rule 4: Phone a friend, especially when times are taxing

However, here is a new difficulty. Astonishingly, as the charity TaxAid puts it: 'Anyone can set up in business offering accounting and tax advisory services, even if they have no professional qualifications or experience.'[7]

We would expect a good financial planner to be extremely reliable and knowledgeable in advising you on tax matters but you will have to reassure yourself that they have useful and relevant qualifications, as well as good experience. You should always check whether your financial adviser is on the FCA's list of regulated people by searching for their name on the Financial Services Register. (Our workbook will help you do this.) However, being regulated as a financial adviser by the FCA does not mean that they are qualified in tax matters. For example, FCA regulation only qualifies an adviser to advise you on investments, pensions, retirement income products and 'general financial planning'.

Your adviser may also be qualified to advise you on mortgages or on insurance products. If so, they will also need to be registered for these qualifications on the FCA Register as these are considered separate areas of expertise.

Restricted or Independent

A very important thing to know about regulated advisers is that some of them don't advise on all products. These are known as restricted advisers. So they might limit themselves to the products from a particular commercial provider, or a few such providers. By contrast, Independent Financial Advisers are meant to look much more widely to find the best product for you. An adviser is required to let you know which of these categories they fall into.

Given our emphasis on finding the lowest fees, and on the pace of innovation that keeps on lowering fees, it's hard for us to see circumstances in which going to a restricted adviser would be in your best interests if you are looking for comprehensive advice. Especially if you are looking for it over the long term. So in this chapter, our focus is on IFAs.

Document yourself clearly

All good IFAs will offer a free short initial meeting. There are lots of ways you could use this time with them. We set out some questions we think you should ask in the next section but we believe there's real value in putting together a spreadsheet or document set summarizing your financial world. You then can send it to them before the meeting. We think this brings two advantages to your meeting with a potential adviser:

- The adviser will know that they don't have to spend hours drawing this information out of you. This may (should!) shape the bargain you drive with them about what they charge for onboarding. Many advisers will assume a worst-case scenario (a very time-consuming process) because some people come to them with very chaotic financial lives.
- With luck, they may prove their worth in this initial consultation by coming up with an opportunity or a saving that you didn't know about. They are unlikely to do this before they have seen your 'big picture'.

There's a further value to you in doing this. If you suddenly died, how would your executors know exactly which financial products you owned? Most people think it won't happen anytime soon and happily, they are right. But the exceptions are always unexpected so having a regularly updated index of all your financial assets is useful at all times, to your family as well as your adviser.

So what should this document (or rather, library of documents) contain? Ideally (deep breath), you should collate everything in the table on the next page. Our downloadable workbook will help you do it.

So we give this the gloomy alternative nickname of 'death box'. Because when you die, this is the kind of information your executors will be hunting for – and they will thank you for it. But it will also be a goldmine to a comprehensive financial adviser and the more clearly it is organized, the more value they can add while you are alive.

It will also be a goldmine to scammers. So when you have collated it, make sure you keep it protected and that only you transfer it to

---

My 'financial world' summary
aka 'death box'

- Your current pre-tax and post-tax income
- If applicable, a copy of your last tax return
- All your current bank accounts (account numbers and balances)
- All your current savings accounts or savings/investment products (account numbers, balances and fees)
- Details of any outstanding debts
- Details of any income protection or life assurance policies
- Your state pension estimate and the age at which you can take it
- Details of any DB or DC pensions you hold, including current values and the fees you pay
- The amounts of your regular pension contributions and those from your employer and HMRC
- Your desired retirement income and when you hope to start enjoying it
- Your best estimate of your longevity
- The value of your home if it were sold, the amount you still owe on any mortgage, alongside the mortgage account number and the rate details
- Similar details for any other properties
- A copy of your will and details of any inheritances you may expect to receive in your lifetime
- A summary of the accounts and regular debits you set up as a result of Chapter 3 (*Manage Your Money*, see pages 42–66) (so, your budgets for essential and variable expenditure, holidays and so on)
- Information about any trusts linked to you
- Details of any large gifts you have made in recent years

Of course, this list needs to bring in relevant details for your partner if you are married or in a relationship, and include relevant details about any children or other dependants.

an adviser through a digitally secure method. Advisers should have a special portal for this purpose.

Find a first-rate adviser

You are going to pay high costs to get any form of regulated financial advice so we suggest you try to find the best person you possibly can and then bargain to get the best price. This isn't easy. The qualities you are looking for are not the kind you can simply assess by trawling an adviser's website, you will need to meet the adviser. You may need to go through 10 or a dozen meetings before you find someone who's really good *and* offering you a good fee arrangement.

We suggest three routes to casting your net wide. It is worth asking around to see if friends or relatives can recommend someone. We say this slightly cautiously, because although a personal recommendation is valuable, it shouldn't override your objective assessment of the adviser (more on this in the next section). Then there are two digital directories of advisers you can use to widen your search.

MoneyHelper offers a non-commercial Retirement Adviser Directory. The main advantage is that you can browse it anonymously. And there has been a deliberate effort to draw in advisers who are not seeking the wealthiest clients.

The equivalent commercial directory is unbiased.co.uk. This too is free for you to use. It's very comprehensive. The main minus point is that if you try the 'best match', rather than geographical search, you won't see any results until you have given your contact details. While you can look through the geographical search without giving your personal details, it will only show a small selection of very local results.

In these days of Zoom you can have a perfectly satisfactory consultation with an adviser without ever meeting them. We would encourage you to look into finding the best adviser for you wherever they are in the UK.

Ask tough questions and get a good price
When you meet the adviser, we suggest there are four questions you will want to answer for yourself from the first, free, initial consultation:

1 Do they feel like someone I can work with – is the chemistry right?
2 Are they aligned with the fundamental principles in this book?

3 Are they experienced and qualified in the areas where I need help?

4 Can I already see added value?

We won't say much about the first area because we can't generalize about your personal dynamics, but we would suggest (and this overlaps with the second point) that everyone should look out for someone who is a natural educator. Seek someone who enjoys sharing their knowledge and is clearly good at doing it because this will empower you. Or to put it another way, we would recommend you steer clear of people who enjoy the power that financial jargon has to bewilder and confuse, and subtly use it to emphasize the inequalities between adviser and advised. They certainly shouldn't give the impression that any question is a stupid one. And of course, given the importance of advisers being there to help compensate for any weaknesses in your behaviour as an investor, we encourage you to think about the behavioural areas where you would be weakest and see whether you think the adviser is stronger than you.

With regard to the second point (alignment with the principles in this book), here are some direct questions you might want to ask, directly or indirectly:

- Do you take a largely active or largely passive approach to selecting investments?
- Do you believe that active investors can consistently outperform the markets? If so, why?
- What do you think are your own behavioural biases and weaknesses that you particularly need to guard against when managing clients' money?
- One of the most important things to me is keeping fees low. What do you do to reduce the fees charged on investments you recommend? And what do you do to keep your fees going down, rather than up?
- How have you responded to the competitive pressures on fees from the wider marketplace?
- Do you help your clients to get to the point where they can manage their own money? Can you give an example?

- How do you keep up with the evidence base for successful investing? What's the most important thing you've learned recently?
- What are the biggest financial shocks you have had to manage and how did you work with your clients to get them the best result?
- How do you ensure you are keeping up to date with all the innovations in the marketplace and helping your clients use them?
- Do you have specialist qualifications in tax?
- If you save your clients money, which are the areas where you most often achieve this and how?
- Are you just as happy to do work paid by the hour as to take on comprehensive management of a client's money?

We are confident that an adviser who can give good answers to all these questions truly will be first-rate! It may sound a bit arrogant to say that you need to check that the adviser lines up with the principles in this book but as you can imagine, we wouldn't have gone to the trouble of writing a whole book if we didn't strongly believe in the evidence behind it.

And there is real financial harm looming if you latch onto an adviser who is still a 'flat-earther' as far as active investing is concerned. The damage that advisers are causing was highlighted in a 2018 study in Canada.[8] Researchers found, for example, that advisers traded too frequently, chased returns, preferred expensive, actively managed funds and under-diversified. All of those things have been shown, time and again, to lead to lower returns. On average, the clients of the advisers analysed underperformed the market by around 3 per cent a year – a staggering margin. So we think that you need an adviser who is going to recommend a highly diversified approach to passive investing *and* keep your fees as low as possible.

Showing added value
Probe their skills in the areas where you need help and see if the adviser can already bring forward some valuable ideas about your circumstances. To do this, you will need to give them what you have

prepared in advance: the statement of your needs and your 'death box' of financial facts.

It may be that in an initial conversation there is not enough time to cover both of these and get a useful response from them. If so, there's no harm in asking them to follow up with their best thoughts in writing – the worst they can do is say no.

Getting a good price

With many advisers, you'll have to ask about fees, because you won't find a simple rate card on their website. However, you can turn this to your advantage because it does mean that everything is negotiable. Remember that the average client who hands over their money for ongoing management has £150,000 invested and that the average fee charged for ongoing money management is 0.8 per cent. This will help you understand the strength of your hand in negotiations. But don't be afraid to ask for the price that will make it work for you. Again, the worst you can get is a 'no'!

Robin writes: A good financial plan should be as rich as a tapestry

If you asked the average person to define a financial plan, chances are they'll nominate an investment strategy. And for many people who call themselves advisers, that's what it amounts to, more or less. But a real financial plan should be so much more than that.

To be sure, an investment strategy will form part of a financial plan but a strategy that is not moored to each individual's goals, risk tolerance, financial situation, family circumstances and values is not a strategy at all. It is more likely just a product that is being sold off the shelf. A real financial plan – as drawn up and constantly reviewed by an independent and licensed planner – is a living and breathing creation that begins with each person's goals and aspirations and works back from there. The goals determine the strategy, not vice versa.

Another identifying feature of a substantial plan is there is not one goal or one strategy. Most people will have a long-term goal, such

---

as generating sufficient income to look after their consumption needs in retirement. But they will also have medium-term goals, like funding children's education or paying off a mortgage or securing the care of elderly parents. And they will have short-term goals, like a holiday next year. Each goal will come with a strategy.

Life insurance, disability protection and income protection insurance should all be part of the mix, as will cash management needs in a crisis. You also need to think about your legacy, so how your estate is managed after you are gone has to be considered as well. So a financial plan serves a wide range of functions. It connects your short-term, medium-term and long-term aspirations to different strategies, taking account not only of those goals but of your preparedness to live with the inevitable volatility involved in getting you there. A financial plan, therefore, is not a static document, but an organic one. It changes as your life and circumstances evolve. Careers change, children come along, education costs increase, children leave home, health challenges arrive, families merge, retirement looms.

You could think of a financial plan as a tapestry composed of many individual panels that are woven together into a whole. It may start as one thing, but frequently evolves in style and content as our life story evolves. It can combine many different themes but within an overarching story. In some ways, it is never finished.

When it comes down to it, a great financial plan is a great life plan. The best kinds of advisers are not just technicians, they combine their knowledge and expertise with a subtle form of life coaching, helping you to weave together your personal and financial goals so that you can achieve, as the title of our book has it, *the life you want*.

It's business, not personal

There are lots of benefits to a long-lasting relationship with a trusted adviser. Some find that their clients confide in them on money matters that even the client's partner doesn't know. A side-benefit of having an adviser managing your money for the remainder of your life is that when it comes to your death, there will be a single professional person your executor can turn to for all the financial facts. We're not saying this alone is a reason to pay adviser fees – there are plenty of other people who could fulfil such a role – but we do note it as an added-value benefit. If you are paying for ongoing, comprehensive money management, bear this in mind and plan for it.

Longstanding trust brings benefits, but of course it has its pitfalls ... if loyalty lets you become blind to fees increasing, or service decreasing. Some questions you might want to ask your adviser regularly are:

- Can you recommend any new ways of reducing the investment fees I pay?
- What is the latest evidence on the merits of active and passive investments?
- What other new evidence should I be aware of?
- Are there any recent innovations that can help me manage my money better?
- What mistakes have you made recently and how are you learning from them?
- Do you think I still need you to manage my money?
- How is the financial advice profession changing?

Most advisers charge you monthly so in practice there is a one-month termination period. Remember, at root, this is a financial relationship: you are paying substantial sums of money. So don't be embarrassed about seeking better value elsewhere.

Now take action

This is the final call to action. Congratulations on getting all the way here! Our downloadable workbook will now help you to:

- Identify your needs for information, advice and behavioural support;

- Review the fees of your current adviser, if you have one, and look them up on the FCA Register;
- Collate your 'financial world' summary;
- Start your hunt for a first-rate adviser.

Our Six Rules and the Downloadable Workbook

1. Summary of our six rules

Before we introduce the downloadable workbook itself, here we set out our six rules – the rules that take the mystery out of money. They are woven through the main body of the book and so inform all the thinking behind the workbook as well.

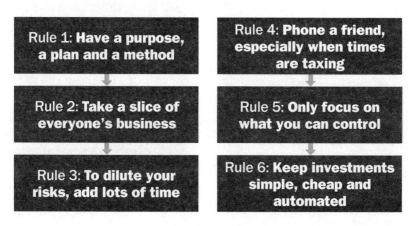

Here's a summary of what each one means.

The purpose of money is to support the life you want, so you need to work out what kind of life you want (where you want

Rule 1: Have a purpose, a plan and a method

it, who you want to spend it with and so on) – a purposeful life, full of human connection and great experiences. So our first few chapters started with this. Your purposes should drive a financial plan (for example, when you will wind down working or stop, and how much money you think you'll need at what stage).

As well as that, you need a day-to-day, month-to-month method of managing your money. In Chapter 3 (*Manage Your Money*, see page 42) we set one out that we think is simple, effective and as automated as possible.

The great writer on investing, John Bogle, wrote, 'In the long run, investing is not about markets at all. Investing is about enjoying

> Rule 2: **Take a slice of everyone's business**

the returns earned by businesses.' It's about getting a share of human enterprise and its continual growth and ingenuity. In Chapter 4 (*Capture Market Returns*, see page 67), we set out the right way to do it: a way that is based on historical evidence, simple and affordable to apply. The gist is rather than trying to pick winners, get a very thin slice of everyone's business and then let the winners grow as markets change.

We return to our third rule throughout the book. In the short term, risks are scary and investing is a roller-coaster ride. The longer

> Rule 3: **To dilute your risks, add lots of time**

you can invest, and the longer the view you can take, the more time will smooth out your risks.

But throughout a long period of investment, we will all discover blind spots and moments when we can't master our feelings. Running

> Rule 4: **Phone a friend, especially when times are taxing**

decisions by trusted friends can be an enormous help. Friends can help you spot scams, calm your feelings when the markets plummet. Or they can (at the simplest level) double-check that you've entered the right bank details when transferring a life-changing sum from one account to another.

Good financial advisers can be even better than a friend because of course they know more and are qualified, but their expertise comes at a high cost. In Chapter 9 (*Find a First-Rate Adviser*, see page 202), we set out how to find a really good adviser and where you might get best value from their expertise.

For some people, it will be best to hand over their money for an adviser to manage precisely because the adviser doesn't have the same gut-emotion feelings about the money, so won't over-react when times are getting 'taxing' and the market is down. For others, a great deal of the value of advice is not about how to apply the simple rules of investing, but more about how to manage the complex rules and sequences of taxes.

Worry and control is a theme that runs through Chapters 4–9, but we do a deep dive into it in Chapter 8 (*Face Your Feelings*, see

Rule 5: Only focus on what you can control

page 187). There are some very obvious things you can't control, such as whether markets will rise or fall, exactly how long you will live and whether politicians will invent entirely new taxes. If you try to anticipate these, you can invest a lot of mental anxiety, and waste a lot of money, by buying and selling assets in a fruitless quest to be two moves ahead on the chessboard.

The best way to address these unknowns is to *monitor* them on a fairly infrequent basis and use all the time and money you save for more interesting and profitable pursuits. These profitable pursuits will include – for at least part of your time – focusing on things you *can* control, to ensure you are on top of them. These include the costs you pay to manage your investments, the tax laws in place that will affect your current money decisions (Chapter 7 – *Manage Your Mix*, see page 152) and keeping up to date with the most recent and cunning scams (Chapter 5 – *Avoid Sharks and Charlatans*, see page 87).

Investment should be about applying simple rules at the lowest possible cost. The great news is that digital automation keeps on

Rule 6: Keep investments simple, cheap and automated

stripping out costs so over the period you will be investing, you can probably expect costs to keep on falling. We focus on automating your current, day-to-day money management in Chapter 3 (*Manage Your Money*, see page 42). We also talk a lot about the easiest platforms and solutions for getting as automated as possible with all your investments. In Chapters 4, 8 and 9, we set out how to put this rule into practice.

So those are our six rules. We think they're highly practical and we hope they are simple and memorable. We think you *will* need to read the whole of the book to get the best out of them, but our aim is that this will be the very last full book you'll need to read on the subject.

2. The workbook

In this printed book we can only provide a glimpse of our downloadable workbook. Go to **www.evidenceinvestor.com/workbook** to download your own PDF version of the workbook. Within the workbook you will also find live links to the many tools and calculators we have recommended you use.

The workbook is password-protected. The password you need to use is:

EvidenceBased!nvesting

You will get the best results if you are able to print each worksheet on A3 paper. This will give you much more room to write on. But you could also print it on A4, then use the worksheets as the jumping-off point for notes you make on the back, or elsewhere.

We think that the average person will take about 25 hours to use the workbook to full advantage, based on asking advance readers to try it out. Note that about a third of the time within this estimate is time to discuss your conclusions with a trusted friend or partner. We strongly advise for all the reasons that led us to Rule 4 (**Phone a friend, especially when times are taxing**). But we reckon that doing your independent work on the workbook will take about 16–18 hours. Two long days would do it. If you do engage a financial adviser, the workbook will be invaluable in your discussions with them as well.

We believe that a lot of the value of the workbook will be from writing *something* down, rather than writing down your '*perfect answer*'. That's why we think it may help you to print out the sheets a few times over your lifetime. Return to them as your life changes.

The first worksheet may be the most challenging – it asks you some fundamental questions about what motivates you. You may feel you don't know the best answer – you probably don't! But you will know *some* elements of *an* answer so writing your first impressions down will help a lot, especially if you revise them in future.

Other parts of the workbook require only simple fact-finding. If you are put off by one sheet, move on and do work that you find easier. The structure of the workbook is as follows:

Our free downloadable workbook

Each worksheet in our workbook is cross-referenced to the chapters you've already read. It's designed to help you reflect on what you've learned, then go deeper.

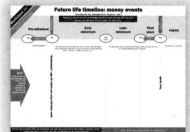

Like the start of this book, the start of our workbook encourages you to think about your purposes and goals.

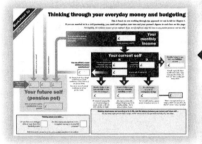

It will help you to gather information about your finances, then apply simple maths to work out how far they will take you.

The workbook then helps you to enter key information into the best free tools we've found. They do complex modelling on your behalf.

Most of the tools we point to are financial tools. But we also encourage you to think through your behaviours, with the help of a psychological profiling tool.

The final sheet of the workbook integrates all of your information into a summary. This has two uses – for you, and for a financial adviser if you choose to engage one.

Worksheet	Which chapters it will help you to work on	Roughly how long we think it might take you	What you should know
1a – **Purposes for your future life** 1b – **Future life timeline: life events** 1c – **Future life timeline: money events**	*Your money or your life?*	Three hours' reflection and notes plus one hour discussion with a friend or partner	*This may not feel easy or meaningful the first time you do it. We think you will get more and more benefit if you return to it every few years and alter it in keeping with your financial progress.*
2 – **Investing in your earning power**	*Invest in … yourself*	Three hours' reflection and notes plus one hour discussion with a friend or partner	
3a – **Thinking through your everyday money and budgeting** 3b – **Approximating your pensions 'mountain'**	*Manage your money*	Six hours' reflection and notes plus one hour discussion with a friend or partner	*If you already budget, you won't need anywhere near six hours. But if you don't, we consider these to be essential foundations for funding the life you want.*
4 – **Health-checking your products and security**	*Avoid charlatans and sharks*	One hour research and notes	
5 – **Choosing and checking your asset mix**	*Take the right risks*	Four hours' research, reflection and notes plus one hour discussion with a friend or partner	*This is the vitally important springboard for making your money grow.*
6 – **Managing your mix and your behaviours**	*Manage your mix* *Face your feelings*	Two hours' reflection and notes plus one hour discussion with a friend or partner	
7a – **Finding an adviser** 7b – **Financial summary on a page**	*Find a first-rate adviser*	One hour, then the time you take to meet with potential advisers Two hours' information gathering, then discussion with an adviser	*It may take a while to put together your financial summary the first time, but it will be much easier to update in the future.*

Jargon-Buster

Words in italics are explained in a separate entry. See also the index to find sections of the book that focus on longer explanations of key concepts.

Accumulation, saving, investing
Accumulating money could involve **saving**, when your *capital* is not at risk but *interest* rates will likely give lower *growth*. Or it could involve **investing**, where you put your money into other assets other than cash, always involving some risk, to see if you can make it grow more.

Active investing
Active investing means trying to spot investments, especially in *equities*, that are undervalued by other investors – or paying an active fund manager to do it for you. An active investor succeeds when, net of costs, his or her net returns exceed the market average.

Advice/guidance/information
Regulated financial **advice** offers a personalized course of action (positive recommendations) and the adviser is liable for the suitability of her recommendations. This is different from **guidance** and **information** – these are not comprehensively defined in law, but usually involve explanation, perhaps ruling out some options, or providing basic facts and data.

Allowance
When you are taxed, the **taxable allowance** is the amount of money you are able to make before the tax is calculated on income or a gain. For example, you can currently earn £1,000 of interest from savings accounts before you have to declare anything for tax.

Annuity

A guaranteed income, one that stops paying when you die. Some **annuities** are linked to *inflation*, some pay fixed amounts and some provide for your partner when you die. See also *pension*.

Assets/asset classes

In markets, **assets** are your ownership of *shares* in companies or *bonds*. In personal terms, assets are everything you own, including your property, car and valuables. An **asset class** is a category of asset such as government bonds or micro-company shares, used to *diversify* your *investments*.

Basis point

One-hundredth of 1 per cent. **Basis points** are often used to talk about fees as they are a quicker and less unwieldy shorthand – 0.7 per cent = 70 basis points.

Bear market, bull market

Shorthand for falling and rising markets. A **bear market** is one in which *stocks* experience a drop in prices over an extended period. A **bull market** is the opposite – a long period of rising stock prices.

Bills/notes/bonds

Different ways of lending, typically to the UK or US governments, but the same language is used for lending to companies (which is much less secure). The language is confusing because they are all 'bonds', but **bills** are bonds that have a shorter-term lending span of a year, **notes** are bonds that mature within two to 10 years, while **bonds** mature over an even longer time period. When all these mature, you get your *capital* back.

Capital, principal/growth, return, interest

When you invest, the money you invest is your **capital**, otherwise known as your **principal**. The **growth** you get on it is called your **return**, except for savings accounts on which **interest** is paid. **Interest** is a formal commitment from a lender to give you profit if you lend them your money. With all risk-based investments, the **growth** or **return** is variable and can even be negative.

Cash, liquidity
Cash is the most **liquid** form of money, which is to say that you can get hold of it very quickly if you need to spend it. Holding money in cash no longer means possessing physical notes and coins; it usually means keeping money in a savings account. However, the more stocks and shares are enabled by electronic trading, the more liquid they become, so the liquidity gap between cash and other forms of investment keeps on getting narrower.

CGT
Capital Gains Tax, often referred to as **CGT**, is a tax on the profit you make when you sell an asset. This can apply to property (except your main home), shares, antiques, the rare car that goes up in value – almost anything you buy or sell. There is an *allowance* so you don't pay CGT on all the profits you make in a year.

Compounding, compound interest
When your *interest*, or *returns*, are **compounded**, it means that they are reinvested and become part of your *capital*. This new, larger amount of capital becomes the baseline for more investment, leading to a very valuable virtuous circle of growth.

Costs, fees
The **costs** or **fees** you pay are how the investment industry makes a living out of you and there are many different ways these are levied – they can be percentages of the amount you invest, percentages of a transaction you make, fixed costs per transaction or annual subscription charges.

Crystallization
When you **crystallize** all or part of a *pension*, you are formalizing whether and how that part of the pension is going to be taxed, based on its value at the time, and beginning the process of drawing money from that part of your pension *pot*.

DB
A **defined benefit (DB)** *pension* is one where the amount of income you receive in retirement is guaranteed by the organization

or company paying it. These are otherwise known as 'final salary' schemes, because they used to be paid as a proportion of the salary you were earning at the point of retirement. These days they mostly depend on a less generous 'career average' of your salary. From the consumer's point of view, they work in more or less the same way as an *annuity*.

DC
A **defined contribution** (**DC**) *pension* is one that invests a pot of money for your retirement and therefore the amount you can pay yourself in retirement will depend on the performance of your investments. There are many laws and rules that dictate the way this pension product can be paid into and used, which makes it more advantageous, but more restricted, than other *investments*.

Decumulation, withdrawal, drawdown
When you **decumulate**, you are **drawing down** or **withdrawing** money from a *DC pension*.

Diversify, diversification
A fundamental principle of *investing* is to **diversify** your investments to reduce risks. You do this by buying a wide range of very different investments. You can diversify across different *asset* classes, across different geographies and most importantly, by buying small slices in a very large number of investments – the fundamental principle of **passive investing**.

Dividend
A **dividend** occurs when a company decides to pay out some of its profits to shareholders, rather than reinvesting profits. Dividends are treated as income and subject to income tax.

Equities, shares, stocks
Equities are **shares** (or **stocks**) in a company. In effect, by buying an equity, you own a very small slice of the company and therefore the right to share in its future profits, which can be paid out as *dividends*.

ESG

ESG stands for **Environmental, Social and corporate Governance**. In practice this means that a company taking ESG seriously will consider not just profits, but its impact on nature and society, as well as the rules, practices and processes by which a company operates. At the opposite end of the spectrum from companies that take **ESG** seriously, there are *'sin stocks'*.

ETF

An exchange-traded fund (**ETF**) is the most common and convenient vehicle for *passive investing*. Although there are many technical complexities about how it is different from other *funds*, the best way to think about an ETF is that it is an owner of many equities in many different companies, bought using *indexing* principles. You can then buy your slice of that ETF as these slices are freely traded on the stock exchange as if they also were equities.

Fund

There are many types of **fund**. What they all have in common is that they allow investors to pool money to buy assets they all have an interest in buying. Mutual funds, hedge funds and exchange-traded funds (*ETFs*) are some of the most common types of funds that invest in equities. We think passively managed mutual funds and ETFs are the most convenient way to apply the principles in this book.

Indexing, tracking

A *fund* that **tracks** an **index** is designed to *passively invest* in *equities* (or *bonds*) that are an accurate reflection of a *market*, or a segment of a market. An example is the FTSE All-Share Index, which comprises around 600 companies listed on the UK stock exchange. Some funds exist to buy equities in these companies in proportion to their value in the FTSE All-Share, so they are tracking that particular index.

Inflation

When prices go up faster than incomes, people's money has less purchasing power. **Inflation** is the way this decline in purchasing power is measured.

Investing/investment

When you lend other people *capital* in the hope of making your money grow you are *investing*. Investing is usually associated with companies but bonds are a form of investment too.

Investment Trust/Unit Trust

Investment trusts and **unit trusts** are common types of *fund* that tend to be used by *active* investors to invest in companies that the fund managers think will outperform the market. For technical reasons, **investment trusts** have more limits on how rapidly they can take on board new investors' money, whereas **unit trusts** have more freedom to grow quickly.

Lifetime Allowance

Despite its misleading name, the **Lifetime Allowance** is in fact a tax on *pensions savings*. It is levied when you draw down a DC pension, on any parts of it not drawn down by your 75th birthday and at other less common events such as when you move your pension to another country. You get an *allowance* of £1,073,100. Below this no tax is payable.

Markets

Although the word **market** is used in many ways, 'the markets' is usually used to refer to the stock exchanges of different countries, where equities can be bought and sold and prices therefore rise and fall in line with supply and demand. Or it can refer to the analogous bond markets for government and company lenders. Within those broad **markets**, there can, for example, be an individual **market** for all the companies over a certain size listed on that stock exchange.

Passive investing

Passive investing takes place when investors buy many small slices of all the companies that exist in a particular market and hope to replicate the overall success of that market, rather than buy individual companies that could beat the market average (*active investing*).

Pension

What a lot of trouble this seemingly simple word brings! **Pension** used to mean a guaranteed income paid in retirement. That was simple. It still means that for many people, but for others it means something very different. The product you buy as a 'container' for your defined contribution (*DC*) investments is a 'pension' product but these products give you anything but a guaranteed income. By contrast, these days if you want to buy a guaranteed income you have to buy an *annuity*.

Pension pot

Pension pot is a quite slippery word. Some professionals use it to refer only to the value of all the *investments* in your *DC pension*. In this book, we use **pot** and *portfolio* to mean the same thing – all the *liquid assets* you can draw on to fund your retirement.

Platform

A trading **platform** is a software system that allows investors to buy and sell equities, bonds and other financial investments such as exchange-traded-funds (*ETFs*). Some platforms will have tens of thousands of investments on offer, so it is often helpful to think of them as a kind of supermarket for investors.

Portfolio

Your **portfolio** is the range of different *investments* you hold. It's quite a slippery word, used often by advisers and commentators in slightly differing ways. We recommend you count up your portfolio to include all your *liquid* investments, so essentially your *cash*, *pension*, other investments, but excluding non-liquid a*ssets* such as the equity in your home, antiques, car and so on. This will give you a reasonable view of the mix of assets you can depend on to fund your retirement.

Post-tax, net

Your **net** income is what is left for you to spend after taxes have been deducted.

Pre-tax, gross

Your **gross** income is the amount you earn, or draw down from your pension, before taxes are deducted. The same principle applies to assets you sell – you will have a **gross** gain before a capital gains tax is deducted, for example.

Real terms, nominal

When you see figures for the rate of *interest* or rate of *return* on *cash* or an *investment*, you need to consider what your **real-term** gain will be. This is the figure minus *inflation*. The figure before inflation, the 'raw' figure, is known as the **nominal** figure.

Regulator, regulations

Regulators are given powers by governments, through law, to control markets and protect investors. In the UK, the main regulator is the Financial Conduct Authority (FCA). It works with the Financial Ombudsman Service, which resolves disputes between consumers and firms, and the Financial Services Compensation Scheme, which refunds consumers who have been objectively badly treated or defrauded by firms **regulated** by the FCA.

Sin stocks

A fairly imprecise expression used in discussion of *ESG*. It usually refers to shares in companies that are viewed as actively harming people through their core business activities – the clearest examples being weapons, alcohol, tobacco or gambling businesses.

Endnotes

We have checked and re-checked the many facts and figures in this book. As you will appreciate, some of the data is always changing. Pension rules and tax laws in particular are subject to revision.

We will welcome any corrections submitted via www.evidenceinvestor.com/corrections.

We also recommend that you now take a look at that page to see if we have published any corrections there.

INTRODUCTION

1 *'A 2002 study'* – Ariely, Dan, and Klaus Wertenbroch. 'Procrastination, Deadlines, and Performance: Self-Control by Precommitment', *Psychological Science* 13, no. 3 (May 2002): 219–24. https://doi.org/10.1111/1467-9280.00441

2 *'An independent review of debt advice'* – Wyman, Peter. *Independent Review of the Funding of Debt Advice in England, Wales, Scotland and Northern Ireland* (London: Money Advice Service, 2018): 11. https://www.moneyadviceplus.org.uk/wp-content/uploads/2018/02/Peter_Wyman_Review_of_Debt_Advice_Funding_2018.pdf

3 *'people warp their reasoning because of their motivations'* – Smith, Megan K., Trivers, Robert and von Hippel, William. 'Self-deception facilitates interpersonal persuasion', *Journal of Economic Psychology*, Vol. 63 (2017): 93–101. https://doi.org/10.1016/j.joep.2017.02.012.

CHAPTER 1

1 *'the case of Jonathan Frostick'* – 'Jonathan Frostick', *LinkedIn*, accessed 20 December 2021. https://www.linkedin.com/posts/activity-6787207960864014336-juUs/

2 *'population-level estimates of "subjective lifespan" in six countries'* –
O'Connell, Alison. 'How Long Do We Expect to Live? A Review of
the Evidence'. *Population Ageing* 4 (2011): 185–201. https://doi.org/10
.1007/s12062-011-9049-1

3 *'According to the UK's Office for National Statistics'* – 'National Life
Tables, UK', *Office for National Statistics*, accessed 20 December 2021.
https://www.ons.gov.uk/peoplepopulationandcommunity/birthsd
eathsandmarriages/lifeexpectancies/datasets/nationallifetablesunite
dkingdomreferencetables

4 *'A 2017 YouGov survey found'* – 'How many Brits like their jobs and
their wages?', *YouGov*, 2017, accessed 20 December 2021. https://
yougov.co.uk/topics/politics/articles-reports/2017/08/03/love-wage
-balance-how-many-brits-their-job-and-the

5 *'34 per cent of Britons were unhappy in their current jobs'* – '66 per cent Of
The British Workforce Enjoys Their Job, What's Going Wrong For The
Remaining 34 per cent?', *SMELOANS*, accessed 20 December 2021.
https://www.smeloans.co.uk/blog/motivation-in-the-workplace
-statistics/

6 *'levels of happiness had barely improved'* – Easterlin, Richard. 'Does
Economic Growth Improve the Human Lot? Some Empirical
Evidence', in *Nations and Households in Economic Growth*, editors
David, Paul and Reder, Melvin (Academic Press, 1974): 89–125.

7 *'happiness brings money when income satisfies basic needs'* – Czapiński,
Janusz. 'The economics of happiness and the psychology of wealth',
English version of the paper 'Ekonomia szczęścia I psychologia
bogactwa' published in *Nauka* 1 (2012): 51–88. https://mpra.ub.uni
-muenchen.de/52897/1/MPRA_paper_52897.pdf

8 *'money buys happiness, but it buys less than most people think'* – Dunn,
Elizabeth, Gilbert, Daniel and Wilson, Timothy. 'If money doesn't
make you happy, then you probably aren't spending it right', *Journal of
Consumer Psychology, 21* (2011): 115–125. https://doi.org/10.1016/j.jcps
.2011.02.002

9 *'subtle reminders of wealth impair people's ability to savor everyday experiences'*
– Aaker, Jennifer Lynn, Rudd, Melanie and Mogilner, Cassie. 'If
Money Doesn't Make You Happy, Consider Time', *Journal of Consumer
Psychology* (2011): 126–30. http://dx.doi.org/10.2139/ssrn.1706968

10 *'A highly influential piece of academic thinking about experiences and
happiness'* – Dunn, Elizabeth, Gilbert, Daniel and Wilson, Timothy. 'If
money doesn't make you happy, then you probably aren't spending it
right', *Journal of Consumer Psychology*, 21 (2011): 115–125. https://doi
.org/10.1016/j.jcps.2011.02.002

11 *'Consumption spending has much in common with a military arms race'* – Frank, Robert. 'How not to buy happiness', Daedalus (spring 2004), accessed 20 December 2021. https://www.amacad.org/publication/how-not-buy-happiness

12 *'seventh equal in a list of 130 countries'* – 'The Henley Passport Index', *Henley & Partners*, accessed 20 December 2021. https://www.henleyglobal.com/passport-index/ranking

13 *'costs about 38 per cent of a similar standard in the UK'* – 'Cost of living', *Numbeo*, accessed 20 December 2021. https://www.numbeo.com/cost-of-living/

14 *'just one fifth of the average pot of a man the same age'* – Portas, Jane et al. *Solving women's pension deficit to improve retirement outcomes for all*, Chartered Institute of Insurance, London, 2018: 7. https://www.cii.co.uk/media/10120355/moments-that-matter-pensions-life-journey-for-women.pdf

15 *'women still earn, on average, 15.4 per cent less than men for every hour worked'* – 'Gender pay gap in the UK: 2021', *Office for National Statistics*, accessed 20 December 2021. https://www.ons.gov.uk/employmentandlabourmarket/peopleinwork/earningsandworkinghours/bulletins/genderpaygapintheuk/2021

CHAPTER 2

1 *'this "graduate premium" nearly halved over the 25 years to 2016'* – Boero, Gianna et al. *The Return To A Degree: New Evidence Based On The Birth Cohort Studies And The Labour Force Survey*, Higher Education Statistics Agency, Cheltenham, 2019: 3. https://www.hesa.ac.uk/files/Return_to_a_degree_main_report.pdf

2 *'a long-term average rate of return of 14.8 per cent'* – 'Asset Class Returns', *Portfolio Visualizer*, accessed 28 July 2022. https://www.portfoliovisualizer.com/historical-asset-class-returns

3 *'They must contribute 3 per cent of the value of your salary to your pension'* – 'Qualifying earnings', *Now Pensions*, accessed 20 December 2021. https://www.nowpensions.com/employers/learn-about-workplace-pensions/qualifying-earnings/

4 *'a powerful general look at how to maximize your career'* – Fetherstonhaugh, Brian. *The Long View*, Diversion Publishing, New York 2016.

5 *'the UK figure might be nearer 80 per cent'* – 'Total individual wealth (including and excluding private pension wealth) by age-band, summary statistics: Great Britain, April 2016 to March 2018', *Office for National Statistics*, accessed 20 December 2021. https://www.ons.gov.uk/peoplepopulationandcommunity/personalandhouseholdfinances

/incomeandwealth/adhocs/11503totalindividualwealthincludingande
xcludingprivatepensionwealthbyagebandsummarystatisticsgreatbritainap
ril2016tomarch2018

6 Table of savings by age – 'How much do I need to retire?', *Fidelity*,
accessed 20 December 2021. https://www.fidelity.com/viewpoints/
retirement/how-much-do-i-need-to-retire

7 *'just 9 per cent of the people they surveyed had this kind of insurance'* –
'Income protection explained', *Which?*, September 2021, accessed 20
December 2021. https://www.which.co.uk/money/insurance/life
-insurance/income-protection-explained-aum068h7cqr3

8 *'People over 50 are three times more likely'* – 'Over-50s three times more
likely to be long-term unemployed, analysis reveals', January 2021,
CIPD, accessed 20 December 2021. https://www.peoplemanagement
.co.uk/news/articles/over-50s-three-times-more-likely-to-be-long
-term-unemployed

CHAPTER 3

1 *'the "trap" of thinking in "rigid categories"'* – Carson, Shelley and Langer,
Ellen. 'Mindfulness and self-acceptance', *Journal of Rational-Emotive
and Cognitive-Behavior Therapy*, Vol. 24 (2006): 29–43. https://doi.org
/10.1007/s10942-006-0022-5

2 *'that number had risen to nine million'* – 'What is the PACE debt advice
pilot?', *Money and Pensions Service*, accessed 20 December 2021. https://
www.moneyandpensionsservice.org.uk/our-debt-work/pace/

3 *'a regularly updated guide to the "Best bank accounts"'* – 'Best bank
accounts', *moneysavingexpert.com*, 16 December 2021, accessed 21
December 2021. https://www.moneysavingexpert.com/banking/
compare-best-bank-accounts/

4 *'and looked at how much they spent'* – 'How much will you need to retire?',
Which? (May 2021), accessed 20 December 2021. https://www.which.co
.uk/money/pensions-and-retirement/starting-to-plan-your-retirement
/how-much-will-you-need-to-retire-atu0z9k0lw3p

5 *'An alternative view is provided by a trade body, the Pensions and Lifetime
Savings Association'* – 'Picture your future: Retirement living standards',
Pensions and Lifetime Savings Association (2021), accessed 20 December
2021. The general information is at https://www.retirementlivingsta
ndards.org.uk/ but we highly recommend the more detailed report
https://www.retirementlivingstandards.org.uk/Retirement-living
-standards-in-the-UK-in-2021.pdf if you want to think through your
future lifestyle in some detail.

6 *Calculators* – https://www.pensionbee.com/pension-calculator
   and   https://www.which.co.uk/money/pensions-and-retirement/
   options-for-cashing-in-your-pensions/income-drawdown/income
   -drawdown-calculator-making-your-money-last-awvp49g8uq6l

7 *'take the switching decisions out of your hands'* – 'Is energy auto-switching
   right for you?', *Which?*, 3 March 2020, accessed 20 December 2021.
   https://www.which.co.uk/news/2020/03/is-energy-autoswitching
   -right-for-you

8 *'80 per cent of higher rate taxpayers miss out on this money'* – 'Higher and
   additional rate taxpayers likely to be missing out on £1 billion in
   unclaimed tax relief', *PensionBee*, accessed 20 December 2021. https://
   www.pensionbee.com/press/higher-and-additional-rate-taxpayers
   -likely-to-be-missing-out-on-1-billion-in-unclaimed-tax-relief

9 *'What it found was this'* – *Listening Document*, Money and Pensions
   Service, London, 2019: 28. https://www.financialcapability.gov.au/
   files/listening-document.pdf

10 *'a regular savings habit as the critical "lead indicator"'* – 'Financial Capability
   in the UK: results from the 2018 survey', *Financial Capability Strategy*
   (2018), accessed 20 December 2021. https://www.fincap.org.uk/en/
   insights/financial-capability-in-the-uk--results-from-the-2018-survey

CHAPTER 4

1 *'the stock market is not the economy'* – 'Why stocks soared while America
   struggled', *Vox* (10 May 2021), accessed 20 December 2021. https://
   www.vox.com/business-and-finance/22421417/stock-market
   -pandemic-economy

2 *'Mark Hebner sums it up like this'* – Hebner, Mark. *Index Funds: the
   12-step Recovery Program for Active Investors*, IFA Publishing, 2018: 232.

3 *'according to the principles of Sharia-compliant finance'* – 'Working With
   Islamic Finance', *Investopedia* (20 May 2020), accessed 29 December
   2021.   https://www.investopedia.com/articles/07/islamic_investing
   .asp

4 *'The most commonly cited academic paper is one from 1986'* – Brinson,
   Gary, Hood, L. Randolph, and Beebower, Gilbert. 'Determinants
   of Portfolio Performance', *Financial Analysts Journal* 42, no. 4 (1986):
   39–44. http://www.jstor.org/stable/4478947

5 *'explained by the Nobel Prize-winning economist William Sharpe'* – Sharpe,
   William. 'The Arithmetic of Active Management', *The Financial
   Analysts' Journal*, Vol. 47, No. 1 (January/February 1991): 7–9. https://
   web.stanford.edu/~wfsharpe/art/active/active.htm

6   *'the relentless rules of humble arithmetic'* – Bogle, John. 'The Relentless Rules of Humble Arithmetic', *Financial Analysts Journal*, Vol. 61, no. 6 (2005): 22–35. http://www.jstor.org/stable/4480712

7   *'In his famous book'* Winning the Loser's Game' – Ellis, Charles. *Winning the Loser's Game: Timeless Strategies for Successful Investing, Eighth Edition*, McGraw Hill, 2021.

8   *'A useful comparison site for broker fees'* – 'Best trading platforms and stock brokers', *Monevator* (December 2021), accessed 21 December 2021. https://monevator.com/compare-uk-cheapest-online-brokers/

CHAPTER 5

1   *'Use a password manager'* — 'The Best Password Managers', *The New York Times* (December 3, 2021), accessed January 3 2022. https://www.nytimes.com/wirecutter/reviews/best-password -managers/

2   *'just how plausible every step of the process seemed'* – 'I lost £95,000 in a bank scam after my solicitor's email was hacked', *Guardian* (29 February 2020), accessed 21 December 2021. https://www.theguardian.com/ money/2020/feb/29/bank-scam-solicitors-email-hacked

3   *'the £239,000 scammed in 2021 from Catriona Oliphant, a city lawyer'* – 'Psychological tricks that meant Catriona didn't stand a chance when a scammer set out to steal her £241,000 savings', *This Is Money* (21 February 2021). Accessed 21 December 2021. https://www .thisismoney.co.uk/money/beatthescammers/article-9281605/How -highly-sophisticated-scam-cost-Catriona-241-000.html

4   *'a lasting power of attorney (LPA)'* – 'Make, register or end a lasting power of attorney', *GOV.UK*, accessed 21 December 2021. https:// www.gov.uk/power-of-attorney

5   *'not claiming the pension credits they are entitled to'* – '£1.8 billion in pension credit left unclaimed – how to check if you or someone you know is eligible', *moneysavingexpert.com* (28 May 2021), accessed 21 December 2021. https://www.moneysavingexpert.com/news/2021 /05/pension-credit-bank-holiday-billions-unclaimed/

6   *'women who reached state pension age before 2016'* – 'Are you one of 100,000+ women missing out on £1,000s of state pension?', *moneysavingexpert.com* (24 September 2021), accessed 21 December 2021. https://www.moneysavingexpert.com/reclaim/married -women-missing-state-pension-boost/

7   *'Bernie Madoff'* – 'Bernie Madoff', *Wikipedia*, accessed 21 December 2021. https://en.wikipedia.org/wiki/Bernie_Madoff

8   *'Dolphin Investments (now known as German Property Group) scandal'* – "'I was told it was as safe as houses": savers owed thousands as firm fails', *Guardian* (20 February 2021), accessed 21 December 2021. https://www.theguardian.com/money/2021/feb/20/i-was-told-it-was-as-safe-as-houses-savers-owed-thousands-as-firm-fails

9   *'the FCA was regulating LC&F's marketing activity, and not its products'* – "'One of the biggest financial scandals around": FCA criticised over LC&F', *Guardian* (29 March 2019), accessed 21 December 2021. https://www.theguardian.com/business/2019/mar/29/one-of-the-biggest-financial-scandals-around-fca-criticised-over-lcf

10   *'With well-functioning markets I do not see intuition having a role in investment'* – 'Daniel Kahneman: Why I'm Against Active Investing', *The Evidence-Based Investor* (29 June 2018), accessed 21 December 2021. https://www.evidenceinvestor.com/daniel-kahneman-im-active-investing/

11   Historical probability of loss decrease by holding equity longer – Data from Macrobond, MSCI World Equity Mid and MSCI Large Cap Total Return in GBP, 1 January 1972—December 2021, as published in 'The facts about long-term investing', *Nutmeg* (2 June 2020), accessed 21 December 2021. https://www.nutmeg.com/nutmegonomics/increasing-your-chances-of-positive-portfolio-returns-the-facts-about-long-term-investing/

12   *'The full dataset is many times richer and it's worth exploring'* – 'SPIVA® data: results by region', *S&P Dow Jones Indices* (30 June 2021), accessed 21 December 2021. https://www.spglobal.com/spdji/en/research-insights/spiva/#/reports

13   *'Their Active/Passive barometer tells a very similar story'* – 'Morningstar European Active/Passive Barometer', *Morningstar* (Midyear 2021), accessed 21 December 2021. https://www.morningstar.com/en-uk/lp/european-active-passive-barometer

14   *'UK active funds over that longer, 10-year timescale'* – Blake, David et al. 'New Evidence on Mutual Fund Performance: A Comparison of Alternative Bootstrap Methods', *Journal of Financial and Quantitative Analysis* 52, no. 3 (2017): 1279–99. https://www.cambridge.org/core/journals/journal-of-financial-and-quantitative-analysis/article/abs/new-evidence-on-mutual-fund-performance-a-comparison-of-alternative-bootstrap-methods/D8A96C14EFAE4144EA29433CF4AA6BBE

15   *'£25 billion of assets'* – 'Neil Woodford', *Wikipedia*, accessed 21 December 2021. https://en.wikipedia.org/wiki/Neil_Woodford

16   *'halved in value, losing billions'* – 'Woodford bullish on chances of reviving performance', *Money Marketing* (15 March 2019), accessed

21 December 2021. https://www.moneymarketing.co.uk/news/woodford-bullish-on-chances-of-reviving-performance/

17 *'20 per cent of the assets into companies that could not easily be bought and sold'* – 'Revealed: the real risk of Woodford', *The Sunday Times* (3 March 2019), accessed 21 December 2021. https://www.thetimes.co.uk/article/revealed-the-real-risk-of-woodford-rr79jvtpm (paywall)

18 *'receiving between 46p and 59p in the pound back'* – 'Woodford investors to get as little as 50p in the pound back', *Evening Standard* (28 January 2020), accessed 21 December 2021. https://www.standard.co.uk/business/woodford-investors-to-get-as-little-as-50p-in-the-pound-back-a4346611.html

19 *'continued to take multi-million-pound management fees'* – 'Woodford's latest social media salvo failed to answer your key concern: Why is he STILL charging fees on a closed fund?', *Daily Mail* (6 July 2019), accessed 21 December 2021. https://www.thisismoney.co.uk/money/investing/article-7219817/Why-Woodford-charging-fees-closed-fund.html

20 *'By the end of last year, we'd reviewed 84 potential closet tracker funds'* – 'The Beginning Of The End For Closet Trackers?', *The Evidence-Based Investor* (5 March 2018), accessed 21 December 2021. https://www.evidenceinvestor.com/closet-trackers/

21 *'the price of tulip bulbs dropped much more spectacularly'* – 'Tulip Mania', *Wikipedia*, accessed 21 December 2021. https://en.wikipedia.org/wiki/Tulip_mania#Available_price_data

22 *'in the network environment, significance precedes momentum'* – 'New rules for the new economy', *Wired* (9 January 1997), accessed 21 December 2021. https://www.wired.com/1997/09/newrules/

23 *'had lost 78 per cent of its value'* – '5 Successful Companies That Survived the Dot-Com Bubble', *Investopedia* (15 August 2021), accessed 21 December 2021. https://www.investopedia.com/financial-edge/0711/5-successful-companies-that-survived-the-dotcom-bubble.aspx

24 *'about as much as a successful corner shop'* – 'Where did it go wrong for Clickmango.com?', *Accountancy Age* (4 September 2000), accessed 21 December 2021. https://www.accountancyage.com/2000/09/04/where-did-it-go-wrong-for-clickmango-com/

25 *'thematic funds have trailed the overall equity market'* – 'The Dark Side of Thematic Funds', Morningstar (19 May 2021), accessed 21 December 2021. https://www.morningstar.co.uk/uk/news/211463/the-dark-side-of-thematic-funds.aspx

26 *'huge fees for their managers while delivering largely mediocre performance'* – 'Review of twenty years of research in private equity & more', *Private*

Equity Laid Bare, accessed 21 December 2021. https://pelaidbare.com/where/

27   *'expensive investments express parts of our identity'* – 'What Returns Should Investors Expect from Private Equity', *Alpha Architect* (7 November 2019), accessed 21 December 2021. https://alphaarchitect.com/2019/11/07/what-returns-should-investors-expect-from-private-equity/

28   *'Let them laugh; the joke's on them'* – Bernstein, William. *The Four Pillars of Investing*, McGraw Hill, 2011.

29   *'index funds account for less than 5 per cent of trading volume on US exchanges'* – 'A drop in the bucket: Indexing's share of US trading activity', *Vanguard* (March 2019), accessed 21 December 2021. https://advisors.vanguard.com/iwe/pdf/ISGINDX.pdf

CHAPTER 6

1   *'more accidents happen when people come down mountains'* – 'Death on Mount Everest: The perils of the descent', *Scientific American* (10 December 2008), accessed 21 December 2021. https://blogs.scientificamerican.com/news-blog/death-on-mount-everest-the-perils-o-2008-12-10/

2   *'the average rate of inflation in the UK since 1900 has been 3.6 per cent'* — Elroy Dimson, Paul Marsh and Mike Staunton, *Credit Suisse Global Investment Returns Yearbook 2022 Summary Edition*, Credit Suisse, 2022, page 12, accessed 28 July 2022. https://www.credit-suisse.com/media/assets/corporate/docs/about-us/research/publications/credit-suisse-global-investment-returns-yearbook-2022-summary-edition.pdf (For the full yearbook email prowham@london.edu.)

3   *'a 2000 paper by William P. Bengen'* – Bengen, William. 'Determining Withdrawal Rates Using Historical Data', *Journal of Financial Planning* (October 1994): 171–180. https://www.retailinvestor.org/pdf/Bengen1.pdf

4   *'Wade Pfau asked'* – 'Does The 4 per cent Rule Work Around The World?', *Retirement Researcher*, accessed 21 December 2021. https://retirementresearcher.com/4-rule-work-around-world/

5   *'the returns delivered by different asset classes'* – Elroy Dimson, Paul Marsh and Mike Staunton, *Credit Suisse Global Investment Returns Yearbook 2022 Summary Edition*, pages 37–38, accessed 28 July 2022. See note 2 above for access details

6   *'a very interesting paper called "Stocks for the long run?"'* – Anarkulova, Aizhan, Cederburg, Scott and O'Doherty, Michael S., 'Stocks for the Long Run?

Evidence from a Broad Sample of Developed Markets', *Journal of Financial Economics*, forthcoming. http://dx.doi.org/10.2139/ssrn.3594660

7 Asset class table: Portfolio Visualizer sourced asset classes – 'Asset Class Returns', *Portfolio Visualizer*, accessed 28 July 2022. https://www.portfoliovisualizer.com/historical-asset-class-returns

8 Asset class table: Gold – 'A History of Gold Returns', *A Wealth of Common Sense* (21 July 2015), accessed 21 December 2021. https://awealthofcommonsense.com/2015/07/a-history-of-gold-returns/

9 Asset class table: Bills and Bonds – 'Elroy Dimson, Paul Marsh and Mike Staunton, *Credit Suisse Global Investment Returns Yearbook 2022 Summary Edition*, pages 37–38, accessed 28 July 2022. See Chapter 6, note 2 above for access details

10 Asset class table: Property – 'Historical Returns of Gold and Real Estate', *Mindfully Investing* (6 August 2020), accessed 21 December 2021. https://www.mindfullyinvesting.com/historical-returns-of-gold-and-real-estate/

11 *'surprisingly ineffective at balancing risk in portfolios'* – Levine, Ari et al. 'Commodities for the Long Run', *Financial Analysts Journal*, Vol. 74(2) (2018): 55–68. https://www.nber.org/papers/w22793

12 *'more their prior beliefs about investing styles'* – Sivarajan, Sam and De Bruijn, Oscar. 'Risk Tolerance, Return Expectations, and Other Factors Impacting Investment Decisions', *The Journal of Wealth Management*, 23 (4) (2021): 10–30. https://jwm.pm-research.com/content/23/4/10

13 *'The typical RTQ does not address these issues'* – 'How Useful Are Risk Tolerance Questionnaires?', *The Evidence-Based Investor* (24 April 2021), accessed 21 December 2021. https://www.evidenceinvestor.com/how-useful-are-risk-tolerance-questionnaires/

14 *'predicting lower returns in the future than investors have enjoyed in the past'* – 'Young people stand to make dismal returns on their investments', *The Economist* (15 March 2021), accessed 21 December 2021. https://www.economist.com/graphic-detail/2021/03/15/young-people-stand-to-make-dismal-returns-on-their-investments (paywall)

15 *'Some people say it took only four-and-a-half'* – '25 years to bounce back from the 1929 crash? Try four-and-a-half', *Mint* (26 April 2009), accessed 21 December 2021. https://www.livemint.com/Money/Oww1BVK1roWvXRUCdoVjIJ/25-years-to-bounce-back-from-the-1929-crash-Try-fouranda.html

16 *'It gives portfolios advocated by six experts'* – '6 Expert Investment Portfolios You Can Implement Today', *Forbes* (26 July 2018), accessed 21 December 2021. https://www.forbes.com/sites/simonmoore

/2018/07/26/six-expert-investment-portfolios-you-can-implement
-today

17 'MoneyHelper offers a tool that enables you to contrast and compare' –
'Understand and compare your investment pathway options (for
pension drawdown)', *MoneyHelper*, accessed 21 December 2021.
https://comparison.moneyhelper.org.uk/en/tools/drawdown
-investment-pathways

18 For print readers, the full hyperlinks to the sites and mentioned in the
rest of this chapter are:
https://www.nestpensions.org.uk/schemeweb/nest/aboutnest/
investment-approach/nest-retirement-date-funds.html
https://www.nestpensions.org.uk/schemeweb/nest/aboutnest/
investment-approach/other-fund-choices/nest-guided-retirement
-fund.html
https://www.vanguardinvestor.co.uk/investing-explained/what-are
-target-retirement-funds
https://www.vanguardinvestor.co.uk/investments/vanguard-target
-retirement-2040-fund-accumulation-shares?intcmpgn=blendedtarg
etretirement_targetretirement2040fund_fund_link
https://www.vanguardinvestor.co.uk/what-we-offer/life-strategy
-products
https://www.nutmeg.com– https://www.aviva.co.uk– https://www
.ii.co.uk
https://www.scottishwidows.co.uk/index.html
https://www.pensionbee.com
https://www.fidelity.co.uk
https://www.standardlife.co.uk
https://www.legalandgeneral.com
https://www.hl.co.uk/

CHAPTER 7

1 'contrived, artificial transactions that serve little or no purpose' – 'Tax avoidance:
an introduction', *GOV.UK*, accessed 22 December 2021.

2 'the basic tax principles' – 'Income Tax Rates and Personal Allowances',
GOV.UK, https://www.gov.uk/income-tax-rates; 'Capital Gains Tax
Allowances' https://www.gov.uk/capital-gains-tax/alloawances; 'Tax
on your private pension contributions' https://www.gov.uk/tax-on
-your-private-pension/lifetime-allowance; all accessed 22 December
2021.

3 Jonathan thanks Rob Handford of Handford, Aitkenhead and Walker
financial advisers for introducing him to this metaphor (as well as
the 'death box' label in Chapter 9) – but takes full responsibility for
mixing in the concrete here.

4 *'handy* Which? *calculator'* – 'Pension tax calculator', *Which?* accessed 22
December 2021. https://www.which.co.uk/static/tools/new-reviews
/pension-withdrawal-calculator/pension-withdrawal-calculator.html

5 *'more likely to get divorced than switch to a new bank'* – 'Why we
are more likely to get divorced than switch bank accounts', *The
Scotsman* (17 October 2019), accessed 22 December 2021. https://
www.scotsman.com/future-scotland/fintech/why-we-are-more
-likely-get-divorced-switch-bank-accounts-1404992

6 *'academic studies from Harvard …'* – Eccles, Robert, Ioannis Ioannou
and George Serafeim. 'The Impact of Corporate Sustainability on
Organizational Processes and Performance', *Management Science*
60, no. 11 (November 2014): 2835–2857. https://dash.harvard.edu/
bitstream/handle/1/15788003/eccles,ioannou,serafeim_the-impact
-of-corporate-sustainability_SSRN-id1964011.pdf?sequence=1 – *'…
and Hamburg'* – Friede, Gunnar, Busch, Timo and Bassen, Alexander
(2015) 'ESG and financial performance: aggregated evidence from
more than 2000 empirical studies', *Journal of Sustainable Finance &
Investment* 5:4(2015): 210–233. https://www.tandfonline.com/doi/pdf
/10.1080/20430795.2015.1118917?needAccess=true

7 *'studies from Princeton …'* – Hong, Harrison and Kacperczyk, Marcin,
'The price of sin: The effects of social norms on markets', *Journal
of Financial Economics* 93 (2009): 15–36 http://pages.stern.nyu.edu/
~sternfin/mkacperc/public_html/sin.pdf – *'… and Larry Swedroe'*
– 'ESG Strategy Performance', ETF.com (10 April 2019), accessed
22 December 2021. https://www.etf.com/sections/index-investor
-corner/swedroe-esg-strategy-performance

8 *'slightly lower volatility when measured over a nine-year period'* – 'Which
Performs Better, The S&P 500 Or The S&P 500 ESG Index?', *The
Evidence-Based Investor* (27 October 2019), accessed 22 December
2021. https://www.evidenceinvestor.com/which-performs-better
-the-sp-500-or-the-sp-500-esg-index/

9 *'implementing ESG strategies can cost nothing'* – Lindsey, Laura Anne,
Pruitt, Seth and Schiller, Christoph, 'The Cost of ESG Investing', *Social
Science Research Network* (30 November 2021). https://ssrn.com/abstract
=3975077 or http://dx.doi.org/10.2139/ssrn.3975077

10 *'Merryn Somerset Webb made this point very well'* – 'Want a greener world?
Don't dump oil stocks', *Financial Times* (12 March 2021), accessed 22

December 2021. https://www.ft.com/content/bbe0f957-5db1-4a2e-b01c-66b4a96d84be

11 '72 per cent of institutional investors and 77 per cent of fund selectors' – 'ESG Investing:
Everyone's on the bandwagon', *Natixis Investment Managers*, accessed 22 December 2021. https://www.im.natixis.com/uk/research/esg-investing-survey-insight-report

12 'focusing your pension savings on sustainable funds was, on average, 21 times more effective' – 'Pension fund carbon savings research: a summary of the approach', *Make My Money Matter* (July 2021), accessed 21 December 2021. https://makemymoneymatter.co.uk/wp-content/uploads/2021/07/Summary-of-21x-research.pdf

13 'Nest's Sharia fund' – 'Nest Sharia Fund', *Nest Pensions*, accessed 24 December 2021. https://www.nestpensions.org.uk/schemeweb/nest/aboutnest/investment-approach/other-fund-choices/nest-sharia-fund.html

14 'a 16.3 per cent (pre-inflation) return over 10 years' – According to Nest, this fund 'passively tracks the Dow Jones Islamic Titans 100 index, a global equity index screened so as to be in accordance with Sharia principles.' For performance figures see 'Nest Quarterly Investment Report', *Nest Pensions* (September 2020), accessed 24 December 2021. https://www.nestpensions.org.uk/schemeweb/dam/nestlibrary/Nest-quarterly-investment-report.pdf

15 'more competitive returns in both rising and falling markets' – Qoyum, Abdul et al. 'Does an Islamic-SRI portfolio really matter? Empirical application of valuation models in Indonesia', *Borsa Istanbul Review*, Vol. 21, Issue 2 (2021): 105–124. https://www.sciencedirect.com/science/article/pii/S2214845020300417/pdfft?md5=dffe696be38b97f11ab977366c998aa9&pid=1-s2.0-S2214845020300417-main.pdf

16 'They predict it will be a common approach by 2025' – 'Custom Indexing: The Next Evolution of Index Investing', *Canvas* (December 2020), accessed 22 December 2021. https://canvas.osam.com/Commentary/BlogPost?Permalink=custom-indexing-the-next-evolution-of-index-investing

17 'about 39 per cent of their portfolios in Singaporean equities' – 'Investing solely in your home country is like juggling live dynamite', *Business Insider* (8 August 2016), accessed 22 December 2021. https://www.businessinsider.com/investing-in-home-country-like-juggling-dynamite-2016-8

18 'outweigh any temporary problems caused by the ups and downs of exchange rates' – 'Global equity investing: The benefits of diversification and

sizing your allocation', *Vanguard Research* (April 2021), accessed 22 December 2021. https://personal.vanguard.com/pdf/ISGGEB _042021_Online.pdf

19 *'you can rapidly check your state pension forecast'* – 'Check your State Pension forecast', *GOV.UK*, accessed 21 December 2021. https:// www.gov.uk/check-state-pension

20 *'pension credits that are left unclaimed'* – '£1.8 billion in pension credit left unclaimed – how to check if you or someone you know is eligible', *moneysavingexpert.com* (28 May 2021), accessed 22 December 2021. https://www.moneysavingexpert.com/news/2021/05/pension-credit-bank-holiday-billions-unclaimed/

21 *'There are additional top-ups for special circumstances'* – 'Pension Credit', *GOV.UK*, accessed 22 December 2021. https://www.gov.uk/pension -credit/what-youll-get

22 *'1 in 6 people aged 80 or older live in a residential care home'* – 'Facts and stats', *MHA*, accessed 22 December 2021. https://www.mha.org.uk/ get-involved/policy-influencing/facts-stats/

23 *'nearly 3 in every 6 adults over the age of 80 do not feel the need'* – *Focus On: Social care for older people*, (Nuffield Trust/Quality Watch, March 2014): 16. https://www.nuffieldtrust.org.uk/files/2018-10/qualitywatch-social-care-older-people.pdf#page=16

24 *'higher-quality private nursing care in a home can cost up to £60,000 a year'* – 'How much does care cost?', *Paying For Care*, accessed 22 December 2021. https://www.payingforcare.org/how-much-does-care-cost/

25 *'prices vary from region to region of the UK'* – 'Care home fees', *Which?* (December 2021), accessed 22 December 2021. https://www.which .co.uk/money/pensions-and-retirement/financing-later-life-care/ care-home-finance/care-home-fees-asntd3w1s3bg

26 *'the average length of stay'* – 'End of Life Care in Frailty: Care homes', *British Geriatric Society* (12 May 2020), accessed 22 December 2021. https://www.bgs.org.uk/resources/end-of-life-care-in-frailty-care -homes

27 *'Two hours … 24-hour support'* – 'Paying for care at home', *homecare .co.uk*, accessed 22 December 2021. https://www.homecare.co.uk/ advice/paying-for-care-at-home

28 *'the UK government's official publication about the change in the rules'* – 'BUILD BACK BETTER: Our plan for health and social care', *GOV. UK* (September 2021), accessed 22 December 2021. https://assets .publishing.service.gov.uk/government/uploads/system/uploads/ attachment_data/file/1015736/Build_Back_Better-_Our_Plan_for _Health_and_Social_Care.pdf

29 *'as Age UK puts it'* – 'Paying for care in a care home if you have a partner', *Age UK* (April 2017), accessed 22 December 2021. https://www.ageuk.org.uk/globalassets/age-ni/documents/factsheets/fs39_paying_for_care_in_a_care_home_if_you_have_a_partner_fcs.pdf

30 *'the council must offer you a form of equity release'* – 'Property and paying for residential care', *Age UK* (August 2021), accessed 22 December 2021. https://www.ageuk.org.uk/globalassets/age-uk/documents/factsheets/fs38_property_and_paying_for_residential_care_fcs.pdf

31 *'using the MoneyHelper "Compare guaranteed income products tool"'* – 'Compare guaranteed income products (annuities)', *MoneyHelper*, accessed 22 December 2021. https://www.moneyhelper.org.uk/en/pensions-and-retirement/taking-your-pension/compare-annuities

32 *'Your cognitive abilities are in a continuous state of decline from your mid-twenties'* – 'The biology of ageing: cognitive changes with ageing', *Boston University School of Public Health* (December 2013), accessed 22 December 2021. https://sphweb.bumc.bu.edu/otlt/mph-modules/ph/aging/mobile_pages/Aging5.html

CHAPTER 8

1 *'I was going to focus on the simple problem of helping people behave correctly'* – Richards, Carl. *The Behavior Gap: Simple Ways to Stop Doing Dumb Things with Money*, Portfolio Books, 2012.

2 *'the example of a highly educated doctor'* – Housel, Morgan. *The Psychology of Money*, Harriman House, 2020.

3 Transactions turnover table – Barber, Brad M. and Odean, Terrance 'The Courage of Misguided Convictions', *Financial Analysts Journal* 55, No. 6 (1999): 41–55. http://www.jstor.org/stable/4480208

4 *'Landmark research by Kahneman and his partner Amos Tversky'* – 'The Two Friends Who Changed How We Think About How We Think', *The New Yorker* (7 December 2016), accessed 22 December 2021.

5 *'It is in the nature of a man's mind'* – Kahneman, Daniel, Knetsch, Jack and Thaler, Richard, 'Anomalies: The Endowment Effect, Loss Aversion, and Status Quo Bias', *The Journal of Economic Perspectives*, 5 (Winter 1991): 193–206. https://scholar.princeton.edu/sites/default/files/kahneman/files/anomalies_dk_jlk_rht_1991.pdf

6 *'the US stock market story since 1955'* – 'Is There Such A Thing As A "Normal" Stock Market?', *The Evidence-Based Investor* (24 June 2020), accessed 22 December 2021. https://www.evidenceinvestor.com/is-there-such-a-thing-as-a-normal-stock-market/

7 Historical returns chart – 'S&P 500 Historical Annual Returns', *Macrotrends*, accessed 28 July 2022. https://www.macrotrends.net /2526/sp-500-historical-annual-returns

8 *'to synthesize some simple, practical methods you can use'* – for good overviews see 'Why Investors Are Irrational, According to Behavioral Finance', *Toptal.com*, accessed 22 December 2021. https://www.toptal .com/finance/financial-analysts/investor-psychology-behavioral -biases and 'Overcoming Six Emotional Biases to Have a Successful Investing Experience', *Echo Wealth Management* (28 February 2019), accessed 22 December 2021. https://www.echowealthmanagement .com/blog/overcoming-six-emotional-biases-to-have-a-successful -investing-experience and '6 Tips for Investors to Overcome Behavioral Bias', *US News and World Report Smarter Investor blog* (19 April 2017), accessed 22 December 2021. https://money.usnews.com /money/blogs/the-smarter-mutual-fund-investor/articles/2017-04 -19/6-tips-for-investors-to-overcome-behavioral-bias

CHAPTER 9

1 *'Its 2020 report on the marketplace it regulates'* – 'Evaluation of the impact of the Retail Distribution Review and the Financial Advice Market Review', *Financial Conduct Authority* (December 2020), accessed 22 December 2021. https://www.fca.org.uk/publication/corporate/ evaluation-of-the-impact-of-the-rdr-and-famr.pdf

2 This seems to be widely agreed on, but the only statistical source that backs it up is the dramatic fall in the number of advisers. It appears that the regulator didn't measure, or didn't publish, the before-and-after difference in consumer takeup of advice, according to its Impact Review. – 'Impact of the Retail Distribution Review on consumer interaction with the retail investments market', NMG consulting for the Financial Conduct Authority (September 2014), accessed 22 December 2021. https://www.fca.org.uk/publication/research/ impact-of-rdr-consumer-interaction-retail-investments-market.pdf

3 *'The average is £150/hour, or £1,100 a day'* – 'Independent financial adviser fees – how much does a financial adviser cost?', *unbiased.co .uk* (13 October 2021), accessed 22 December 2021. https://www .unbiased.co.uk/life/get-smart/cost-of-advice

4 For print readers, the full hyperlinks to the practical sites and tools mentioned in the rest of this chapter are: https://www.evidenceinvestor.com/home-uk/ https://www.moneysavingexpert.com/ https://www.moneyhelper.org.uk/

https://www.which.co.uk/
https://www.investopedia.com/
https://www.moneyhelper.org.uk/en/pensions-and-retirement/
pension-wise
(former TPAS helpline)
https://www.moneyhelper.org.uk/en/pensions-and-retirement
(*Which?* Money Helpline)
https://www.which.co.uk/about-which/our-products-and-services
/271/which-money-helpline
https://www.nutmeg.com/
https://www.moneyfarm.com/uk/
https://www.wealthify.com/
https://www.open-money.co.uk/
https://www.vanguardinvestor.co.uk/financial-advice
(Financial Services Register)
https://register.fca.org.uk/s/— (Retirement Adviser Directory)
https://www.moneyhelper.org.uk/en/pensions-and-retirement/
taking-your-pension/find-a-retirement-adviser
https://www.unbiased.co.uk/

5 '*over £150,000 of assets under advice*' — 'Evaluation of the impact of the Retail Distribution Review and the Financial Advice Market Review', *Financial Conduct Authority* (December 2020), accessed 22 December 2021. https://www.fca.org.uk/publication/corporate/evaluation-of-the-impact-of-the-rdr-and-famr.pdf

6 '*can call themselves a financial planner (which is not)*' — 'Financial advisor or financial planner — what's the difference?', *The Frazer James Blog* (December 2021), accessed 22 December 2021. https://frazerjames.co.uk/financial-advisor-financial-planner-the-difference/

7 '*Astonishingly, as the charity TaxAid puts it*' — 'Choosing an accountant or tax adviser', *TaxAid* (2021), accessed 22 December 2021. https://taxaid.org.uk/guides/taxpayers/choosing-an-accountant-or-tax-adviser

8 '*a 2018 study of advisers in Canada*' — Linnainmaa, Juhani, Melzer, Brian and Previtero, Alessandro, 'The Misguided Beliefs of Financial Advisors', *Journal of Finance*, Kelley School of Business Research Paper No. 18–9 (16 May 2018), accessed 22 December 2021. http://dx.doi.org/10.2139/ssrn.3101426

Acknowledgements

We would like to thank the many people who offered encouragement, counsel or detailed readings of this book over its long gestation. We are particularly grateful for the different ways in which the following people have helped us along the journey: Iona Bain, Sandy Bell-Ashe, Dr Tim Edwards, David Haigh, Artash Hakobyan, Andrew Hallam, Anas Hassan, Hannah Hubbard, Richard Hubbard, David Jones, Jackie Leiper, Paul Lewis, Mark Northway, Abraham Okusanya, Professor Ludovic Phalippou, Larry Swedroe, Philippa Thomas, Alasdair Wight and Steven Williams. We'd also like to thank all the friends and colleagues who gave endorsements, seen at the beginning of this book. But all mistakes and omissions remain, of course, our own.

We'd also like to thank our agents, Chris Newson and Nick Wallwork, for their instant enthusiasm for our book and our editors, Ian Hallsworth and Allie Collins at Bloomsbury, who shared their vision – for a single, comprehensive, highly practical book that demystifies everyday money, pensions and investing.

Index

INDEX